PRAISE FOR *REIMAGINING LUXURY*

T0289613

Diana was leading the way on sustainable luxury w̲   ̲.̲.̲.ion or ESG was nascent and far from the buzzword it is today; her vision for the industry – embracing authenticity, transparency and demonstrating success with measurable impact – has proven to be the key to sustainable success. Diana shares her vision in *Reimagining Luxury* in practical terms that companies can apply to their businesses to start their transformational journey.
Alyssa Auberger, Chief Sustainability Officer, Baker McKenzie

Reimagining the way we live is a critical step towards taking the action that is needed – shifting from talking about impact to achieving a positive outcome for nature and society. Diana's book offers a North Star for the luxury industry that could do so much and still has so far to go.
Dame Polly Courtice, Founder Director, University of Cambridge Institute for Sustainability Leadership

Diana brings a credible and commanding voice to the movement for a more sustainable luxury industry. She offers a well of actionable insight for building a future in which people and nature thrive together, and we're all better off heeding her wisdom.
M Sanjayan, CEO, Conservation International

Inspiration for action – this book will give you great insights into the future of luxury and sustainability.
George Weissacher, Creative Director, POAN, Former Head of Menswear Vivienne Westwood

Diana is a pioneer when it comes to ESG and sustainability, she has been leading the way for ethical practice in the Luxury sector for over two decades. Her priceless learning is laid throughout these pages for us all to benefit from and more importantly implement.
June Sarpong, actress, environmentalist, broadcaster and author

An invitation to the luxury and entertainment industries to reimagine a collective vision of the future. Compelling and hopeful, Diana Verde Nieto show the opportunities that lie ahead.
Paul Polman, business leader, campaigner and co-author of *Net-Positive*

By adopting sustainable practices, businesses can unlock innovative opportunities that benefit the planet, their teams and their brand. Embracing sustainability as an innovative opportunity will enable companies to create unique and engaging offerings, cultivate purpose-driven teams and foster communities of passionate brand supporters. *Reimagining Luxury* showcases sustainability and innovation as avenues for growth and provides guidance for all companies seeking to pursue this path.
Hannah Jones, Chief Executive Officer, The Earthshot Prize

Diana Verde Nieto helps you see sustainability in a fresh light: Not as a burden to bear, but rather as an unparalleled opportunity to create value for humanity. *That* is a real luxury!
April Rinne, global futurist and author of *Flux: 8 superpowers for thriving in constant change*

Diana is a remarkable experiences leader within the sustainability industry. She effortlessly combines luxury, tradition and innovation with conscious responsibility. This book inspires action, reflects on what change is possible and provides clear examples of how we can create a better future for all, being catalysts for impact together.
Cristina Ventura, General Partner and Chief Catalyst Officer, White Star Capital

Diana makes clear the role – if not the responsibility – that even the most exclusive and luxurious brands can play in creating a more inclusive and sustainable world. The examples and insights she shares are sure to spark conversation and inspire action.
Shamina Singh, Founder and President, Mastercard Centre for Inclusive Growth

Diana's grasp of the role sustainability will play in the evolution of luxury is unparalleled – an essential read for anyone who sees their future in the sector.
Robin Swithinbank, Journalist, Author, Luxury Industry Specialist

Reimagining Luxury

Building a sustainable future for your brand

Diana Verde Nieto

First published in Great Britain and the United States in 2024 by Kogan Page Limited

2nd Floor, 45 Gee Street	8 W 38th Street, Suite 902	4737/23 Ansari Road
London	New York, NY 10018	Daryaganj
EC1V 3RS	USA	New Delhi 110002
United Kingdom		India

www.koganpage.com

Kogan Page books are printed on paper from sustainable forests.

ISBNs

Hardback	978 1 3986 1365 2
Paperback	978 1 3986 1363 8
Ebook	978 1 3986 1364 5

British Library Cataloguing-in-Publication Data
A CIP record for this book is available from the British Library.

Library of Congress Control Number
2023950549

Typeset by Integra Software Services, Pondicherry
Print production managed by Jellyfish
Printed and bound by CPI Group (UK) Ltd, Croydon, CR0 4YY

To the ones that bravely reimagine a world where we can live in harmony with each other and with nature

CONTENTS

ACKNOWLEDGEMENTS

A special thank you to Lara Grobosch, writer and journalist, for editing, researching and overall making a lonely journey fun, Stephen Armstrong, award-winning journalist and author, for his mentorship and Fiona Fung, graphic designer and sustainability expert, for her creative input and direction.

I would like to thank Fflur Roberts, Head of Luxury at Euromonitor International, and Maria Indeka, cultural research analyst and trend forecaster at The Future Laboratory, for their special contribution, research and insights.

My heartfelt thanks to the many industry leaders who generously gave their time and shared priceless insights and perspectives during the interview process. In particular, Marysol Antón, Alyssa Auberger, Elizabeth Aubrey, Alejandro Bataller, Judith Batchelar, OBE, Tom Beagent, Sylvie Benard, Roy Bernheim, Tina Bhojwan, Lara Bonnel, Domitilla De Luca Bossa, Igor Boyadjian, Paul Bunje, Tony Burdon, Lea Brizio, Caroline Brown, Matteo Capellini, Dan Carter, Carolynn Chalmers, Rachael De Renzy Channer, Laure Charpentier, Denise Chen, Doina Ciobanu, Gabriela da Costa, Prof Carole Collet, Dame Polly Courtice, Marie Claire Daveu, Jenny Davis-Peccoud, Jessica DeBruyne, Sabrina and Idris Elba, OBE, Kodzia Edenharder, John Elkington, Dr Richard Federowski, Mathieu Flamini, Chantal Gaemperle, Sarah George, Santiago Gowland, Sylvain Guyoton, Kurt Haegeman, Linda Hewson, Nikita Jayasuriya, Hannah Jones, Livia Kalossaka, Valerie Keller, George Kern, CEO Breitling, Dina Khalifa, Daniel Klier, Professor John Kotter, Eva Kruse, Claudia Lazzari, Jerome Luciat-Labry, Nathan MacKenzie, Rachel MacLeod, Keith McCambridge, Elizabeth McMillan, Susan McPherson, Joanne Milner, Jaime Nack, Elisa Niemtzow, Devin Nieusma, Natalia Noguera, Joe O'Sullivan, Prof Olivier Oullier, Belinda Parmar, OBE, Lauren Gloster Pendleton, Leigh Pezzicara, Stephanie Phair, Emmanuelle Picard-Deyme, Anne Pitcher, Paul Polman, Nina Rawal, Jess Redgrave, Tonia Ries, April Rinne, Christine Rique, Karen Roberts, Susannah Rodgers, MBE, Dean Sanders, Dr M Sanjayan, June Sarpong, OBE, Corinne Sawers, Marie-Pia Schlumberger, Jennica Shamoon Arazi, Isabelle Sultan, João Paulo Testa, Christian Toennesen, Martin Townsend, Georg Weissacher, Joe Wilkinson, and Sue Williams.

I would like to also express my immense gratitude to his Excellency Mr Javier E Figueroa, Ambassador of the Argentinean Republic to the United Kingdom, and Mariana Plaza, Minister of the Argentinean Republic to the United Kingdom, Nancy Oakley and Suzanne Walters from Purple PR, Andrew Richardson, CEO of Home House, Joost de Kruiff, General Manager and Jessica Barwell, Marketing Communications Manager of Home Grown, Jeylan Ramis, Donna Goddard and the Kogan Page team for giving me this opportunity and breathing life into *Reimagining Luxury*.

Karen Hanton MBE, John Elkington and Jonathan Porrit, MBE for their mentoring since the very start of my career, Amy Nelson Bennett, CEO of Positive Luxury and the team who kept the business thriving while I was on sabbatical writing, and the World Economic Forum and the Young Global Leaders community for their support.

Words cannot express my appreciation to Anthony Kleanthous for showing me the ropes in life and in business, Sandra Marcuzo and J A Verde Nieto, the Fergusons, the Dawes, the Delucas, the Johnsons, the Fernandez Juanateys, the Alvarezes, the Armstrongs, the Websters, the Lacys, Daniela Vega, Adam Schulman, Menchie Gonzalez and Fenia Bougla for their unwavering support.

Finally, I am profoundly grateful to family on both sides of the Atlantic Sandra, Juan, Vanina, Fernando, Lola, Julieta, Hamish, and Rufus. Thank you for your love, support, guidance and patience all these years. You have truly helped shape me into the person I am today.

And thank you to all the readers who will dare to reimagine their business and leave the world better than they found it.

Introduction

How do you create value for others? Finding the answer has been my drive for many years since I started my career in sustainability almost 25 years ago. It wasn't written in the stars; it was written in my surname – Verde, the Spanish word for green.

Finally now, we have arrived at a place where there is fertile ground to have this conversation. I don't know if we will solve the climate crisis – what I do know is that if every person in every business in every sector did their bit to restore nature and invest in people, everybody would be better off. Don't try to fit in, there is no joy in that. Reimagine the world that we live in and play your part in designing it.

Back in 2011, I had found myself sitting next to David Attenborough at an awards dinner. I had the 'job' of giving him his Lifetime Achievement Award, a pleasure in itself, but I also got to dine with one of my great heroes. And he lived up to every expectation. He told me the story of the British blue butterfly, one of the most successful insect reintroductions that ever happened. The moral of the story? We can drive species to extinction, or use the power of our collective will to restore nature.

The big change that we have seen in the last year is how legislation is mushrooming, not just in Europe but from all corners of our planet, all against a backdrop of major challenges on all fronts – politically, economically and finally environmentally. But legislation alone is just compliance.

Today we can answer a question that we have not been able to answer before. What is the business case for sustainability? And I mean money.

In 2009, I attended former USA Vice President Al Gore's programme formerly called 'The Alliance for Climate Protection', held in Mexico City. It was autumn. The rest of the participants were from all over the world, and everybody held the same enthusiasm and hunger for knowledge. I wasn't sure what to expect. In the first session, Gore opened his presentation with a picture of Earth Rising, a picture taken by astronaut William

Anders from a lunar orbit on 24 December 1968 during an Apollo 8 mission. The photos were mesmerizing. By the end of the week, we were clear about one thing: the human race is like a messy teenager without the ability to clean up after themself; the problem is that there is nobody coming after us to clean up.

Why are we in this mess? Why is nature rapidly decreasing? Why are there no just societies? The answer is tragically simple: 1) Our economies are built on a resource consumption-extractive system and natural resources are not endless; 2) There is little incentive in our economic system to reward the right actions.

In the future, transparency and accountability will be the norm and reporting on impact will be a compliance matter. However, the companies that truly make the sustainability business case will be the ones that stand out. Those are the companies that will really see the difference in their bottom line.

We do not need more sustainability people, we need good operators, good procurement, good designers, good salespeople, good marketers, who can all do their jobs in a sustainable manner. We need to break the silos and make sustainability the new normal. Collective action is at the heart of progress.

We all need to accelerate the transformation and lead with solutions in order to change the mindsets and heartsets of organizations and individuals.

Why am I writing this book now, you may ask? I woke up on the first day of my fifth decade in my dear Buenos Aires and for a moment, the world stood still. I saw my humble beginnings in the Global South and how with a lot of effort, hard work and help from a 'village' of incredible people that I bumped into on my journey, I'm privileged to sit at the 'dinner table' in the Global North.

While working on this book over the last six months, I had the honour of speaking with more than 90 industry leaders, entrepreneurs, innovators and educators from the world of luxury and beyond, rounding up to a total of 11 full days of interviews bringing together their combined wisdom to share with you.

We have the opportunity to influence the future, just like Messi in the second half of the World Cup Final in 2022. This is our moment, a moment in history that may never come back, a moment that will defy the wellbeing of the next generations. We can influence the scoreboard. Argentina won the World Cup on penalties, in extra time.

We are in that moment – tired, nervous, defying, excited – we are looking into the future about to take that shot...

I hope this book gives you the tools, curiosity, the super charge that we need to reimagine the future and take the shot that will make humanity score the most important penalty of our lifetime.

01

The world has changed
for a sustainable future

We assume that luxury companies are obsessed with tradition.

There is nothing further from reality. They are investing in innovative materials, processes, reshoring, innovative business strategies, leaning into technology upstream and downstream, and keeping their finger on the pulse for consumer trends.

Luxury companies are constantly reimagining the norms, extending their brand halo to influence culture. A can-do mindset, collective action for a positive future and dash of innovation are at the heart of reimagining luxury. Change is never gradual and/or linear, nor is it based on a proportional relationship between cause and effect. Change is not controllable, it can be created or accelerated, can involve threats or opportunities and, just like luxury, is a dance with paradoxes.

When we think about sustainability it is hard not to think about change, but sustainability is a team sport, and, very much as a team, we all collectively can build the businesses, the culture, the society of tomorrow with a regenerative mindset, where humans and other living species rely on one another for health and our co-evolutionary reciprocal relationships-based respect and care to thrive.

In 2024, climate change does not need a publicist, most people are aware that the weather patterns are erratic and disruptive, therefore redefining luxury and our world is not an option but a must. As the European Union is tightening the rules across many sectors, the question arises of how luxury can differentiate if all brands, regardless of the sector, will need to apply the same principles as luxury when it comes to design, durability, quality, consumer use and end of life.

Gabriela da Costa is Partner at the international law firm K&L Gates and a competition and trade regulation practitioner advising luxury and consumer products brands. She confirmed the EU legislation is rapidly expanding to address the whole lifecycle of many products, from responsible design, production, labelling, packaging and marketing through to efforts to encourage sustainable consumption. These include proposals being explored to promote a culture of reuse and digital tracking of products through the value chain. Additionally, whilst the proposed new laws in the EU and other regions generally limit consumers' extended rights to repair to certain electronic goods, luxury producers will increasingly come under pressure to enable repairs for relevant goods and extend lifespans. Designing for obsolescence is no longer an option, as durability and transparency are at the top of the legislators' agenda. This begs the question: are four to eight per season per year going to be a thing of the past?

Luxury culture is being democratized, but the product remains exclusive. One can go to the Bulgari or Louis Vuitton Hotel for a drink, a visit, a stay or an Instagram photo or eat at the Prada restaurant and experience the ethos of brands.

Going back to go forward

Would you have believed someone if they told you in January 2020 that the world would stand still, we would fall into a global pandemic and we would vaccinate nearly the entire world in less than two years and then resume activities almost as normal?

Humans are innovative and resilient, and we all have a deep survival instinct. The state of our world from social, economic and environmental perspectives can be changed. We just need to work together, just like we did with the pandemic, and have a collective vision of what 'good' looks like.

To solve a problem, you must first define it. Climate change has been defined in many ways – chemically, meteorologically, historically… It is a human problem with human solutions. To solve it, we must change ourselves, our mindset and our heartset. And that has its own problems.

We live in the most connected and yet fragmented of times. In 2024, the world is more interconnected, interdependent and transparent than it has ever been. We understand more about the way business works, the way people think and the way the planet's life unfolds than ever before.

And yet, despite this knowledge and the ability to connect, we are more polarized than ever. Economic anxieties, institutional imbalances, class divides and the collapse of trust in the media and political leaders mean we are more aware of our problems and yet feel more helpless in facing them. And so we turn to social media, the most untrusted communicator, where our fears are only reinforced.

We are paralysed by the enormity of the challenge and defeated by the lack of positive feedback – the changes we make appear to have no effect. You recycle, you switch the lights off, nothing gets better.

'The problem is too big, I can't make a difference, we don't have time', we think to ourselves, so why bother? We should have started sooner. If only they'd told us earlier…

And yet, they did. As Carl Sagan (1980) once famously put it, 'You have to know the past to understand the present.'

The first person to spot the danger was the American scientist Eunice Newton Foote, born in 1819. In a paper, she showed that rising CO_2 levels would change atmospheric temperature and impact the climate. Nearly 170 years ago, she tried to tell us what was coming (Newton Foote, 1856).

Further warnings came in 1896, 1938 and in 1972, the latter the year I was born. The meteorologist John Sawyer, who spent World War II forecasting the weather for the Royal Air Force, published *Man-made Carbon Dioxide and the "Greenhouse" Effect* (1972). Sawyer was no radical – if anything, he was most interested in the way air flowed over mountains and the effect that had on rainfall. In his paper, he accurately predicted the rate of global warming that would occur between 1972 and 2000.

I like the detail of this story – Sawyer was one of the first weather forecasters to master computers and he outlined our peril from his office in Bracknell, an optimistically designed postwar new town in rural Berkshire, England.

Finally, in July 1977, the topic moved on from the worried scientists to an active politician. President Carter's chief science adviser Frank Press warned of the possibility of catastrophic climate change in a memo with the subject line 'Release of Fossil CO_2 and the Possibility of a Catastrophic Climate Change' (Pattee, 2022).

Frank Press warned of the 'catastrophic' knock-on effect that greenhouse gases would have on our climate. He outlined a future of large-scale crop failures and the consequent threat of starvation, adding like Cassandra – the Trojan prophet cursed to be always correct and always ignored – 'The urgency of the problem derives from our inability to shift rapidly to non-fossil fuel sources once the climatic effects become evident not long after the year 2000' (Press, 1977).

It's not worth discussing the insanity of a species warned repeatedly for nearly 200 years that something terrible would happen if they didn't tweak their behaviour, refusing to tweak that behaviour. That's the nature of being human. If word came to us that aliens were on their way, they would be here in 170 years and they'd kidnap anyone with a moustache, there would, no doubt, be moustache clubs cropping up in the final decades as obstinate humans sprouted facial fuzz just to prove a point.

We have been reminded, in detail, at least once every five to six years of the impending climate issue in the IPCC Assessment Reports. The 2001 report was the first to make a direct connection between the rise in global temperatures and human activities (IPCC, 2001). Its infamous hockey stick graph showed an abrupt historical temperature rise just as greenhouse gas emissions rose.

Finally in 2005, the Kyoto Protocol made a stab at lowering global temperatures, but without China, India or the United States it made very little difference beyond offering the tantalizing prospect of future agreements.

Does this remind you of anything?

In 1986, a report on genetic mutations in viruses warned of the threat of a pandemic from a mutated flu virus. Joshua Lederberg (1988), then president of Rockefeller University, said that the world had learned nothing from previous pandemics and even the health establishment was blind to the threat of new viral disease. It was tempting to think that we will never learn and for a while I felt something close to despair.

But then, in 2020, the global pandemic made us realize for the first time that we are not invincible.

The new fragility

In November 2021 the unexpectedly positive outcome of COP26 seemed to show that we are learning from the effects of ignoring specific signs. The scientific consensus on climate change is no longer in doubt – those business and political leaders who tried to defend their refusal to change by trying to spread uncertainty have finally accepted the years of evidence.

For the first time ever, it is accepted that global temperatures are now more likely than not to breach 1.5 degrees Celsius (2.7 degrees Fahrenheit) of warming by 2030, said the World Meteorological Organization (WMO). According to Jacqueline McGlade, Professor for Resilience and Sustainable Development at University College London (2021), the overall emphasis placed on the need for nature-based solutions to protect and restore nature and ecosystems to achieve 1.5°C, 'the work to be undertaken on a global adaptation goal, the new balancing of adaptation and mitigation financing, the phasing-out of inefficient fossil-fuel subsidies and the inclusion of non-carbon dioxide greenhouse gases including methane' were all welcome. All this speaks volumes to the science and evidence.

There was also greater recognition of the role of communities and Indigenous peoples – for the first time in the history of the United Nations Framework Convention on Climate Change (UNFCCC), 28 indigenous peoples were nominated from each of the seven United Nations UN indigenous socio-cultural regions as Indigenous experts with governments.

This crystalized the acceptance of the importance of Indigenous people as protectors of the planet. As the World Economic Forum wrote in the report 'How to Include Indigenous Communities in Climate Action' (El-Katiri, 2022), Indigenous people make up a small minority of the world's population, yet they have played a critical role in sustaining the world. There are just 476 million Indigenous people across 90 countries representing 5,000 different cultures (Center for Disaster Philanthropy, 2021). Much of our world's non-commercially exploited land and many of its remaining mineral and forest resources, major rivers, fossil fuels and sources of renewable energy are in their territory (United Nations, 2021).

In 'Climate Change 2022: Mitigation of Climate Change' (IPCC, 2022), the International Panel on Climate Change highlighted that empowering Indigenous communities 'not only strengthens climate leadership in many countries, but also changes broad social norms by raising knowledge of Indigenous governance systems which supported sustainable lifeways over thousands of years'. With many Indigenous livelihoods and cultures being inextricably linked to their lands, territories and resources, the IPCC (2022) also stated that, worldwide, Indigenous people bear the brunt of environmental and climate injustices because of their geographic location in extraction and energy 'sacrifice zones', areas most impacted by extreme weather events, and/or through inequitable energy access.

Private finance creates its own Green Deal

COP26 also saw private companies take the lead over laggard governments in tackling climate change. Mark Carney, former governor of the Bank of England and UN special envoy for climate action and finance, helped found the Glasgow Financial Alliance for Net Zero (GFANZ) (which we will look at in more detail in the next chapter). Carney announced the deal, warning in a Bloomberg opinion piece together with former New York City mayor Michael R Bloomberg (2021) that the transition to a net-zero economy will require 'trillions of dollars in new investment — likely in the ballpark of $100 trillion', and that most of that investment 'will have to come from the private sector, especially after the enormous toll that the pandemic has taken on governmental budgets'.

'Make no mistake, the money is here if the world wants to use it,' Carney (2021) said at the climate summit COP26.

In leading edge businesses, however, this is nothing new. Larry Fink, founder of BlackRock, the world's largest investment firm, has been pushing in this direction since 2018, when he urged corporate leaders to evaluate the impact of their businesses and consider climate change (Fink, 2018). In January 2022, he stated in his annual letter to CEOs that 'Stakeholder capitalism is not about politics. It is not a social or ideological agenda. It is not "woke". It is capitalism, driven by mutually beneficial relationships between you and the employees, customers, suppliers, and communities your company relies on to prosper. This is the power of capitalism' (Fink, 2022).

In the aftermath of the closure of Silicon Valley Bank, many pointed to its impressive ESG performance as proof that the bank had been killed by wokery. This, of course, is not correct. SVB made bets on long-term government bonds that caused its initial losses and had got away with a weak investment strategy by specifically ducking oversight by regulators thanks to the 2018 roll-back of the Dodd-Frank act. No ESG screening would pick that up, which is why it's part of the due diligence and not the only tool in the box.

'There's two mega trends going on which impact any capital allocators in terms of what they do and how they do it,' Corinne Sawers, ESG and Climate Principle at global investment firm KKR, told me. 'Society, regulators, and customers are expecting more from a business in terms of what responsible behaviour looks like. And in some ways, this is something that we're starting to measure – assessing companies based on their non-financial impacts. But we are also looking at the incentives at every level from C-suite down for achieving those targets when we make an equity investment. I don't think European investing is going to reverse that. It is a fundamental cultural shift that will only get more embedded as the younger generations increasingly control the wealth in our society.'

Good COP, bad COP

The 12 months that followed COP26 saw energy conservation legislation passed in India, the Bahamas introducing climate financing that would encourage richer countries to pay to help protect the fragile islands, legally binding emissions targets cemented into law in Australia and net-zero laws introduced in Nigeria. As this chapter will discuss, further sweeping regulations are planned or have already followed.

Those of us who still believe that change for the better is possible need to act while the ripples from these moments are still disturbing our pool of complacency. We will explore how later in the book.

Where are we today? The historic extractive nature of our species has led scientists to call this ecological era the Anthropocene, after our dominating influence over animals and plants. Climate change has a branding and positioning issue. As a complex system, it is difficult for most people to get feedback from the planet for the small changes they make. For years that meant that warnings were ignored. Now, however, the effects we have been warned about for so long are visible to all.

It is not only the temperature that is changing. Global ice caps and glaciers are melting, and our sea levels are rising while the increasing amount of carbon dioxide in the atmosphere is being absorbed by our oceans, leading to a rise in acidity levels. Our weather systems are also being affected. Extreme weather events are increasing in frequency and intensity – and are far harder to predict. Undoubtedly one of the most important changes in our world is the loss of animals and plants at an unprecedented rate, due to pollution, land use changes, pesticides and overall human activity. The United Nations predicts that there will be a 'sixth extinction' by 2039, wiping out over 75 per cent of all species – approximately 1 million animals and plants (Morrish, 2023).

Biodiversity is crucial for food security, human wellbeing, both physical and mental, the tourism industry, most supply chains and climate mitigation. Thankfully the private sector is recognizing the impact that this loss will have on them, and most businesses are committing to protecting, managing and restoring nature.

It is an enormous task. We have been very efficient in exploiting natural resources and have created a global bio monoculture. Some 70 per cent of all the birds on the planet are farmed poultry like chickens, 60 per cent of all mammals are livestock like pigs, sheep and cows and a further 35 per cent of mammals are humans. Only 4 per cent of mammals live in the wild (Carrington, 2018).

Industrial agriculture lowers the diversity of animals, impacting natural food chains as more land is being used to feed the very livestock I mentioned. In turn, this causes habitat loss around the world further impacting biodiversity.

Perhaps the most heartbreaking fact is that half of the planet's animals and plants have been lost over my lifetime – 50 years.

Although there are many local and international treaties around the world to protect biodiversity, animals and plants corruption threatens those treaties. We need to go beyond the law and appeal to business to be the guardians of our future, as the lack of balance in nature will affect supply chains, and of course the top and bottom lines of businesses.

Business activity, directly or indirectly, has an impact on our natural world through supply chain activities, whether it is on water, animals, land use, forestry, etc. This is the very reason businesses and people all over the world are exploring how to conserve, restore, protect and re-wild our planet. Climate change has moved from scientific theory to real life experience – i.e. the destruction of our communities, displacing people, disrupting supply chains and increasing the overall cost of doing business.

On 30 July 2022, for instance, London firefighters had their busiest day since London was bombed in World War II. Temperatures topped 40°C, there were 2,670 emergency calls and more than 40 houses were destroyed by grass and open land fires. Almost exactly a year earlier, London was drowning after one month's rainfall poured down on parts of the capital in just one hour. The Fire Brigade evacuated 120 homes in Kensington & Chelsea, rescued people from cars stuck in flood water and helped hospital patients escape to safety (Hancock, 2021).

In the spring/summer of 2022, Spain and Portugal faced an unprecedented heatwave, reaching temperatures of over 40.7°C and claiming 1,700 lives, according to the World Health Organisation (2022), causing the Spanish government to ban outdoor work.

Business is responsible for much of this pollution – but in the fragmented, trust-free world we inhabit, it is one of the few actors that can have a significant, direct effect in reducing it.

I have dedicated almost my entire working career to encouraging companies to act – sometimes successfully, sometimes less so. In the last 12 months, however, the conversation has started to head towards actions and outcomes instead of just commitments. In writing this book, I spoke to senior people at some of the world's largest and most influential companies to understand how organizations are evolving to meet this challenge. I have also spoken to entrepreneurs and changemakers to understand how they see our future.

I wanted to know if the pandemic had influenced their thinking, how they were moving from paying lip-service into activating real purpose and what sort of change this requires. I asked them how the wave of regulations sweeping the world will change the way they think and act.

It is time for business to step up and fight – for its future, for its customers and for the children of its staff and management. For one thing, that's what consumers and employees want businesses to do, according to the Edelman Trust Barometer Special Report 'The New Cascade of Influence' (2022), 63 per cent of people agree with the statement 'I buy or advocate for brands based on my beliefs and values'. Moreover, among employees, 69 per cent of people agree that 'having societal impact is a strong expectation or deal breaker when considering a job (avg)' as stated in the Edelman Trust Barometer Special Report 'Trust in the Workplace' (2022).

'Consumers and employees want companies to act right, not greenwash,' Tonia Ries, Executive Director, Thought Leadership, at Edelman told me. 'Not talking but acting is extremely important. Consumers and employees will vote with their wallet or look for jobs with companies that are more sustainable. So, it becomes an employee retention problem if you don't take these things seriously.'

Edelman's research, she explained, highlights an information overwhelm as one of the barriers companies face when encouraging people to act. The terms are too jargony and confusing, the problem is so big that it seems impossible to tackle, we're all going to die, so what can I do?

Nature strikes back

'Covid shed light on the inequalities across fashion's entire value chain – everything from the supply chains and the grievances workers were going through to the retail and delivery workers continuing to serve,' said Elizabeth Aubrey, ESG and Sustainability Strategist. 'With consumers stuck at home on their computers, there was tremendous transparency and an increased understanding of the impact of individual purchasing decisions on each other and our ecosystems. Fashion is a beautiful system that is hardwired to redesign itself. It holds boundless potential to build and pioneer more regenerative systems – but we must find the collective will and mechanisms to enable this shift.'

Aubrey had hoped this rush of awareness would lead to a reimagining of business models but has found the post-Covid world still clinging a little to the past. 'I do think it has gotten the industry thinking about what the value they bring to the world is and how we can re-evaluate our relationships with the raw material supply chains and the people who work across that supply chain. So, I do think it helped. It was a horrible crisis to go through that people are still going through, but I do think that there are some lessons learned that we can draw from it.'

Aubrey talked about people, rethinking supply chains, understanding the interconnected nature of our environmental, social and economic systems, and seeing first-hand the interdependence. She noted the increase of hyper-localized supply chains across the world, as people became dependent on what the 100-mile radius around them in the Covid lockdown could do to keep them alive and healthy.

For corporations, these lessons have to be learned at every level, and it is not enough to just have a Chief Sustainability Officer or an ESG Director. Addressing sustainability is often seen as just the CSO or the CEO job, but it is not realistic to think that one function can drive the sustainability of the entire business. To succeed, companies need an integrated approach, hardwired into the everyday performance of the organization. This is easily said but harder to get done – when done right, this can drive not only impact but deliver a competitive advantage. The only way that we will be able to re-engineer the system is to truly transform the organization.

Transformation generation

The main challenge companies face in becoming a sustainable business is integrating sustainability into their way of thinking and working. Leaders must motivate and encourage their co-workers to make decisions and act in ways that support this goal. It involves building awareness and understanding, achieving alignment on a shared mission, values and strategy, making sure everyone throughout the organization feels responsible and empowered to make a difference and addressing any critical skill or knowledge gaps.

The most avant-garde companies, such as Edrington, are in the process of reimagining sustainability into specific functions or at certain levels of management. This empowers leaders to integrate sustainability into their strategies or governance structures as a first step – usually at its best if coupled with the right financial incentives.

'The difference between pre and post Covid is a realization of the importance of sustainability from a consumer's perspective,' Tom Beagent, Partner, sustainability at PwC, said. 'At a lot of the companies that I talked to, this turbocharged the importance of integrating sustainability into all the ways in which businesses are run – including the products and services on offer. It was a moment to double down on sustainability as opposed to pulling back.'

The greatest impacts lie within the supply chain and consumers. As society increasingly holds multinational companies accountable for their environmental and social impacts, companies have to start engaging and educating their suppliers and customers towards sustainability.

'While value for money is important,' stated Fflur Roberts, Head of Luxury at Euromonitor International, 'nowadays consumers also value sustainability.'

Consumers are reframing value, as the cost-of-living crisis and inflation is common all over the world. They are now considering multiple factors, including sustainability, as well as how the product/service makes them feel. As a result, consumers are becoming more selective and careful with their spending. For brands to capture people's attention nowadays, they must authentically reflect and be aligned with people's values and beliefs.

And this is an important point as sustainability and the value of it is not the same all over the world. In certain areas of Europe, people perceive recycled cashmere not only as a luxury item but as a positive luxury item, for which people would be prepared to pay more.

The same cashmere is not perceived the same way by Americans and Asian consumers, especially Chinese.

Luxury brands will also need to review their selling strategies and innovate into new retail models or perhaps diversify their portfolio to experiences, either digital or physical. New consumption patterns via resale and rental are being explored as luxury beyond ownership rises. Those types of platforms and business models have been catapulted into a digital age of growth.

Daniella Vega, former Chief Sustainability Officer at Selfridges, coined the expression 'buy less, buy better' in 2017 when Selfridges deliberately made a stand not only about their role as a retailer but as a curator. Luxury brands followed by withdrawing their use of fur and exotic skins, mirroring Selfridges more and signalling to consumers that they were listening. Today, people are buying less and are buying better. Leaning into luxury investment pieces that they can re-sell or rent. Equally, they are not necessarily buying new, but pre-loved, especially in categories such as watches, jewellery and furniture.

According to the latest data from Euromonitor International (2023) 58 per cent of high-income consumers (those with an annual income of more than $100,000) state that they are willing to buy pre-owned goods. This is versus the global average of 51 per cent. Meanwhile, 51 per cent of high-income consumers state that they are willing to rent goods. This is versus the global average of 46 per cent.

Technology has made it easier to sell pre-loved fashion and luxury and is now going mainstream, with many key players already partnering with third-party platforms to launch luxury consignment stores as well as investing in their own pre-loved/re-sale platforms and taking this initiative in-house.

Sustainability as core to business success

Today there is a clear business case for the value addressing sustainability delivers for an organization – something that was not always visible back when I started my career.

I interviewed Dame Polly Courtice, the Founder Director of the University of Cambridge Institute for Sustainability Leadership, where she was also Founder Director of the Prince of Wales's Business & Sustainability Programme and served as Academic Director of the University's Master of Studies in Sustainability Leadership. Polly was very generous with her time and thoughts, and although soft spoken the fire of her narrative and her eyes made the conversation magnetic and mesmerizing.

She started by saying:

> 25+ years ago, working with the corporate sector, we had to sell them the problem. We had to convince them that climate change, and the social and environmental destruction that we were witnessing, were not only bad for society, but bad for business as well. People were either simply not aware

(and there were times when I was shocked at just how unaware they were), or they were simply in denial, sceptical about the facts about climate change and the consequences of environmental destruction, and totally not convinced that it was business's problem. Back then all this wasn't showing up on the P&L, resources were less constrained, and none of this carried as much reputational risk as it does now. We were amongst the 'doom and gloom merchants', trying to persuade people of the enormity of the problem and the need to act. This was a necessary step in the process, and it was important both to intellectualize it as well as to hold people's feet to the fire. But that time has passed and thankfully there has been a noticeable shift in the last 5 to 10 years. People, especially at the leadership level, both in business and the finance sector, now mostly accept the scientific evidence, and the risks facing their businesses. They have come to recognize that we can't continue the current trajectory, that we need to look for solutions, and that we will have to work together in wholly different ways. But of course, how to react, and when to do so, remains a difficult decision for most of them. Nobody should assume that the action that is being taken now is remotely sufficient to the task, but it is a start.

She is right to say that sentiment has changed, and negative narratives don't work today. Radical collaborations can accelerate to find solutions, and co-investment can help accelerate innovation to get us out of this mess. The luxury industry is in a privileged position to set those standards and aspirations that can change the climate narrative, but, most importantly, to lead by example.

The opportunity for companies, whether luxury or not, is to treat sustainability programmes and sustainability innovation with the same level of importance as other business initiatives, have them meet the same business case requirements and use the same performance improvement processes. This is key to integrating sustainability into the overall business strategy and ensuring that it is given the attention and resources it needs to succeed.

Naturally, there are still questions about how sustainability drives profits. Sustainability and technology are driving efficiencies throughout the value chain, especially through AI. There are many start-ups popping up in all corners of the globe, revolutionizing prototyping, enabling companies to cut down on the use of raw materials, reduce waste, gain time and reduce their carbon emissions. As luxury, especially fashion, is getting more vertically integrated, AI can optimize production lines, reducing waste and increasing efficiencies throughout, predicting demand, adjusting production schedules and minimizing overproduction.

Many CEOs cannot always see how sustainability innovation is connected to value creation and sustainable economic growth – some still see it as a cost instead of an investment in the health and resilience of the business as well as a reputational issue linked to risk management. Granted that the returns may not come the next quarter, but the cost of inaction or not meaningful actions will be greater in the long run.

ESG and sustainability innovation are a defence against the volatile supply chains, fluctuating cost of energy, water scarcity and human inequalities that are crippling businesses today. Sustainability is not separate from business strategy – in fact, it should be seen as a core part of that strategy rather than an add-on or afterthought. By doing this, it can create more value – not only for the company itself but for its suppliers, shareholders, customers and the wider world. Sustainability in the long term can be a win-win situation for everyone involved.

As Georges Kern, CEO of Swiss watchmaker Breitling, explained, sustainability is deeply connected with economic success and growth: 'A company who is not strong in ESG cannot be successful. I would even say that if you don't invest in sustainability economically and socially, you will go bankrupt.'

Regulation and legal action

CASE STUDY
Torres Strait

In 2017, after a violent storm hit the scattered sandy Torres Strait Islands some way off the coast of Queensland, Yessie Mosby found the skeletal remains of his great-great-grandmother beneath a tree on the beach of Masig Island.

Originally inland and a good distance from the shore, her sacred burial ground had crept closer to the sea as erosion ate away the low-lying land. Yessie spent the day with his children gathering his ancestor's bones as the storm washed away the site's last defences.

In some respects, the islanders were lucky. The local population is little more than 10,000 strong, living on 16 of the 274 small islands dotted along the surface of the coral reef between Australia and Papua New Guinea claimed by Captain James Cook in 1770.

And whilst the culture is a colourful fusion of the ancient – ancestors aren't exactly worshipped, but the dead are still considered part of the family and their bodies are a little like living kin – and the modern, with houses painted in the garish colours of rugby league teams, it's an area most Aussies have barely heard of.

Fortunately for the islanders, a young lawyer called Sophie Marjanac had taken a junior job in the Australian government department that oversees Indigenous land rights in the Torres Strait after graduating from the University of New South Wales in 1999. She got to know the islanders and their culture.

In 2017, Sophie joined ClientEarth, a London-based environmental NGO that uses the law to persuade or force companies and governments to abide by legislation designed to protect the plant and its people. It has forced companies to close old power stations, prevented new gas plants being built and helped governments draft eco-friendly laws.

When the Australian government's response to the rising seas was to offer to move the whole community to the mainland, forcing them to leave their life – and their ancestors – behind, Sophie helped eight islanders file a complaint with the United Nations using an interpretation of the Universal Declaration of Human Rights in a way that had never been tried before – but, if successful, would set a huge global precedent.

The Universal Declaration of Human Rights includes a clause on the protection of minority groups and their culture. Sophie's challenge was to argue the islanders' right to life with dignity was violated by the Australian government's inaction. In September 2022, the United Nations Human Rights Committee in Geneva decided that:

- Climate change was impacting the claimants' daily lives to the extent that their rights were being violated.

- Australia's poor climate record was a violation of the islanders' right to family life and right to culture under the International Covenant on Civil and Political Rights.

- Australia had violated Article 27, the right to culture, and Article 17, the right to be free from arbitrary interference with privacy, family and home.

The Committee's decision obliged the Australian government to compensate the Indigenous people from the Boigu, Poruma, Warraber and Masig islands for 'the harm they have suffered, to engage in meaningful consultations to assess their needs and take measures to secure their communities' safe existence'.

Armstrong (2023)

Similar campaigns are starting to affect companies and industries as pressure groups like ClientEarth use innovative legal challenges. In 2019, the pressure group complained to the Organisation for Economic Co-operation and Development OECD over BP's 'Possibilities Everywhere' ad campaign, which focused on clean energy investments, despite the company spending 96 per cent of its expenditure on oil and gas. In a ruling that set a precedent for corporate greenwashing complaints, the UK branch of the OECD Guidelines for Multinational Enterprise agreed that ClientEarth's complaint had been 'material and substantiated', and BP withdrew its ads before the case could proceed (ClientEarth, 2020).

In January 2020, the charity ShareAction, advised by ClientEarth, pressured Barclays Bank to align its financing activities with the Paris Agreement. ClientEarth's legal letters to Barclays board suggested that investing in fossil fuels was placing the company directors in breach of their fiduciary duty.

Under the UK Companies Act 2008, the fiduciary duty of a company's directors includes acting 'in the best interests of the company' (Armstrong, 2023). This has traditionally meant 'ensuring it is profitable now and in the future'. Gordon Gecko's infamous 'greed is good' speech is based on this premise – the so-called shareholder primacy theory. ClientEarth took that law and flipped it. In early 2022 it began civil proceedings against the 13 directors of Shell plc, holding them personally responsible for the company's failure to move to carbon neutrality. ClientEarth is arguing a board's fiduciary duties are owed to the long-term existence of the company itself, not the short-term pockets of shareholders. In April 2020, Barclays agreed and announced its ambition to target net-zero emissions by 2050.

And then there's the wave of new legislation either passing or on the way. This has appeared – in legislative terms – very quickly. The idea of a Green New Deal was not on the US political agenda in 2016. By 2021 it was part of US President Biden's infrastructure and jobs plans. In the same year, the European Union adopted proposals aimed at making the EU's climate, energy, transport and taxation policies reduce net greenhouse gas emissions by at least 55 per cent by 2030, compared to 1990 levels (Shankar et al, 2021). Similar legislation is in various stages of consideration in the United Kingdom and South Korea, amongst others.

Up to now, businesses have been complacent in building sustainability teams, setting up targets and telling inspirational stories with creative flair, instead of working towards operationalizing sustainability in every department of the organization and empowering every employee to be the custodians of their sustainability strategy. That time is over, as regulation is here to stay, and the pressure to break the silos is mounting.

The International Sustainability Standards Board (ISSB) is an independent, private-sector organization responsible for developing and approving IFRS Sustainability Disclosure Standards (IFRS SDS).

It has proposed a new definition for sustainability: 'the ability for a company to sustainably maintain resources and relationships with and manage its dependencies and impacts within its whole business ecosystem over the short, medium, and long term' (ISSB, 2022).

Legislation enforcing these ideas has arrived. The EU Strategy for Sustainable Textiles, the Circular Economy Action Plan and the European Green Deal all promote sustainable practices and are designed to reduce the damaging environmental impact of any and all economic activities. The new Corporate Sustainability Reporting Directive (CSRD) – part of this effort – was passed in January 2023. It requires qualifying organizations – from the very large through to small and medium-sized enterprises (SMEs) in various sectors, including fashion, to report on ESG metrics following defined standards that can be verified through external audits (Le Rolland, 2023).

'After years of little concrete action and company-led voluntary initiatives, the EU Strategy for Sustainable and Circular Textiles signals that the EU intends to pass laws to tackle the fashion industry's overproduction and drastically reduce waste, pollution, and labour right infringement,' reported Marguerite Le Rolland (2023), Apparel and Footwear Industry Manager at Euromonitor International.

The EU Strategy for Sustainable and Circular Textiles is designed, in the words of the EU release announcing its launch, to 'help the EU shift to a climate-neutral, circular economy where products are designed to be more durable, reusable, repairable, recyclable and energy-efficient' (European Commission, 2022).

Created in part to support an industry still recovering from the Covid-19 crisis, it involves EU-backed investment, research and innovation and takes a holistic approach to the entire fashion lifecycle. This impacts every stage of the supply chain from production and sales to disposal with proposals on taxing carbon emissions and imports, introducing legal minimum eco-design requirements, and implementing an EU-wide framework of Extended Producer Responsibility (EPR), which holds companies responsible for the waste they produce.

This is going to have a real impact on what is being communicated to consumers and how, as only certifications with real governance, such as

FSC, the Butterfly Mark and the Leather Working Group, with real audits and assurance processes, will be a safe bet.

A good example of this is when the Norwegian Consumer Authority (NCA) and Netherlands Authority for Consumers and Markets (ACM) issued a joint document outlining how the Higg Materials Sustainability Index (MSI) tool developed by the Sustainable Apparel Coalition (SAC) – one of the most well-known sustainability rating systems – should improve the underlying data behind its claims or it would breach the countries' marketing legislation and therefore become illegal (Le Rolland, 2023).

Companies that want to stay ahead will need to invest now in software that will enable them to understand their ESG risks and opportunities, map their value chain and understand their carbon footprint. France is in the process of developing a new law that would require fashion brands to add 'carbon labels' to their products, indicating an environmental 'score' from A to E, just as white goods are labelled.

And the US is not staying still either, the Garment Worker Protection Act in California, the New York Fashion Sustainability and Social Accountability Act and the federal FABRIC Act are all demonstrating a growing trend towards greater oversight and accountability in the fashion industry.

'What I see today is that basically there is a regulatory wave happening from the EU and the USA,' said Sylvain Guyoton, Chief Rating Officer at EcoVadis, a globally recognized assessment platform that rates businesses' sustainability. 'The more mature companies, who have been looking at the supply chain issues before the regulatory wave arose, are now in a leadership position as they have been genuinely working to make their supply chain more sustainable because they firmly believe that it creates value, reduces risk and creates efficiencies and cost reductions.'

The global context and the role of luxury

Let's start by defining luxury. Luxury is anything over and above the basics of what you require to live. It can be a soft carpet, a pink handbag, a bigger car or just moments of absolute sheer joy during a wonderful experience.

In every generation, luxury is reimagined. New ideas and ideals and new possibilities create new values and new goals. Today, especially for younger people, luxury is about experiences, exploring, discovering, tasting, sharing, listening, travelling. The music in a store, the smell of the place, the person you are with, the empathy displayed by the salesperson – these all affect how you feel about the product you are buying, what value it bears for you, and that memory is imprinted in your brain, explained Professor Olivier Oullier, neuroscientist and founder of neuroscience AI start-up Inclusive Brains. This same multi-sensory experience does not yet happen when you buy something online. This is why luxury brands invest so much in the metaverse, in order to offer, in the near future, the ultimate multi-sensory online experience that the physical world can offer.

But luxury is also about time – and the beautiful tension between history, the present and the future. As Chantal Gaemperle, Group Executive Vice President Human Resources & Synergies at LVMH, put it, luxury is about 'dancing with paradoxes'.

Many brands are rooted in history and have their own DNA but they are at risk of no longer being relevant in today's world. 'The ideal dance is a balance between disrupting and pioneering while not forgetting where we are coming from,' said Gaemperle. 'Just like life, full of paradoxes, of tensions.'

But being relevant in the present is not enough. Luxury also means thinking about time in terms of a long future. For years, luxury brands have talked about the rise of Gen Z and Millennials driving conscious consumption. However, climate change, inequality and a globe linked by dangerously insecure supply chains mean social conscience is no longer a youthful fad.

Sustainability is now an issue for people of all generations, from Boomers to Gen X, Millennials, Gen Z and even Alphas. In fact, Alphas will be to climate change what Millennials were to digital technology – they are growing up as 'sustainability natives'. For brands that choose to greenwash and make false claims about their sustainability practices, there will be no financial return. However, for brands that genuinely understand the importance of the matter, there is a significant opportunity for both financial and reputational benefits. In the coming decade, business transformation towards sustainable practices will be a key opportunity for brands to differentiate themselves and appeal to consumers valuing sustainability (Positive Luxury, 2022).

Brands are increasingly looking for purpose, but consumers are looking for trust – brands that reflect their values. Bobby Duffy, Professor of Public Policy and Director of the Policy Institute at King's College, London and author of *Generations: Does When You're Born Shape Who You Are* oversaw research at KCL into generational attitudes to climate change and found the headlines about culture wars and generation clashes were wildly inaccurate when it came to climate change and brand boycotting. Whilst younger consumers do typically expect more from brands in terms of good citizenship, older consumers are not only just a few percentage points away in their opinions but are far more likely to boycott brands they disapproved of (Positive Luxury, 2022).

Euromonitor's Passport Megatrends survey (2022a) found that climate activists account for 34 per cent of the global population with Baby Boomers and Generation X over-represented. One in four global consumers, according to the survey, say that spending on eco/ethically conscious goods makes them feel good.

All businesses know that understanding customers is crucial to any successful strategy. Deciding where to play, how to win and how to differentiate yourself from your competition are essential questions for every business. The label systems that are being introduced through the legislation described above will be incredibly laborious to implement, will definitely grab the headlines for a short while and then will become so much a part of everyday life that they will be as exciting as staring at the calories on the back of a can or soup or packet of sandwiches.

Combining the two – understanding the consumer and spotting the opportunity beyond compliance – to get a competitive advantage in sustainability is crucial.

Becoming a mission-driven company

In the following chapters, I will showcase the role a company plays in the world, including a look at employment. We are going to go back to what is known in Britain as the Quaker organizations, those companies that invested in the wellbeing of all their stakeholders as people and have an emotional connection with products and organizations that they perceive are sustainable or good.

Companies should leverage the rational appeal with the emotional one. For Baby Boomers and Generation X, the environmental legacy – what the planet will leave to their (grand)children – is very important (Euromonitor International, 2022b). Emphasizing the future consequences and framing the information in monetary terms might cater to those seeking legacy and loss aversion. Millennials and Generation Z make purchasing decisions based on values and principles (personal, social and environmental), creating the purpose-driven consumer (Euromonitor International, 2023).

Nearly a fifth of all consumers are purpose driven. These are consumers who buy products and services from brands that support social and political issues that are aligned with their values. The shift towards buying from purpose-driven brands is particularly evident among those in higher income groups as highlighted in Euromonitor International's 'Passport Voice of the Consumer: Lifestyles Survey' (2023).

Purpose-driven consumers, according to Euromonitor (2022c), are mainly Millennials (22.4 per cent) who fall into the higher income segment (26.4 per cent of consumers with an annual household income of $80,001–100,000 are purpose-driven consumers) who are educated to graduate and/or postgraduate degree level (23.4 per cent), with India and the United Arab Emirates having the highest population concentration (38 per cent and 37 per cent, respectively).

Euromonitor International's research (2022c) identifies 2020 as a year of awakening in the luxury and fashion industries as the global pandemic highlighted the plights of textile workers around the globe and the adverse impact of human activity on our planet.

Becoming a mission-driven brand that recognizes the importance of bringing value beyond profits has become increasingly important to attract people, whether consumers or talent, creating goodwill, and loyalty. Issues related to reducing energy consumption, working with environmental NGOs, recycling and reducing plastic use as well having strong Diversity, Equality and Inclusion ethics have particularly come to the fore in the last year. While concerns over climate change are escalating, so too are issues around green- and social-washing. This gap could trigger the boycotting of brands as consumers become increasingly vocal about their values and beliefs.

Luxury across all sectors, fashion, beauty, automotive, drinks, etc is in a prime position to influence positive social change.

In that context, having a strong mission that recognizes the importance of bringing value beyond profits is becoming increasingly important to gain consumer favour and avoid reputational damage. In a post-pandemic world, luxury and fashion brands are in a prime position to use their influence to be better agents of social change and to lead corporate action, while those which do not might be left out and suffer a significant backlash in the near future.

Polarization and the new denial

In 2022, *Nature* published research from a team of sustainability scientists in London and Italy called 'Growing polarization around climate change on social media'. They established, by following discussions on social media, that 'a prominent opposition to the dominant pro-climate discourse has established itself since late 2019, resulting in a highly polarised online climate debate' (Falkenberg et al, 2022).

'The two biggest drivers of polarization that might affect luxury goods are distrust in government and a lack of shared identity,' Tonia Ries, Executive Director, Thought Leadership, at Edelman explained to me. She continued:

> The sense that the social fabric is weak, that we're not interconnected so that really, it's better for me to focus on my needs in order to win at any cost as opposed to making sure that everyone is taken care of and that will make everybody more prosperous. The final driver is systemic unfairness.

> The sense that the system is designed to work for some people but not for everyone. The third-tier drivers are economic pessimism about societal concerns such as climate change as well as distrust in the media. If we go back in time to 50 years ago, most people really didn't pay that much attention to luxury brands. That has changed for better and for worse.

Historically, luxury has been very exclusive, which perhaps reinforces the feeling of inequality, and creates complications for luxury brands. Today, a polarized world could well put luxury brands in the crosshairs.

This book is designed to minimize that risk, as we are in the middle of a transitional decade, the decade of delivering. This is the time when sustainability is a core strategic imperative for businesses to drive innovation, impact and attract and retain talent.

The cultural and operational transformation involved in embedding sustainability means breaking down the silo and truly equipping the rest of the business to play its part.

There is an ambition and reality gap as most organizations see cooperation to embrace this challenge as a burden, outside the scope of their job descriptions or impossible because there is a skills gap.

Sustainability can have a positive influence on revenue, cost reduction and employee satisfaction when systematically implemented. For this, Chief Sustainability Officers need to empower and inspire other functions to collaborate in the delivery of the strategy. As a company transforms so will the CSO role. Within the next seven years, the sustainability function as we know it will lie in a sustainable finance department and in every function of every employee in the organization – including the CEO. Just as we have seen the democratization of IT and digital functions, we will see the democratization of sustainability. Don't get me wrong, the technical areas will require experts, and those technical areas will multiply towards the end of the decade, however a combination of technology, innovation and bridging the skills gap will welcome 2040 with an unprecedented maturity in the field.

Do you want to understand how you can be part of the solution?

References

Armstrong, S (2023) Meet the Earth's Lawyers, Wired, 6 January, www.wired.com/story/clientearth-lawyers-defending-environment/ (archived at https://perma.cc/DCH7-M5XV)

Bloomberg, M R and Carney, M (2021) To fight climate change, put markets to work, Bloomberg, 3 November, www.bloomberg.com/opinion/articles/2021-11-03/mike-bloomberg-and-mark-carney-on-climate-finance (archived at https://perma.cc/3CAV-X5RB)

Carney, M (2021) COP26 Finance Day [Speech]. UN Climate Change Conference UK 2021, Glasgow, 3 November

Carrington, D (2018) Humans just 0.01% of all life but have destroyed 83% of wild mammals – study, *The Guardian*, 21 May, www.theguardian.com/environment/2018/may/21/human-race-just-001-of-all-life-but-has-destroyed-over-80-of-wild-mammals-study#:~:text=The%20new%20work%20reveals%20that,pretty%20staggering%2C"%20said%20Milo (archived at https://perma.cc/9XAY-ZNHZ)

Center for Disaster Philanthropy (2021) Indigenous Peoples, 21 November, https://disasterphilanthropy.org/resources/indigenous-peoples/ (archived at https://perma.cc/F4FY-PETX)

ClientEarth (2020) BP greenwashing complaint sets precedent for action on misleading ad campaigns, 17 June, www.clientearth.org/latest/latest-updates/news/bp-greenwashing-complaint-sets-precedent-for-action-on-misleading-ad-campaigns/ (archived at https://perma.cc/TQG5-497Z)

Edelman (2022) Trust Barometer Special Report. The Cycle of Distrust, 10 March, www.edelman.com/trust/2022-trust-barometer (archived at https://perma.cc/B6NP-ACTZ)

El-Katiri, L (2022) How to include Indigenous communities in climate action, World Economic Forum, 19 September, www.weforum.org/agenda/2022/09/how-to-include-indigenous-communities-climate-action/ (archived at https://perma.cc/H5C7-SLZX)

Euromonitor International (2022a) Passport Megatrends Survey

Euromonitor International (2022b) Passport Voice of the Consumer: Lifestyles Survey

Euromonitor International (2022c) Passport Briefing: Diversity, Equity and Inclusion in Luxury and Fashion: What's Here and What's Next?, 10 August

Euromonitor International (2023) Passport Voice of the Consumer: Lifestyles Survey

European Commission (2022) EU strategy for sustainable textiles. About this initiative, 30 March, https://ec.europa.eu/info/law/better-regulation/have-your-say/initiatives/12822-EU-strategy-for-sustainable-textiles_en (archived at https://perma.cc/C4YK-5K44)

Falkenberg, M, Galeazzi, A, Torricelli, M. et al (2022) Growing polarization around climate change on social media, *Nature Climate Change*, 12, 1114–21, https://doi.org/10.1038/s41558-022-01527-x (archived at https://perma.cc/6KHQ-VPE4)

Fink, L (2018) Larry Fink's annual letter to CEOs: A sense of purpose, BlackRock, October, https://aips.online/wp-content/uploads/2018/04/Larry-Fink-letter-to-CEOs-2018-BlackRock.pdf (archived at https://perma.cc/8GT5-7RDZ)

Fink, L (2022) Larry Fink's 2022 letter to CEOs: The power of capitalism, BlackRock, 21 January, www.blackrock.com/corporate/investor-relations/larry-fink-ceo-letter (archived at https://perma.cc/C6FP-KD85)

Hancock, S (2021) London flooding news – live: Tube travel chaos after parts of capital receive month of rain in one day, *The Independent*, 13 July, www.independent.co.uk/news/uk/home-news/london-flooding-live-today-news-b1883004.html?page=2 (archived at https://perma.cc/84VC-APET)

IPCC (2001) Climate Change 2001: The Scientific Basis. Contribution of Working Group I to the Third Assessment Report of the Intergovernmental Panel on Climate Change [Houghton, J T, Ding, Y, Griggs, D J, Noguer, M, van der Linden, P J, Dai, X, Maskell, K and Johnson, C A (eds.)], Cambridge University Press, Cambridge, UK and New York, www.ipcc.ch/report/ar3/wg1/ (archived at https://perma.cc/8UZB-LY7W)

IPCC (2022) Climate Change 2022: Mitigation of Climate Change. Contribution of Working Group III to the Sixth Assessment Report of the Intergovernmental Panel on Climate Change [Shukla, P R, Skea, J, Slade, R, Al Khourdajie, A, Diemen, R, McCollum, D, Pathak, M, Some, S, Vyas, P, Fradera, R, Belkacemi, M, Hasija, A, Lisboa, G, Luz, S, Malley, J (eds.)], Cambridge University Press, Cambridge, UK and New York, www.ipcc.ch/report/sixth-assessment-report-working-group-3/ (archived at https://perma.cc/N87M-K5PP)

ISSB (2022) ISSB describes the concept of sustainability and its articulation with financial value creation, and announces plans to advance work on natural ecosystems and just transition. IFRS, 14 December, www.ifrs.org/news-and-events/news/2022/12/issb-describes-the-concept-of-sustainability/ (archived at https://perma.cc/9J44-TGD7)

Lederberg, J (1988) Medical science, infectious disease, and the unity of humankind, *JAMA*, 260(5), 684–5, https://doi.org/10.1001/jama.1988.03410050104039 (archived at https://perma.cc/5TJ7-TR3U)

Le Rolland, M (2023) New environmental regulation and a greenwashing crackdown: So what does that mean for fashion?, *FashionUnited.uk*, 21 March, https://fashionunited.uk/news/fashion/new-environmental-regulation-and-a-greenwashing-crackdown-so-what-does-that-mean-for-fashion/2023032168588 (archived at https://perma.cc/V5VS-U4SV)

McGlade, J (2021) A step-change in urgency, UCL University College London, www.ucl.ac.uk/climate-change/cop26/cop26-reflection (archived at https://perma.cc/76CK-W25F)

Morrish, K. (2023) Protecting nature helps your bottom line as well as the environment, *The Sunday Times*, 26 January, www.thetimes.co.uk/article/protecting-nature-helps-your-bottom-line-as-well-as-the-environment-7gpb7npd8 (archived at https://perma.cc/M77J-QF6S)

Newton Foote, E (1856) Circumstances affecting the heat of the sun's rays, *The American Journal of Science and Arts*, Second Series, Vol. XXII, November (Whole Volume), 382–3, www.sothebys.com/en/buy/auction/2021/history-of-science-technology-including-fossils-minerals-meteorites/foote-eunice-newton-circumstances-affecting-the (archived at https://perma.cc/6MKF-H9XV)

Pattee, E (2022) The 1977 White House climate memo that should have changed the world, *The Guardian*, 14 June, www.theguardian.com/environment/2022/jun/14/1977-us-presidential-memo-predicted-climate-change (archived at https://perma.cc/WW7P-CRFC)

Positive Luxury (2022) 2022 Predictions Report,13 January, www.positiveluxury.com/content/uploads/2022/01/PL_PredictionsReport2022_embargo13Jan.pdf (archived at https://perma.cc/3U8C-DNCC)

Press, F (1977) Release of Fossil co2 and the Possibility of a Catastrophic Climate Change. Executive Office of the President. Office of Science and Technology Policy, 7 July [Memorandum], https://uploads.guim.co.uk/2022/06/02/SSO_148878_031_07.pdf (archived at https://perma.cc/J9V8-W5SN)

Sagan, C E (author and presenter) (1980) Episode 2, One Voice in the Cosmic Fugue [Television series]. In Adrian Malone (Producer), *Cosmos: A Personal Voyage*, Arlington, VA: Public Broadcasting Service

Sawyer, J (1972) Man-made Carbon Dioxide and the "Greenhouse" Effect, *Nature*, 239, 23–6, https://doi.org/10.1038/239023a0 (archived at https://perma.cc/57AL-BC42)

Shankar, P, Lei Win, T and Hekman, L (2021) Lobbies undermine EU's green farming plan, *DW Deutsche Welle*, 19 October, www.dw.com/en/exposed-how-big-farm-lobbies-undermine-eus-green-agriculture-plan/a-59546910 (archived at https://perma.cc/83YH-F26T)

United Nations (2021) Indigenous peoples continue to face barriers to realizing rights to lands and territories, March, www.un.org/sw/desa/indigenous-peoples-continue-face-barriers-realizing-rights-lands-and-territories (archived at https://perma.cc/YH8V-APAN)

World Health Organisation (2022) Heatwave in Europe: local resilience saves lives – global collaboration will save humanity, statement by WHO Regional Director for Europe, Dr Hans Henri P. Kluge, July 22, www.who.int/europe/news/item/22-07-2022-heatwave-in-europe--local-resilience-saves-lives---global-collaboration-will-save-humanity (archived at https://perma.cc/E7YS-F5HM)

02

Is sustainable finance
the new normal?

A seismic change is taking place within the luxury industry, driven from the top and from the ground up – leaving no space for those who ignore or delay action. The call for companies to make and honour commitments to environmental, social and governance issues are coming from government legislation, a wave of activist investors and a new generation of luxury consumers with a conscience. The link between truly sustainable business operations, commercial performance and company valuation cannot be ignored.

While innovation remains essential for brands, the definition of innovation is changing – away from a demanding lifecycle of product introductions and toward genuine innovations in environmental practices: sustainable material, ingredients, packaging, production, manufacturing techniques and business models alongside progressive social practices addressing inequality of opportunity and boosting creativity.

Authenticity is no longer just about a brand's compelling story or niche positioning; it is now about the strength of a company's sustainable operations across the entire business, including its entire value chain.

This is too good an opportunity for luxury to miss.

Companies must be courageous, urgently adopting ESG metrics without compromise whilst ensuring these new ideas of creativity, innovation and authenticity are at the very heart of their businesses – from the leadership throughout the organization.

Adopting sustainability and ESG metrics is not just a question of doing the right thing, it is about delivering value to all stakeholders. Under the new reporting directives companies will need to highlight what parts of their balance sheet are at risk due to climate risks as sustainability has become the language of accountants and investors who have had to learn to translate climate data into investor data.

This means that companies will need to take provision in their balance sheet just like they do with financial provisions. Companies disclaiming their CO_2 emissions won't be enough anymore, they will need to say which part of the business is affected by those emissions and how they can then mitigate the risk. ISSB disclosure will be able to directly translate the value at risk for business from the 2025 reporting cycle.

In other words, don't wait to do it because you have to. Do it now. This is how you secure the future – the future for your business, the future for the planet and the future for all the people connected, directly or indirectly to your organization. Commercial success and profit not only coexist alongside climate and social justice; action to commit to and deliver on bold values and targets has been proven to improve both. Earn the trust and respect of the consumer. Act now or be left behind.

What does sustainable investment mean?

Sustainable investment is the process of being aware of environmental, social and governance (ESG) considerations when making investment decisions leading to more long-term investments in sustainable economic projects. Environmental matters include climate change mitigation and adaptation, as well as the conservation, restoration and regeneration of biodiversity, water preservation, animal welfare and the circular economy just to name a few. Social considerations in sustainability involve addressing issues related to people and communities, such as inequality, labour relations and human rights (European Commission, Finance, 2018).

According to the 2018 EU Action Plan on Financing Sustainable Growth 'the governance of public and private institutions – including management structures, employee relations and executive remuneration – plays a fundamental role in integrating social and environmental considerations into the decision-making process' (European Commission, Finance, 2018). Sustainable finance can redirect investments towards more sustainable technologies and businesses and help create a low-carbon, climate-resilient and circular economy.

Although some investors are already reflecting ESG risk factors in the cost of capital this is not a widespread approach across the industry, yet. The savvier investors have identified strategies that enable them to put ESG standards as a condition of business – as the long-term risks to society and the environment accumulate in the long term – while some investors integrate these considerations into their asset choices.

The key pain point is that these considerations are not yet consistently applied, and the criteria are not visible to business.

Financial intermediaries have the power and influence to accelerate the flow of capital into business models that serve the interests of society and benefit our natural world, but entrepreneurs innovating in this space often struggle to access capital. For many businesses across a myriad of sectors their current operating model is not sustainable for the long term; successful businesses will need to align their mission with stakeholders' interest in order to create value while making a positive contribution to social contribution, with neutral or positive impacts on the natural world. The level of disruption that business and financial institutions are facing today calls for a much-needed rebalancing approach to portfolios and business models.

The key insight is that in order to achieve this, employees from all levels of the organization, from the board, to the execs to the frontline workers, will need to be upskilled in sustainability as the decisions and actions that they take will shape the ESG performance of the company and the levels of risk.

In this transitional decade, businesses will need to navigate the trade-offs of focusing on the long term and growing more sustainable activities whilst driving business performance in the short term. In a not-too-distant future, opportunities will arise from reimagining the market boundaries.

Luxury is already doing this by diversifying their business portfolios and managing risk across their businesses and investment.

What are the benefits of ESG investing?

ESG needs a rebranding, not conceptually – perhaps we should call it Governance, Environment and Social metrics so it does not get stained with bad connotations, especially in America. Companies that have sustainability processes and targets tend to be better at forecasting and managing potential future risks and opportunities, are more focused on long-term value creation and are stronger at strategic thinking and innovation.

For investors going through the due diligence process, part of the reason for investing in a company with well-defined sustainability targets and clear ESG performance metrics is that over the long term, prioritizing people and the planet is more profitable because of the company's resilience in the face of environmental and social regulatory challenges.

Sustainable investment is not a new concept

Back in the 1960s, socially responsible investing became a buzzword amongst the investment community, mainly to address the exclusion of entire industries from their portfolios, such as tobacco production and/or the involvement in the South African and West Africa Apartheid regime, a system of institutionalized racial segregation that existed from 1948 to the early 1990s. Although over 30 years have passed, and many things have changed, sustainability and ESG have not evolved as fast.

I started working in the sustainability field last century, and yet I was not the first one. John Elkington, aka the godfather of sustainability, has been discussing how climate change was going to be one of the biggest challenges we'd face going into the 21st century since the late 1970s. I remember the first time I met John, back in 2001. I used to 'pop in' to his old SustainAbility office in [technically] Holborn as a form of mentorship to ensure that I was on the right track whilst consulting with business – he always welcomed me with a cup of coffee and a smile but encouraged me to leave my rollerblades at the door.

John is a true visionary and a prolific author with over 20 books written in this field, including the *Green Consumer Guide* published in the 1980s. He founded SustainAbility in 1987, the first sustainability consultancy, and coined terms such as 'environmental excellence' and 'green consumer'. In 1994, he created the idea of the 'triple bottom line' as a way to encourage companies to include in their mission and objectives how to improve the livelihood of people and the health of the planet. In his own words, the 'triple bottom line' has sometimes been reduced to a way of balancing trade-offs instead of doing things differently. So he announced what the *Harvard Business Review* (who published the piece) called the 'first-ever product recall of a management concept' back in 2018. The idea was to challenge the triple bottom line (TBL) community, including over 6,000 B Corporations worldwide, not to sink the concept with all hands. That said, fast forward to today, and we continue pushing way beyond key planetary boundaries without any signs of slowing down.

In 1999, the G20 created the so-called 'fourth pillar' of the global economy – the Financial Stability Forum and its 2009 successor, the Financial Stability Board (FSB). Operating alongside the IMF, the World Bank and the World Trade Organisation, the FSB's job is to promote global financial stability. For the first decade, the body was charged with keeping the world's financial system stable by coordinating policies and standards across central banks and treasuries. Among the FSB's tasks is identifying vulnerabilities that could destabilize the financial system.

In a critical moment for the concept of sustainable investment, the FSB included mitigating the risk of climate change in its brief in 2015, after the failure of the Paris Agreement – climate change being one of the largest financial vulnerabilities the FSB identified.

How everything changed – from Kyoto to Paris to Glasgow

The term ESG gained the spotlight in 2004 when a report by the UN Global Compact with the bold title 'Who Cares Wins' was published. The late Kofi Annan, United Nations Secretary-General, invited financial institutions to develop recommendations and guidelines to integrate ESG topics in asset management and securities.

The United Nations' attempts to get some sort of global agreement on climate change go back decades, but the first significant treaty aimed at reducing greenhouse gases was 1997s Kyoto Protocol. The largely successful but occasionally fractious agreement – the United States refused to sign, and Canada dropped out in 2011 after facing a $14 billion fine under the terms of the treaty – included the founding of the Conference of Parties, or COP, to monitor and improve the effectiveness of the treaty.

The 2015 Paris Agreement was intended to further mitigate the effects of climate change after a disastrous conference in Copenhagen in 2009 collapsed without producing any agreement. Although the Paris Agreement did, in theory, establish Nationally Determined Contributions (NDCs), which gave each of the 189 nations signing the treaty its own specific set of commitments in a bid to prevent the talks from collapsing again, the contributions were widely recognized as insufficient to keep warming below 2°C or limit it to 1.5°C. There was a lack of transparency and no international standards for countries to demonstrate they were meeting their commitments.

Enter the FSB, which founded the Task Force on Climate Related Financial Disclosures (TCFD) to devise standards for the financial world. The Task Force had a clear message – a crucial moment in the history of sustainable investment: 'Climate change presents financial risk to the global economy,' its founding statement read (TCFD, 2020a). 'Financial markets need clear, comprehensive, high-quality information on the impacts of climate change' (TCFD, 2020a). 'One of the essential functions of financial markets is to price risk to support informed, efficient capital-allocation decisions. To carry out this function, financial markets need accurate and timely disclosure from companies. Without the right information, investors and others may incorrectly price or value assets, leading to a misallocation of capital' (TCFD, 2020b).

In other words, the pricing of risk by financial markets must include a measure of the effects of climate change. This is impossible unless there is transparent information of a uniform standard to allow investors to understand and evaluate the scale and therefore the price of risk.

At a stroke, the interests of investors became aligned with transitioning to a lower carbon economy. Initially voluntary, the recommendations of the TCFD quickly became essential to the regulatory framework for climate disclosure. The European Union, Singapore, Canada, Japan and South Africa all signed up and, following COP26 in Glasgow in 2021, the United Kingdom and New Zealand made TCFD climate-risk disclosure mandatory, whilst China, India, Israel and Nigeria have announced their intentions to follow suit. Brazil, Hong Kong, Switzerland and the USA are all considering legislation. In short, this means companies looking to operate in any of the 35 nations signing or considering signing up to the TCFD standards will need to comply with those regulations or face fines and disinvestment.

The banks vs climate change

COP26 also saw the formation of an unprecedented union of private finance – the Glasgow Financial Alliance for Net Zero. In April 2021, more than 160 financial institutions, including 87 asset managers, 42 banks and 58 asset owners, joined the Alliance, a global forum for financial institutions to accelerate the transition to a net zero economy no later than 2050. For some perspective, this alliance controlled over $70 trillion, roughly the size of the world's 15 largest economies added together. By the end of 2022, membership of the Alliance had grown to 550 organizations with $153 trillion in assets under management – more than the combined GDP of every country in the world.

The Alliance leadership is an impressive collection of experienced central bankers and business leaders. It was established by the UN special envoy on climate action and finance and former governor of the Bank of England, Mark Carney. Michael R Bloomberg, the UN Special envoy for climate ambition and solutions, joined Carney as co-chair, while Mary Schapiro, former SEC chairman and head of the secretariat for the TCFD, serves as vice chair.

The COP26 conference was unsatisfactory in delivering the action and commitments needed to reach the targets set by the Paris Agreement, UN Secretary General Antonio Guterres admitted in his statement at the end of the conference, but it did create the new International Sustainability Standards Board (ISSB) which will set ESG reporting standards for business, and 'for the first time they encourage International Financial Institutions to consider climate vulnerabilities in concessional financial and other forms of support, including Special Drawing Rights,' he said (United Nations, 2021).

The various standards mean the investment community has a comparable set of data to evaluate companies' ESG performance. Green finance, which includes funding from banks, markets, insurance companies and climate-conscious investors, will play a crucial role in promoting action to tackle climate change, thus delivering a better return to their stakeholders.

For companies, this means figuring out what that data is and how to really understand the impact of their businesses so that they can show investors solid reasons to justify their faith and money. Not only are countries' climate commitments being called into question, privately owned companies are also facing intense scrutiny from clients and institutional investors to prove that their net zero commitments are both legitimate and sound – and this extends to ESG too.

In 2023 Kering and L'Oréal, as well as many other organizations, created a new function reporting to the Chief Sustainability Officer called 'Sustainable Finance'. This function is well placed to embrace the new reporting directives under the CSRD where companies will take a double materiality approach. In other words, companies will need to report the impacts of their activities on people and the environment ('outside-in'), as well as how their activities impact society and the environment ('inside-out').

Listed companies will need to release transitional plans on how to achieve sustainability transformation including those net zero plans by 2030. And it is a warning call to the modern equivalent of 'sin stocks' – the wages of sin are fiscal death.

CASE STUDY
BlackRock

BlackRock is the world's biggest investment firm – founded in 1988, initially as a risk management and fixed income institutional asset manager, it has $10 trillion in assets under management (BlackRock, 2022).

Larry Fink, BlackRock's Chief Executive, sends out an annual letter to investors that has become a widely examined bellwether for the finance industry. In 2018, he caused a stir in the investment community and garnered headlines worldwide when his letter included a clarion call to arms to all corporate leaders, asking them to assess the societal impact of their businesses, embrace diversity and consider climate change and its effects on long-term growth.

'Companies must ask themselves: What role do we play in the community? How are we managing our impact on the environment? Are we working to create a diverse workforce? Are we adapting to technological change?,' he wrote (Fink, 2018).

The letter set out BlackRock's policy of sustainable investing, declaring the firm's intention of allocating more capital towards businesses that meet specific environmental and social standards.

In 2020, Fink's letter upped the stakes, announcing that environmental sustainability would be a key goal for investment decisions. In 2021, BlackRock and the Vanguard Group Inc., the world's largest asset managers, urged companies to make changes to address racial and gender diversity.

What surprised Wall Street with all of these statements was Fink's certainty that he could do this and continue to make the returns his investors expected. 'People listen to BlackRock, because they're the biggest investor in every company,' said Daniel Klier, CEO of sustainability data and technology firm ESG Book. 'When they invest into new areas, the rest of the industry will follow. That's just very powerful. I think most investors are now operating a policy where they look at red flags – companies that are particularly poor performers across ESG. A good ESG screen avoids big downsides.'

Traditionally investors examine business fundamentals to establish risk. Fink is leading investors to include the idea that harming the environment, insecure supply chains and unfair employment policies should also be considered a business risk.

Investing with ESG considerations in mind is a challenge, especially in the US, due to the lack of regulatory requirements, and leaves investors under fire from politicians and activists for doing too little or too much. In 2022 Fink came under attack from both right and left, with Republican states withdrawing funds and activist investment firms accusing him of underperforming.

Fink has expressed some public concern that the attacks have become personal. At the end of 2022, however, the company showed no sign of changing tack. BlackRock's 2023 update on its stewardship policies dialled back on Fink's more urgent tone but said the company still considered climate risk as an investment risk. 'We do not anticipate material changes in our voting, and much of our engagement with companies will be continuing the dialogue on material risks and opportunities that we had in 2022,' it said (BlackRock, 2023).

Whilst the trend is strong, BlackRock's battles highlight the need for regulation to back principals.

The new investment landscape

Sustainability used to be a differentiation point for a business. Today it has become a licence to operate. Forbes reported that more than 80 per cent of mainstream investors now consider ESG information when making investment decisions (McPherson, 2019). This has monumental implications for every business. Lines of credit will be attached to carbon emission targets. Investment in unsustainable businesses will crater. It's simple: where the money goes, the world is going to follow.

'Over half of the UK pension industry has made serious commitments to net zero before 2050, including halving emissions this decade. But currently the world is on a trajectory of 2.5C of global warming – this will have a devastating impact on the viability of business,' explained Tony Burdon, CEO of pressure group Make My Money Matter. 'Investors need to move faster and more strongly on driving down emissions, particularly in high polluting businesses like oil and gas, but also to make use of what Mark Carney calls the "biggest commercial opportunity in living memory". The new companies and industries arising from the net zero transition are likely to provide huge returns to investors. This means that for finance it is no longer a morals vs money question.'

Why are investors looking to invest in sustainable businesses? As explained by Claudia Lazzari, ESG officer at independent private equity firm Mindful Capital Partners, investors are increasingly aware of the importance of ESG factors in the long-term success of a business. Therefore, they consider ESG risks and opportunities in the investment process and manage them by playing an important role in incentivizing companies to take specific actions while protecting their investments.

There are three main drivers, according to Montse Suarez, co-founder of investment firm Vaultier7: 'The first is a shift in consumer behaviour – consumers will spend more on a product they believe is sustainable and reduce their spend with products or companies which are not.' 'Secondly, government policies, and finally, the pandemic has seen investors shifting risk and exposure by moving into ESG, with a willingness to focus more on the intangible' (Positive Luxury, 2021).

Thirdly, investors are also seeing proof that sustainable companies are more profitable – S&P Global Market Intelligence analysed 26 ESG funds with more than $250 million in assets under management from 5 March 2020 to 5 March 2021 and found 19 of those funds rose between 27.3 per cent and 55 per cent compared to the S&P 500, which increased by 27.1 per cent (Whieldon and Clark, 2021).

And investor activity is not just focused on the boardrooms of FTSE 100 or S&P 500 listed companies. At the end of 2020 and the start of 2021, a group of mainly European VC funds introduced initiatives to address ESG. London-based Balderton Capital, which focuses on European startups, announced its Sustainable Future Goals in early December 2020, which included internal behaviour change, investment decisions and portfolio support. Balderton is also a leading member of a group of 25 VCs which formed ESG in VC, a community of LPs, fund managers and VCs led by GMG Ventures and Houghton Street Venture, a new firm affiliated with the London School of Economics.

'Investors now expect ESG to be a core part of company strategies, and reducing greenhouse gas emissions should be the top of the ESG priority list for businesses. But there's also more attention paid to employees and in general to the human side of business, so they want companies to promote diversity and inclusion within their employees,' said Lazzari. 'They want to invest in training for employees, specific training regarding ESG topics and they also want to improve their well-being. So, they are trying to adopt and implement welfare solutions for them, such as flexible benefit or healthcare coverage insurances. These are the more common things that investors are asking companies.'

According to Sophia Bendz, Partner at Berlin-based Cherry Ventures, the group is 'really keen' on upping its ESG game. 'I also believe that true impact doesn't result from knowledge silos. It's great that we are learning from and supporting each other to have more societal impacts in our day-to-day roles,' Bendz said, speaking to TechCrunch (Lenhard, 2021).

Susan Winterberg, an ESG consultant at Harvard, credits an increased awareness of how VC activities impact climate change and social justice as well as an awareness of how adopting ESG can advance business goals such as increasing sales, attracting top talent and reducing operating risks. Given investor interest in ESG – from global trillion-dollar asset managers to spry early-stage VCs – companies from PLCs to SMEs have an opportunity and a challenge ahead (Lenhard, 2021).

The resistance – is it futile?

In March 2022, Republican senators voted to overturn a rule that makes it easier for retirement fund managers to consider sustainability factors like climate change when making investments (Wick, 2023). The battle over sustainable investing is not yet fully won. Investors, however, are looking at ESG factors in terms of financial risks to a company's value, using them as a framework for risk management and investment rather than a political position.

When legal NGO ClientEarth began civil proceedings against the 13 directors of Shell plc in early 2022, the novel legal move was to hold the directors personally responsible for the company's failure to move to carbon neutrality on the ground that a board's fiduciary duties are owed to the long-term existence of the company itself, not the short-term pockets of shareholders. 'We are acting in love not anger to stop the company being driven off the cliff by these directors,' Laura Clarke, ClientEarth's CEO, told *Wired* magazine (Armstrong, 2023). 'And we are going for the board of directors' sense of personal responsibility. That is a powerful point of leverage.' 'Fiduciary duty is about prudent risk management,' added Sophie Marjanac, Senior Lawyer and Climate Accountability Lead and ClientEarth. 'Human rights are about the inherent dignity of the individual. The crisis of the modern world is the climate crisis and the biodiversity crisis. It's only natural that the law will step up and adapt' (Armstrong, 2023).

This means a change of mindset from company boards, leadership teams and management as this new additional pressure and added scrutiny means that there is nowhere to hide. And yet, as Caroline Brown, Managing Director at Closed Loop Partners, a New York-based investment firm focused on development of the circular economy, told me, 'We cannot change the entire value chain of a company overnight. That is the path to company failure. These are very complex systems and responsible timing of these changes is critical to its success.'

Brown says investors see the change to a more circular, sustainable future as a positive investment opportunity, irrespective of whether they have been an impact investor in the past or not. 'We are living in a time where major industries are shifting,' she explained. 'How we do business is shifting, supply chains are shifting. And part of that disruption is a meaningful opportunity for businesses and investors alike. But companies need to be really disciplined in choosing which of the many metrics they can focus on for sustainability – maybe it's water waste, maybe it's material use, maybe it's end-of-life recollection of a product – whatever it might be. Choose from that menu, identify priorities, and make sure that's clear throughout the organization so that people making decisions in production, selling and distribution can act on it.'

In her experience – and in mine – even inside large companies there's confusion. One department may focus on embedding transparency tools and another one may focus on bins in the store to get materials back. They negate each other because it's not a concentrated effort. It's about access to capital – investors putting money behind these solutions to give them the resources to pilot with large companies.

Denise Chen, Senior Sustainability Adviser at Melco Resorts & Entertainment, oversees the company's sustainability strategy and invest-ments in startups in the sustainability tech space. 'There is still less choice for Asian VCs in the Asian market in terms of sustainable investments,' she explained. 'But I'm sure this will quickly catch up.'

Looking ahead, things are moving in the right direction. In the years to come, we can expect to see more standardization and harmonization as companies become increasingly committed to fully disclosing the impact of their activities on people and the planet. As a result, investors are becoming more confident in investing in companies that prioritize sustainability for long-term success.

Current regulatory developments, such as the recent introduction of the EU Directive on corporate sustainability reporting, are expected to lead to more clarity and transparency in the future and create a solid baseline for ESG investments.

Is ESG a political or an investment issue?

With the European Climate Law in 2021, EU governments set formal targets for the continent to become climate neutral by 2050 and are setting standards on ESG reporting, auditing and investing (European Commission, Climate Action, no date). In the US, however, politicians and regulators are engaging in political combat over the basic principles involved in ESG criteria (Masters, 2022).

In May 2022, the US Securities and Exchange Commission brought charges against BNY Mellon for falsely claiming investments had been reviewed for ESG risks, whilst conservatives have sued the Nasdaq stock exchange to prevent it from requiring companies to justify having fewer than two board members who are women or members of ethnic minorities (Masters, 2022).

Ensuring a board has a diverse team in polarized times where language is weaponized can seem like a political statement. But when Henry Ford raised the salary of his employees to a generous $5/day, he was no socialist. He needed skilled staff working hard and, at the time, was paying them around the market rate of $2.25 (Worstall, 2012). He suffered from high turnover and his production often halted over staff shortages. The high wages secured their loyalty and labour. Reducing inequality was good business for him.

And in purely bottom-line terms, investing in ESG is like Ford investing in his workforce. In July 2022, for instance, the Corporate Governance Institute published data from the ESG Book showing that, over the preceding five years, investments in companies with good ESG performance yielded higher returns than the average within their broader market (Byrne, 2022).

For investors in these choppy economic times, ensuring a diverse board in companies makes sound business sense. 'Talent from the "developing" or producing world has many years of resilience experience,' explained Carolynn Chalmers, CEO of the South African-based Good Governance Academy. 'We have grown up in times of energy uncertainty, rampant inflation, corruption, and local governments which change several times in a week. Where people in the "developed" or consumer-based countries are horrified by such events and consider them crises – this is normal life for those in production-based countries. There is little operational risk guidance that consumer-based countries can provide to the "producing world" that they have not already experienced. They are fundamentally operationally resilient out of necessity.'

The key for investors when it comes to taking advantage of these opportunities is transparency. We are living in a time where major industries are shifting, how we do business is shifting, supply chains are shifting, and that disruption is a meaningful opportunity for investors. New technologies, new business models and new materials are all great business opportunities and that really changes the dialogue in the investment community.

'A lot of the measurement systems that have been developed in the last couple of years that rate impacts and put metrics behind the claims have enabled investors to participate in companies with full visibility that the company's mission, values, targets and goals are aligning to the commitments that you have made to your fund and your own limited partners,' Caroline Brown explained.

Brown likes to demonstrate the cost benefits and business opportunities of the circular economy using the example of a woman's jacket. Companies spend a lot of money mining raw materials to use them once and have them end up in landfill, she pointed out. She explained:

> If you recapture your materials, that's a huge advantage. Companies now have
> the opportunity to partake in the secondary sale of their product in a way
> that they never have before, partly because consumer sentiment wasn't excited
> about that. But now, if I sell a jacket once, I can get it back and I can sell it a
> second time. The margin on those pieces may be the same because I don't have
> a production margin in the second sale because accounting principles forced
> me to apply the cost of goods in the first sale. Particularly in businesses that
> are heavy on brand and storytelling, the ability to keep a relationship with
> your customer ongoing longer than just the transaction of the credit card in the
> store is a great opportunity to keep that person close to your company. Picking
> smart materials that may be biodegradable and not end up in landfill, picking
> smart designs that can easily be deconstructed, rebuilt, and reused, makes an
> enormous difference in that first stage. But this is a great opportunity to keep
> higher value customers that already know and love your brand connected to
> you and in the loop of your product.

CASE STUDY
Fashion

In 1926 Gabrielle 'Coco' Chanel created a short, simple black dress which she debuted in American *Vogue* and changed luxury fashion forever. In September 2020, the company made another debut – this time in green, issuing its first ever

€600 million sustainability-linked green bond (Reuters, 2020). The money is intended to expand its green commitments by paying for investments in, for instance, start-ups developing plastic alternatives for leather.

Raising the investment money through debt rather than Chanel's operating profits – $3.49 billion in 2019 (Chanel, 2020) – is a tool to bring investor oversight and accountability to the company's activities. The bonds are tied to Chanel's ability to fulfil the goals of Chanel Mission 1.5° – the luxury firm's commitment to decreasing emissions by 50 per cent by 2030. If the company fails to hit its targets, it will have to repay the bonds at far higher interest rates than if it succeeds.

Deloitte's 2020 fashion and luxury private equity and investor survey found roughly 60 per cent of investors have a fashion and luxury asset in their portfolio. Chanel's bond was wildly oversubscribed and came hot on the heels of Burberry, which had issued luxury fashion's first sustainability labelled bond a few weeks before.

Unusually for fashion, the finance sector was ahead of the luxury industry on this. In the first five months of 2021, investors poured $54 billion into bond funds specializing in environmental, social and governance issues, compared with almost $68 billion for all of 2020 (Mooney, 2021).

Double materiality – an idea whose time has come

'When measuring targets and progress these days I'm interested in impact,' I was told by Jerome Luciat-Labry, Partner at CVC Capital Partners, the Luxembourg-based private equity firm with approximately $152 billion of assets under management. CVC's investors are pension funds and sovereign funds with very clear expectations. He has found the ESG agenda a top priority for prospective investors when it comes to raising new funds.

'So now you have two metrics,' he explained. 'You have your money metric – returns, etc – and then the double materiality of this. What is your actual impact beyond the profit line? Have you created 50 jobs, have you invested $20 million, or $200,000,000 or whatever number into new technologies? What have you physically done to improve the world, not just your business or your fund?'

The responsibilities of the companies and their boards have shifted again and again over the years. Stakeholder capitalism versus shareholder capitalism. It's about who bears the risk and who reaps the rewards.

In the context of ESG investing, a material risk refers to a risk that is significant enough to potentially affect a company's financial performance or reputation. The word was first introduced in the U.S. Securities Act of 1933, defined as 'those matters as to which an average prudent investor ought reasonably to be informed before purchasing the security registered' (Katz and McIntosh, 2021).

Currently, companies determine for themselves whether such issues are material or immaterial. European regulators have attempted to address the need for investors to have more information on ESG factors and whether they have financial significance. The concept of double materiality recognizes that corporate information can be important not only for its financial implications but also for its impact on the world at large, especially concerning climate change. Therefore, a company's impact beyond financial performance is material and worth disclosing.

A beginner's guide to sustainable investment

There are no investment returns at all on a planet left uninhabitable by climate change. (Armstrong, 2020)

Governments across the globe are looking to restructure economies to reduce net greenhouse gas emissions to zero and decouple growth from resource use – most see finance and investment as essential tools. The EU has led the way on financial services legislation, but other jurisdictions are picking up the regulatory baton. The Biden administration is moving into standard-setting. The EU and the UK have committed to efforts to increase environmental protection while promoting sustainable trade. Meanwhile, Japan has signed up to the International Platform on Sustainable Finance, which now has 16 members, including Switzerland and Norway.

It's clear that investors and consumers are in lockstep in their expectations. According to business advice consultancy finnCap (2020), 90 per cent of Millennials want to invest in ESG-compliant companies, with 84 per cent already doing so. Large companies with resources and sustainability teams find it easy to draft policies and guidelines, develop green products and enter into high-level agreements to prove both intention and delivery. With current rating efforts by indexes and platforms skewed towards larger firms, ESG-compliant SMEs run the risk of losing out.

Small businesses, on the other hand, can often make decisions faster, have less bureaucracy and are more flexible compared to larger organizations. Additionally, they may have a closer relationship with their customers due to being local and having a product story that resonates with consumers on an emotional level. And despite smaller profit margins, small businesses have the potential to save significant amounts of money by making simple changes such as switching to digital receipts, minimizing packaging sizes and volume, or reusing props from an event.

finnCap (2020) suggests three ways smaller companies can highlight their credentials: obtain environmental data points; demonstrate that they are delivering sustainable, both social and environmental, practices; and promote more diversity at every level – but especially at senior and board levels.

'... ESG concerns are no longer simply a way to signal a company's caring credentials – they are a fundamental part of sustainable business success,' stated finnCap's CEO Sam Smith (2020).

There are already some systems in place that measure performance and show opportunities for both brands and a new wave of investors and VCs. In the US, for instance, white employees comprise 72 per cent of the venture capital workforce and investment professionals overall (Deloitte, 2021). This is both a challenge – homogenous investment teams can lead to selection bias, according to a report by RateMyInvestor in partnership with Diversity VC (2017) – and an opportunity for firms like LA-based Muse Capital, which invests in consumer tech with a focus on underserved markets and advocates for diversity and inclusion in start-ups.

According to research by West River Group (2021), homogenous teams in venture capital are bad for business. Companies with diverse executive teams are 48 per cent more likely to produce a better rate of investment and derive 45 per cent of their revenue from innovation compared to homogenous teams, which derive just 26 per cent of their revenue from new ideas.

Meanwhile, Antoine Baschiera, co-founder of Earl Metrics, which provides data on early-stage companies for investors, has found VCs are becoming increasingly interested in how start-ups are scoring on their ESG policies and practices (Clawson, 2021). Start-ups that don't measure up from the outset may find it difficult to deal with regulatory, legal or reputational issues at a later stage. Investors have been spooked by the difficulties faced by the likes of Uber and Deliveroo, for instance, who have faced court action over their employment policies in the UK (Clawson, 2021).

Anna Sweeting and Montse Suarez, co-founders of Vaultier7, the UK's first female-led specialist investment fund, suggest simple ways start-ups and SMEs can secure the attention of ESG focussed investors.

'Certification can help a business achieve milestones,' says Sweeting. 'I think a big opportunity is amazing tech. A Vaultier7 family brand called Joone has radical transparency as its core value. It is collaborating with DOORZ, a blockchain-based traceability platform that allows real-time, transparent, and secure access to their suppliers and partners.'

'Talent is another opportunity,' adds Suarez. 'By hiring young, diverse talent, you can position yourself to the younger generation. Your business will understand the consumer better if it is more representative of the consumer. Investors are seeing proven results for companies with more ethnic diversity, and positive ESG metrics' (Positive Luxury, 2021).

Sustainable finance

The most progressive organizations are restructuring their leadership and the makeup of their departments. Most companies today are accelerating the restructuring of their sustainability and finance functions. As sustainability is becoming a regulated field, reporting with accuracy is becoming mandatory, and it will be as binding as your financial report.

Most listed companies will need to have a Task Force on Climate-Related Finance Disclosures (TCFD) framework and, depending on their jurisdiction, they will need to comply with Europe's Corporate Sustainability Reporting Directive, the European Financial Reporting Advisory Group, the international Global Reporting Initiative, and SASB.

This framework is based on a comparative ESG metric, which will help companies better understand what needs addressing in order to identify risks and prioritize them.

What this all means is the investment community will have a comparative set of data that will enable it for the first time to properly understand how companies are progressing toward sustainability.

Up to now, ESG and sustainability were interchangeable concepts and, more often than not, external facing for communications to consumers and or other stakeholders.

Today ESG is a framework that enables companies to understand which areas need to be transformed in order to drive efficiencies and how the outcomes of those strategies can be communicated.

This is usually discussed in terms of impact – another one of those over-used words that have no meaning anymore. Impact is really the consequence resulting from an action. It sits in the past, not in the future. Measuring what you have done is hardly something noteworthy. It is a hygiene factor and a necessary step to reimagine the future.

We are entering the action paradigm, where we need to focus on outcomes – whether positive or negative – so companies need to start shifting their mindset and treat environmental and societal risk almost like a balance sheet. They need to ensure that they are in the black, not in the red. As new regulations apply and finance focuses its concerns on ESG metrics, being in the red more than in the black will have implications for businesses.

Brand and investor perspective

'We want to do what's right for the world, but there is a competitive advantage in being a sustainable business. We are profit-driven but sustainability helps create that profit. It turns out that things that are good are also good for business,' said Enrique Lax Banon of White & Blue Capital (Positive Luxury, 2022).

For every product, there is a sustainable way of doing business and an unsustainable way, says Lapo Favilli, Bluegem Capital. 'In a nutshell, a strong ESG proposition is likely to become a key element of a company's long-term success in our sector,' he explained (Positive Luxury, 2021).

New investors like Naval Ravikant, who founded AngelList and democratized early investments, and old school VCs with new school attitudes like Skype founder Niklas Zennström's London-based venture capital firm Atomico are interested in more than just the 'E' in ESG.

'For example, at Conran they pay the London Living Wage,' Enrique Lax Banon explained. 'This has led to more engaged employees and less turnover as a result – a demonstration of how ESG has a commercial advantage. But certification is important. You need a third party to show that this is real – this builds trust with consumers and gives a tangible commercial advantage' (Positive Luxury, 2021).

Getting certification is particularly important for start-ups and SMEs who lack the oversight of a plc or the desire to borrow as extensively as Chanel with such high-risk defaults built in. Amongst other certification programmes, Positive Luxury offers the Butterfly Mark – the luxury industry's leading sustainability certification. There are other options, some specific to markets or to areas in the supply chain. All can offer investors valuable checks on performance.

Those investors still applying the old rules aren't appealing to the new wave of sustainable start-ups who believe innovation is best achieved without undue pressure. These ESG-native start-ups and SMEs are looking to build a new kind of relationship with investors based on trust as much as strategic ambition.

Key actions and takeaways

Sustainability and ESG metrics have finally become essential to measure the E, S and G performance of businesses and for that they rely on ESG metrics to be able to understand where the business is at. What is needed now is for the rating companies to decouple E, S and G metrics instead of blending them in order to give a single score that in my view is meaningless, as it is like comparing bananas and apples. Yes, both are fruit but they are not comparable.

Talking with Martin Townsend at the British Standards Institution (BSI), he explained that standards play an important and sometimes undervalued role in driving change, providing a route to sharing best practice, or providing transparency through associated second or third party audit programmes to assist organizations wherever they are on their environmental, social, and corporate governance (ESG) journey, and will help companies overcome the balance between greenwashing and greenhushing.

The BSI's sustainable finance standard provides a framework for organizations that wish to be sustainable and better aligned with global initiatives like the United Nations Sustainable Development Goals (UN SDGs) and the Paris Agreement. 'The framework recognizes that transformation is needed to equip the industry to address issues across all elements of ESG, including inequality, climate change, environmental degradation, poverty, prosperity, peace, and justice,' stated the BSI (2023) in a press release.

Here's a breakdown of some essentials for companies looking for funding.

Before talking to investors, SMEs should examine all areas of operations and supply chain. It's no longer just about climate change – it's about climate justice, so don't just look at the E in ESG. Honesty is essential. Greenwashing or social-washing is not… going to wash. As Chanel's green bonds show, investors are happy to back companies that report accurately, set honest targets, and strive to meet them.

1 Be committed, bold and resolute
Wherever your business is on its sustainability journey, set yourself ambitious and achievable targets and deadlines. Commit to meeting them. Do it. Failure is not an option.

2 Be transparent and accurate in your reporting
Investors need to know their money is being spent wisely. Honesty is essential. Don't fool yourself. You may have a long way to go, so being aware of where you're starting from is crucial. If you have to play the long game, short-term savings are a false economy. Success is not fleeting, it's your modus operandi.

3 ESG is more than just E
Social means looking at your social impact and examining your own staff. A diverse and inclusive workforce is proven to outperform homogeneous teams and closes the gap between a company and the consumer. Generation Z is increasingly diverse and vocal. A representative workforce and awareness of your supply chain's attitude and impacts will help understand their values, needs and wants. It also helps recruit this dynamic generation.

4 Leadership must live these values
No one likes being tricked by a business. Ensure your company has a clear mission and values as well as being commercially driven. Governance for SMEs means reporting structures are important.

5 Innovation is attractive and profitable
From working with your suppliers to packaging, from circular business models to technology that allows traceability and transparency – innovation at whatever level is attractive to investors. It also has unintended benefits. Innovation powerhouse 3M has over 100,000 patents thanks to its adaptability to problem-solving. Its Pollution Prevention Pays programme was established in 1975 to reduce toxins in factories and has up to now saved the company nearly $1.4 billion thanks to wide-ranging waste reduction inventions (3M, 2023). This takes courage, a measure of risk and a willingness to fail – but the rewards outstrip the risk.

Future gazing

The future of boards is evolving as organizations face new challenges and stakeholders demand increased accountability, transparency and diverse perspectives.

There is a growing recognition of the importance of diversity in boardrooms, including gender, ethnicity, age and professional backgrounds. Diversity is a plus across an organization but especially at a board level as it enhances decision-making, fosters innovation and better represents the interests of various stakeholders, including your customers.

Boards are shifting towards a more stakeholder-oriented approach, moving from focusing just on shareholder value to focusing on stakeholder value, including considering the interests of employees, customers, communities and the environment in their decision-making processes. This broader view of governance reflects a more holistic understanding of business outcomes and sustainability.

ESG metrics are gaining prominence in boardrooms too, as they are expected to oversee and integrate sustainability strategies, manage ESG risks and set long-term sustainability goals and mitigation plans to meet them. This includes addressing climate change, promoting responsible supply chains and ensuring ethical and just business practices.

Another important topic cropping up at the board level is the digital landscape as technology becomes increasingly integral to business operations. They are responsible for overseeing cybersecurity, data privacy and digital strategy, and harnessing the potential of emerging technologies like artificial intelligence, blockchain and automation.

Recent events, such as the Covid-19 pandemic, have highlighted the need for effective risk management, scenario planning and agile decision-making. Boards are expected to ensure robust crisis response plans and the ability to adapt to rapidly changing environments.

In recent years it is evident that they are paying more attention to the composition of boards and ensuring a balance of skills, experiences and backgrounds. They are seeking directors' expertise in areas such as technology, sustainability, finance, governance and risk management. Boards are also increasingly considering a broader range of candidates beyond traditional networks to bring fresh perspectives.

They are adopting practices such as board assessments, director education and development, succession planning and enhanced board refreshment strategies. This helps ensure that boards have the right mix of skills, competencies and dynamics to fulfil their responsibilities effectively.

As stakeholders are demanding greater transparency and accountability, including disclosure of board composition, decision-making processes, executive compensation and ESG performance metrics, today's boards are expected to communicate and engage with stakeholders, address concerns and demonstrate ethical behaviour.

The investment community is perhaps one of the most interested stakeholders in a company's ESG metric, especially now that the standardization of reporting frameworks will enable better comparison, but the elephant in the room is that the 'ESG' label has started to receive negative connotations, especially in America.

The reality is that there has never been a better framework, and although companies, especially luxury ones, are not talking publicly about ESG, they have operational plans and a corporate strategy that have social, environmental, governance and economic metrics.

Climate change is not going away, in fact most companies are building it into their strategies as more and more companies are committing billions if not trillions of dollars to adjust their operations and excel in a low carbon economy. Regulatory bodies are increasingly focusing on governance reforms and raising the bar for board oversight. New regulations and guidelines aim to strengthen board effectiveness, increase diversity and enhance board accountability. Boards need to stay informed about evolving regulations and ensure compliance.

All in all, the makeup of boards will change. In the not-too-distant future, it will include ESG and sustainability-savvy directors who will be able to see the risks and opportunities related to climate ahead. The nomination committees for developed-market boards with an abundance of older men should rethink their approach to board recruiting in order to have a more just representation of who their customers are.

If truth be told, I've struggled to find black, Latin, or any other minority community women at the helm or boards of luxury houses. Amidst the current climate of instability, the Global South appears to possess a higher level of readiness to manoeuvre through the unpredictable twists and turns of the economy and cope with the fluctuating supply chain due to the fact that such turbulence is an accepted aspect of their everyday life.

Women on boards are not just an issue for developed world companies as India has strengthened gender-diversity requirements to include an independent female director in the top 1,000 companies based on market cap. Korean companies will need to appoint at least one female director ahead of a new board-diversity regulation (MSCI, 2022) – and this is only the beginning. The age of women is coming as is the recognition that a more diverse board will pay dividends.

In 2023, we are moving from climate targets to climate transitional plans and implementation. In 2024, we will see how capital, financial and human resources are being allocated against those targets and plans in order to understand the viability of achieving those targets.

According to the MSCI (2022), 'financial-market participants subject to the EU's Sustainable Finance Disclosure Regulation (SFDR) must begin reporting Principal Adverse Impact indicators (PAIs) — the negative environmental or social impacts — associated with their portfolio holdings, and from 2024 they will also need to report year-on-year changes.'

The lungs of the world are being cut at a terrifying rate – the Amazon, that is. We will see from 2023 and accelerating in 2024, companies with high deforestation exposure upping their game on due diligence and supply-chain monitoring programmes as they seek to maintain access to key markets that ask for high levels of transparency.

A brief look at changing legislation

Note: this is a complex and changing area of legislation. Any book is a moment captured in time. The website Climate Change Laws of the World is constantly updated with new and amended legislation.

The 2022 US Inflation Reduction Act earmarked $369 billion for clean energy and climate-related projects and has already prompted BMW, Italian energy group Enel and Norwegian battery group Freyr to boost US investment (Thomas, 2023). The law intends to stimulate investment in emerging clean energy technologies by providing a system of tax credits and also rewards companies for setting up in the US, and for reorganizing supply chains to be located in the US.

The EU's Net Zero Industry Act, announced in spring 2023, sets out targets to 'scale up manufacturing of clean technologies in the EU and make sure the Union is well-equipped for the clean-energy transition'. The Act, according to the Commission, is aimed at increasing the resilience of Europe's clean energy supply chains and preventing the EU from relying on countries like Russia and China. It is intended to guarantee that at least 40 per cent of the bloc's clean tech needs are met domestically by 2030 (European Commission, 2023).

China's Banking and Insurance Regulatory Commission 2022 green finance guidelines are the first time China's financial regulator has specified green finance and ESG requirements for banks, insurance companies and insurance asset management companies. The rules require banks and insurers to 'promote green finance at a strategic level, reduce the carbon intensity of their asset portfolios, and eventually achieve carbon neutrality of asset portfolios' (China Daily, 2022).

The UK's Financial Conduct Authority (FCA) has increased its scrutiny and oversight of ESG 'including investment product sustainability labels and restrictions on how terms like "ESG", "green" or "sustainable" can be used' in a bid to combat greenwashing and 'build trust and integrity in ESG-labelled instruments, products and the supporting ecosystem' according to the FCA (2022). At the time of writing, the final rules had not yet been published by the FCA.

Final thoughts for investors

Do you see sustainability as a risk, an opportunity or a responsibility for your company?

Although ESG has become a central topic in the sustainability discussion, the term itself tends to limit the conversation to financial risks and strategies to mitigate them.

'All too often, companies and business leaders are not getting any insights from ESG analyses because they approach the issue solely as a reporting exercise,' stated Julia Binder, Professor of Sustainable Innovation and Business Transformation at IMD (Binder, 2023). 'While this "tick-box" approach requires an incredible amount of data, it does not offer any insights on how to seize the enormous opportunities of sustainable transformation.' There is so much more to ESG than just finance. Technology can help – and developing such technology is an enormous opportunity.

Shifting away from a risk mindset and embracing sustainability is both an opportunity and a responsibility for your company. Prioritizing sustainability can help you tap into new markets, meet changing customer needs, and attract and retain top talent. A recent study by McKinsey estimated that the transition to net zero alone will provide business opportunities of $12 trillion a year by 2030 (Binder, 2023).

So, do you lead or follow?

References

3M (2023) Sustainability, www.3m.co.uk/3M/en_GB/graphics-and-signage-uk/resources/Sustainability/ (archived at https://perma.cc/9E4P-YY8J)

Armstrong, R (2020) The fallacy of ESG investing, *Financial Times*, 23 October, www.ft.com/content/9e3e1d8b-bf9f-4d8c-baee-0b25c3113319 (archived at https://perma.cc/CG8K-B5EV)

Armstrong, S (2023) Meet the Earth's lawyers, Wired, 6 January, www.wired.com/story/clientearth-lawyers-defending-environment/ (archived at https://perma.cc/NB46-KFTQ)

Binder, J (2023) Let's be clear: ESG is not 'woke' and it's different from sustainability, IbyIMD, Institute for Management Development, 23 February, www.imd.org/ibyimd/magazine/lets-be-clear-esg-is-not-woke-and-its-different-from-sustainability/ (archived at https://perma.cc/G9W9-E5CC)

BlackRock (2022) BlackRock reports full year 2021 diluted EPS of $38.22, or $39.18 as adjusted Fourth Quarter 2021 Diluted EPS of $10.63, or $10.42 as adjusted, Financial Statement, 14 January, https://s24.q4cdn.com/856567660/files/doc_financials/2021/Q4/BLK-4Q21-Earnings-Release.pdf (archived at https://perma.cc/CP5L-HQP6)

BlackRock (2023) Investment Stewardship. 2023 Policies Summary, www.blackrock.com/corporate/literature/fact-sheet/blk-responsible-investment-global-policies-summary-2023.pdf (archived at https://perma.cc/UN7N-33JJ)

BSI (2023) 'Consistency, collaboration and coherence' vital to embedding sustainability in global finance sector, 28 February, www.bsigroup.com/en-GB/about-bsi/media-centre/press-releases/2023/february/consistency-collaboration-and-coherence-vital-to-embedding-sustainability-in-global-finance-sector/ (archived at https://perma.cc/NFW4-S5N8)

Byrne, D (2022) Companies with strong ESG perform better, Corporate Governance Institute, 29 July, www.thecorporategovernanceinstitute.com/insights/news-analysis/companies-with-good-esg-perform-better/ (archived at https://perma.cc/T7HT-3BKH)

Chanel (2020) Chanel Limited financial results for the year ended 31 December 2019 [Press Release], https://services.chanel.com/media/files/chanel_limited_financial_results_for_the_year_ended_31_december_2019.pdf (archived at https://perma.cc/SL4X-YATG)

China Daily (2022) Guidelines in place to support green finance, English.Gov.Cn, https://english.www.gov.cn/policies/policywatch/202206/08/content_WS629fe148c6d02e533532bd53.html (archived at https://perma.cc/8SE3-8J34)

Clawson, T (2021) The citizen startup—why investors are becoming more interested in ESG measures, Forbes, 27 May, www.forbes.com/sites/trevorclawson/2021/05/27/the-citizen-startupwhy-investors-are-becoming-more-interested-in-esg-measures/?sh=18a4d6974ef6 (archived at https://perma.cc/V4KD-DP3U)

Deloitte (2020) Fashion & Luxury Private Equity and Investors Survey 2020, Global Report, March, www2.deloitte.com/content/dam/Deloitte/pt/Documents/consumer-business/deloitte-ch-en-2020-global-fashion-luxury-private-equity-survey.pdf (archived at https://perma.cc/U76D-HRVT)

Deloitte (2021) VC Human Capital Survey, third edition, March, www2.deloitte.com/content/dam/Deloitte/us/Documents/audit/vc-human-capital-survey-3rd-edition-2021.pdf (archived at https://perma.cc/VR5T-Q6RW)

European Commission (2023) Net-Zero Industry Act: Making the EU the home of clean technologies manufacturing and green jobs, 16 March, https://ec.europa.eu/commission/presscorner/detail/en/IP_23_1665 (archived at https://perma.cc/E7QT-RV9L)

European Commission, Climate Action (no date) International climate finance, https://climate.ec.europa.eu/eu-action/international-action-climate-change/international-climate-finance_en (archived at https://perma.cc/7ZZD-AX6Z)

European Commission, Finance (2018) Overview of sustainable finance, https://finance.ec.europa.eu/sustainable-finance/overview-sustainable-finance_en (archived at https://perma.cc/AS2V-HCXW)

FCA (2022) FCA proposes new rules to tackle greenwashing, 25 October, www.fca.org.uk/news/press-releases/fca-proposes-new-rules-tackle-greenwashing (archived at https://perma.cc/TL43-5FRW)

Fink, L (2018) Larry Fink's annual letter to CEOs: A sense of purpose, BlackRock, October, https://aips.online/wp-content/uploads/2018/04/Larry-Fink-letter-to-CEOs-2018-BlackRock.pdf (archived at https://perma.cc/Z7GE-QC3V)

finnCap (2020) An ESG handbook and toolkit, Q4, www.finncap.com/uploads/media/5f5a05b85a87a/esg-focus-q4-2020.pdf?v1 (archived at https://perma.cc/9CSS-KLRL)

Katz, D A and McIntosh, L A (2021) Corporate governance update: 'Materiality' in America and Abroad, Harvard Law School Forum on Corporate Governance, 1 May, https://corpgov.law.harvard.edu/2021/05/01/corporate-governance-update-materiality-in-america-and-abroad/ (archived at https://perma.cc/V3HE-KYR2)

Lenhard, J (2021) European VC funds are building community around ESG initiatives. TechCrunch, 11 February, https://techcrunch.com/2021/02/11/european-vc-funds-are-building-community-around-esg-initiatives/ (archived at https://perma.cc/VRV2-T39E)

Masters, B (2022) Business is caught in political crossfire of ESG disputes, *Financial Times*, 6 December, www.ft.com/content/b050a037-9047-4f77-ad3c-ff40ed4fd5bc (archived at https://perma.cc/WJ3P-P4GS)

McPherson, S (2019) Corporate responsibility: What to expect in 2019, Forbes, 14 January, www.forbes.com/sites/susanmcpherson/2019/01/14/corporate-responsibility-what-to-expect-in-2019/?sh=33b37e1d690f (archived at https://perma.cc/P2MV-SA46)

Mooney, A (2021) Investors pile $54bn in to ESG bond funds in fiery start to 2021, *Financial Times*, 25 June, www.ft.com/content/af62e245-a136-40c1-b53d-89795b507d45 (archived at https://perma.cc/9MSZ-64FP)

MSCI (2022) ESG and Climate Trends to Watch for 2023, www.msci.com/documents/1296102/35124068/ESG+and+Climate+Trends+to+Watch+for+2023.pdf (archived at https://perma.cc/CEX6-CJX7)

Net-Zero Industry Act: Making the EU the home of clean technologies manufacturing and green jobs (2023), https://ec.europa.eu/commission/presscorner/detail/en/IP_23_1665 (archived at https://perma.cc/S22T-JFV7)

Positive Luxury (2021) The Sustainable Finance Revolution, November, www.positiveluxury.com/content/uploads/2021/11/PL_SustainableFinancePaper_Jul21.pdf (archived at https://perma.cc/T6BL-H4YA)

Positive Luxury (2022) Return on Sustainability Investment, July, www.positiveluxury.com/content/uploads/2022/07/PL_SustainabilityReturnsJul13.pdf (archived at https://perma.cc/FDA2-XSCS)

RateMyInvestor and DiversityVC (2017) Diversity in U.S. Startups, https://ratemyinvestor.com/pdfjs/full?file=%2FDiversityVCReport_Final.pdf (archived at https://perma.cc/G2PR-RTM5)

Reuters (2020) Fashion label Chanel issues bond linked to climate targets, 24 September, www.reuters.com/article/us-chanel-bond-idUSKCN26F2ZF (archived at https://perma.cc/SY93-2ZJU)

TCFD Task Force on Climate-related Financial Disclosures (2020a) Climate change presents financial risk to the global economy, 21 September, www.fsb-tcfd.org (archived at https://perma.cc/4VEF-SDLR)

TCFD Task Force on Climate-related Financial Disclosures (2020b) About, 22 September, www.fsb-tcfd.org/about/ (archived at https://perma.cc/QWT8-DL3L)

Thomas, N (2023) Investing in the green hydrogen 'revolution', Investment Week, 06 April, www.investmentweek.co.uk/opinion/4111722/investing-green-hydrogen-revolution (archived at https://perma.cc/2DZJ-46AX)

United Nations (2021) Secretary-General's statement on the conclusion of the UN Climate Change Conference COP26, 13 November, www.un.org/sg/en/content/sg/statement/2021-11-13/secretary-generals-statement-the-conclusion-of-the-un-climate-change-conference-cop26 (archived at https://perma.cc/6BHQ-VBCY)

West River Group (2021) The Power of Diversity: Why homogeneous teams in venture capital are bad for business, 21 September, www.wrg.vc/white-paper (archived at https://perma.cc/GT5B-DR6T)

Whieldon, E and Clark, R (2021) ESG funds beat out S&P 500 in 1st year of COVID-19; how 1 fund shot to the top, S&P Global Market Intelligence, 6 April, www.spglobal.com/marketintelligence/en/news-insights/latest-news-headlines/ esg-funds-beat-out-s-p-500-in-1st-year-of-covid-19-how-1-fund-shot-to-the-top-63224550 (archived at https://perma.cc/SD6F-EJFP)

Wick, B (2023) Republicans swim against tide of ESG money, Reuters, 2 March, www.reuters.com/legal/government/republicans-swim-against-tide-esg-money-2023-03-02/ (archived at https://perma.cc/E2Q9-RWZ5)

Worstall, T (2012) The story of Henry Ford's $5 a day wages: it's not what you think, Forbes, 4 March, www.forbes.com/sites/timworstall/2012/03/04/the-story-of-henry-fords-5-a-day-wages-its-not-what-you-think/?sh=1352be17766d (archived at https://perma.cc/ML6S-A7JV)

03

The legislative context

I thought it would be important to give you a bit of flavour on the legislative context, as a lot of the decision-making of business is being driven by the tsunami of legislation driven by the EU and up to a certain extent the USA.

I had the pleasure of speaking with Rachel MacLeod, Senior Associate, Competition Trade and Foreign Investment and Karen Roberts, Lead Knowledge Lawyer for CG&R, both for Baker McKenzie, one of the leading international law firms helping clients navigate through strategic and operational business challenges, working across borders to find simple, creative solutions in response to legal and commercial developments affecting their business.

Karen started by explaining that 'there is an increasing abundance of legislation around sustainability impacting players in the luxury and fashion industry'. In this chapter we look at legal trends and developments falling within two key themes to help companies navigate their current and future obligations and responsibilities. First, we consider the development of circular economy-driven laws which aim to ensure products are more sustainable and curtail the use of the 'take, make, break and throw away' model. Then we move on to consider the evolving framework of supply chain due diligence legislation aimed at promoting sustainable and responsible business behaviour throughout the entire supply or value chain.

Circular economy

EU Green Deal

The European Union has taken a formative role in sustainability legislation. The European Green Deal is the European Union's flagship decarbonization strategy and was launched in 2019. The Green Deal sets the target of a carbon neutral Europe by 2050 (i.e. 'net zero' – any residual emissions in the EU would be compensated by carbon removals) and aims to mainstream climate and environmental objectives into all sectors of the economy through legislative action. The Green Deal in itself is neither a piece of legislation nor a specific policy. However, the measures and regulations introduced as part of this strategy will be tremendously impactful for consumers and companies throughout the EU.

One of the main objectives of the EU Green Deal when it comes to retail is to encourage a circular economy where the lifecycle of goods and products are fully considered. Two policy plans included in the Green Deal supporting the circular economy, and particularly impacting the fashion and luxury industry, are:

- the EU Circular Economy Action Plan
- the EU Strategy for Sustainable and Circular Textiles

which both aim to promote longer-lasting products that can be repaired, recycled and re-used and to empower consumers to be able to make informed and environmentally friendly choices when purchasing products. These plans are going to be implemented by a number of legislative and non-legislative measures, including many discussed further in the sections below.

The concept of circularity is already resonating with the public. In the Sustainable Products Initiative and Deloitte Sustainability & Consumer Behaviour Survey 2022 it was found that UK consumers are embracing 'circularity' with 53 per cent claiming to have repaired an item instead of replacing it with a new equivalent and 38 per cent paying extra for a more durable or longer-lasting product.

Ecodesign for Sustainable Products Regulation

Building on the Ecodesign Directive 2009, the proposed Ecodesign for Sustainable Products Regulation seeks to establish a framework to set ecodesign requirements for specific product groups to significantly improve their circularity, energy performance and other environmental sustainability aspects. Although currently in draft form, the framework will allow for the setting of a wide range of requirements, including on:

- product durability, reusability, upgradability and reparability
- presence of substances that inhibit circularity

- energy and resource efficiency
- recycled content
- remanufacturing and recycling
- carbon and environmental footprints
- information requirements, including a Digital Product Passport

Textiles and fashion is one of the areas particularly referenced in discussion around this Regulation and it will be on fashion brands to:

- look at product-specific performance requirements to increase textiles durability, reparability, recyclability and fibre-to-fibre recyclability
- provide better information to consumers and along the value chain
- take responsibility for the waste their goods create

We are already seeing fashion brands tackling the issue of circularity with investments into R&D as well as new sustainable textiles, utilizing recyclable waste, providing more information on products and providing in-store used clothing collection facilities.

Greenwashing

Greenwashing is the practice of publishing misleading sustainability claims by companies and is currently a very hot topic for regulators. In a recent study by McKinsey – 'Do consumers really care about ESG?' – the results showed that when you look across a broad set of product purchases, there's a clear link between ESG-related claims and sales growth. Products that didn't have ESG-related claims on their labels grew, on average, 4.7 per cent per year over the course of the past five years, while products that did have ESG claims grew 6.4 per cent. In consumer-packaged goods, which generally grows in line with the economy, that difference is significant. The study also found that putting more than one ESG-related claim on a product label correlated with two times greater growth than putting only one claim on the label. With such an impact on consumer behaviour, the incentive to put sustainability related claims on products and in marketing material is huge. However, companies must ensure the language used is clear and accurate and any claims made are supported by evidence. Failure to do so risks reputational damage, regulatory enforcement and potential financial penalties as well as the possibility of being held to account in litigation.

Many greenwashing claims may be caught by general legislation and guidelines in relation to misleading marketing and advertising claims. However, more and more jurisdictions are implementing greenwashing specific legislation or guidelines.

In March 2023, the European Commission adopted a proposal for a Directive on Green Claims. The proposed Directive requires companies to substantiate any voluntary claims made about the environmental aspects of their products using scientific and verifiable methods and to follow specific rules when presenting such claims to consumers. This followed another proposal published in March 2022 (as part of the Sustainable Products Initiative) which will ban the use of generic and vague environmental claims (such as 'eco' or 'green') except for where the excellent environmental performance of a product can be demonstrated and to ban the use of voluntary sustainability labels where these are not based on a third party verification scheme or established by public authorities.

In 2021, the UK published a Green Claims Code, which serves as a checklist for businesses to consider prior to making any green claims. The UK regulator promised that regulatory action would follow and has already launched investigations into greenwashing claims involving the fashion sector. It is currently reviewing the use of green claims by the FMCG sector and has indicated that it will target travel and transport next. The UK Advertising Standards Authority (ASA) has also published a number of recent rulings criticizing the use of green claims and this is a trend reflected across many EU jurisdictions as well. In the US, greenwashing lawsuits continue to be brought by NGOs, consumers, competitors and investors, primarily under state consumer protection laws and federal securities laws. In California, the Truth in Labelling for Recyclable Materials bill, which will come into force on 1 January 2024, will limit the use of the chasing arrows symbol or the word 'recyclable' to products that actually get recycled (versus being capable of being recycled). While the primary focus of the law is to increase the amount of plastic that actually gets recycled, its ancillary focus is on greenwashing to avoid the illusion of recycling.

It is imperative for businesses to continue to be rigorous in the review of company communications across the board and to be aware of how to speak about ESG issues in product claims and other public documents/disclosures to ensure consistency and accuracy. Be on the lookout for new regulatory developments on the horizon, including in the US where a long-awaited review of the FTC Green Guides and the new proposed SEC rules are anticipated. The latter are expected to mandate public disclosure of a greater amount of climate-related information that could potentially have material impacts on the veracity of claims businesses make on products and packaging.

Guidance on green claims:

• Ensure that you keep up to date with the latest measures and guidance on greenwashing and assess their impact on your business as soon as possible to prepare a strategy for implementing the requirements.

• Analyse your marketing strategy in relation to claims, provide training to your marketing teams and consider implementing sign-off processes and effective controls on the use of green claims.

• Retain product lifecycle data and objective evidence to substantiate any claims made.

• Include ESG data collection and verification provisions when contracting with third party suppliers of product parts and materials.

• Prepare to set up a website that will contain relevant information relating to the substantiation of green claims, including a summary, in easily understandable language.

Plastics

Plastics are being increasingly regulated globally amongst growing public awareness of the impact of the use and disposal of plastic products on the environment. Countries are approaching plastic regulation in different ways with measures ranging from plastic taxes to single use plastic bans to microbead bans to deposit return schemes and consumer charges to discourage consumption (e.g. carrier bag charges).

In the EU, a specific Plastics Strategy has been introduced. One of the measures consists of a Plastics Own Resource known as the EU Packaging Levy (in place since January 2021), which requires Member States to pay a contribution based on the amount of non-recycled plastic packaging waste they generate. This has spawned the development of new plastic taxes in certain Member States such as Spain and Italy. The UK has also introduced its own Plastic Packaging Tax (PPT) payable by UK manufacturers of plastic packaging as well as businesses that import plastic packaging into the UK. Crucially, even if not liable for PPT, downstream businesses in the UK that handle plastic packaging need to undertake due diligence on their suppliers to ensure that they are not found jointly and severally liable for any unpaid tax within their supply chains.

Further at the EU level, the existing Single Use Plastics Directive applies different measures to different products to reduce the use of plastic. These measures are designed to be proportionate and tailored to get the most effective results. Where sustainable alternatives are easily available and affordable, single-use plastic products cannot be placed on the markets of EU Member States. This applies to cotton bud sticks, cutlery, plates, straws, stirrers and sticks for balloons. It will also apply to cups, food and beverage containers made of expanded polystyrene, and on all products made of oxo-degradable plastic.

For other single-use plastic products, the EU is focusing on limiting their use through:

- reducing consumption through awareness-raising measures
- introducing design requirements, such as a requirements to connect caps to bottles
- introducing labelling requirements, to inform consumers about the plastic content of products, disposal options that are to be avoided and harm done to nature if the products are littered in the environment
- introducing waste management and clean-up obligations for producers, including Extended Producer Responsibility (EPR) schemes

Another initiative by the EU is the proposed Packaging and Packaging Waste Regulation. A key objective of the initiative is to ensure that all packaging is reusable or recyclable in an economically feasible way by 2030. It also seeks to increase the use of recycled content in packaging, tackle issues associated with over-packaging and reduce the amount of packaging waste produced in the EU.

On a more global level, earlier this year, 175 nations at the UN Environment Assembly (UNEA-5) endorsed a resolution to end plastic pollution and propose an international legally binding agreement by 2024. The resolution addresses the full lifecycle of plastic including its production, design and disposal and establishes an international intergovernmental negotiating committee to work out the details. With this, we anticipate that more regulatory action is likely to be in the pipeline over the next few years across many jurisdictions.

Such action is forcing brands to be more inventive in order to eliminate plastics from the supply chain where possible.

Guidance on plastics

When reviewing plastic taxes:

- determine the plastics or products that are in the scope of the tax regulation, plus the exceptions noting relevant thresholds
- review taxable operations or transactions
- determine the relevant taxpayer (is it the manufacturer or is it the company who uses the packaging?)
- actively consider alternatives to plastic

Supply chain due diligence

One of the fastest developing areas in ESG legislation is the evolving framework of supply chain due diligence legislation aimed at promoting sustainable and responsible business behaviour throughout the entire supply or value chain. This covers many areas of ESG and places a particular responsibility and burden on businesses.

New and developing legislation around the world is forcing organizations to more closely address issues associated with human rights, forced labour and the environment in both their own businesses and supply chains. Whilst the initial legislative framework in this area was primarily focused on reporting requirements, which is an area that continues to develop, new and proposed legislation is now placing more substantive obligations on organizations in terms of ESG due diligence and supply chain accountability.

Forced labour

Forced labour covers a number of scenarios from compelling someone to work against their will to more subtle scenarios where identity papers are retained or employers apply manipulated debt. The ILO Forced Labor Convention 1930 defines forced labour as 'all work or service which is exacted from any person under the threat of a penalty and for which the person has not offered himself or herself voluntarily'.

Many countries are formally adopting legislation to place more substantive obligations on organizations in terms of human rights due diligence and supply chain accountability in order protect workers against such practices. Below are some examples of such legislation:

- UK Modern Slavery Act
- California Transparency in Supply Chains Act
- French Duty of Vigilance Law
- Australian Modern Slavery Act
- Dutch Child Labour Due Diligence Law
- German Supply Chain Due Diligence Act
- USA Uyghur Forced Labor Prevention Act
- California's Garment Worker Protection Act
- Canada's Fighting Against Forced Labour and Child Labour in Supply Chains Act
- EU's proposed ban on products made using forced labour

Legislation of this nature makes it crucial for brands to know how and by whom their products are made, even if this is outsourced to third parties, and for them to proactively seek information and documentation from their supply chain partners. This is likely to require the insertion of provisions in supply contracts to make both working conditions and the reporting and documentation around such conditions an obligation on the supplier. This is applicable for all products, parts, components and materials.

Breaches of such legislation can have a real impact on a business. For example, suspected infringement of the USA Uyghur Forced Labor Prevention Act will mean that goods are denied entry into the US, having a material impact on supply chain, meeting orders and business continuation, as well as the cost consequences of delays and failing to meet order deadlines.

There is also a rise in class action litigation around workers' rights and conditions. Where workers and/or activists commence litigation against multinationals and brands for breaches of human rights and working conditions. Again, the effect of this is for brands to be actively engaged in monitoring and reviewing workers' conditions and ensuring they comply with acceptable standards, not just in their direct employment but in their full product supply chain.

EU Corporate Sustainability Reporting Directive (the CSRD): The CSRD entered into force on 5 January 2023 and requires large and listed companies to report on the social and environmental risks they face, and how their activities impact people and the environment. The CSRD also makes it mandatory for companies to have an audit of the sustainability information that they report. This provides greater transparency for stakeholders, shareholders and consumers, but also brings the risk of being held accountable for the claims and information they provide. The CSRD is being implemented in phases from 2025 to 2028 and will impact businesses at different times depending on size.

EU Corporate Sustainability Due Diligence Directive (CSDDD or CS3D): When in force this will require the adoption and implementation of effective due diligence policies to identify, prevent, mitigate and bring to an end actual and potential human rights and environmental harms in companies' business operations and value chains (both upstream and downstream). It also aims to impose new duties on company directors in relation to decisions they make that impact sustainability matters. The luxury and fashion sector, due to its long and complex value chains, will undoubtedly be significantly affected by the CSDDD. Moreover, luxury and fashion companies covered by the CSDDD will be required to adopt a plan to ensure that their business model and strategy is 'compatible with the transition to a sustainable economy and with the limiting of global warming to 1.5°C in line with the Paris Agreement'.

EU Deforestation Regulation: Of particular relevance to the fashion and cosmetics industries is the EU Deforestation Regulation which, from 2024, will require companies to undertake due diligence into the source of a wide range of commodities, including cattle, cocoa, coffee, palm-oil, rubber, soya, wood and leather to ensure that they have not been obtained as a result of deforestation. Businesses placing relevant products on the EU market (or exporting them) will be required to ensure that products are 'deforestation-free'. This means that products must be produced on land that has neither been deforested after the 31 December 2020 cut-off date, nor has seen primary and naturally growing forests converted into plantations. Further, products must have been produced in compliance with all applicable and relevant laws in force in the country of production. To comply with the Regulation, businesses will need to ensure that they have due diligence processes in place that include information gathering, risk assessment and risk mitigation measures. Businesses will also need to put in place appropriate processes to ensure that signed due diligence statements can be prepared in respect of all shipments.

Similar legislation is set to be implemented in the UK in respect of 'Forest Risk Commodities' as a result of provisions in the UK Environment Act.

General takeaways

- There is already a large body of existing legislation in this area globally and this is continuously evolving and developing. It has never been more important for companies to ensure that they are ahead of the legislative curve and have the right frameworks in place to enable them to prepare for and meet any future developments. This includes ensuring that companies set the right 'tone at the top'.

- There are many drivers behind these developments and scrutiny will not just come from regulators and governments, but also competitors, stakeholders and consumers. The issues covered by these developments can attract significant media attention, particularly with reference to modern slavery, human rights and other labour abuses in the supply chain.

- Compliance with requirements needs to be considered and planned for at the front end of product development to ensure the sustainability of products throughout their full lifecycle.

- Implementing effective strategies in this space will involve multiple teams within any company and require significant coordination and information sharing. Companies need to ensure that they have the right mechanisms in place to achieve this, Rachel MacLeod, Senior Associate, Competition Trade and Foreign Investment, Baker McKenzie and Karen Roberts, Lead Knowledge Lawyer for CG&R, Baker McKenzie concluded.

DISCLAIMER:
The material in this chapter is of the nature of general comment only. It is not offered as legal advice on any specific issue or matter and should not be taken as such. Readers should refrain from acting on the basis of any discussion contained in this publication without obtaining specific legal advice on the particular facts and circumstances at issue. While the author has made every effort to provide accurate and up-to-date information on laws and regulations, these matters are continuously subject to change. Furthermore, the application of these laws depends on the particular facts and circumstances

of each situation, and therefore readers should consult their attorney before taking any action.

ACKNOWLEDGEMENTS
Baker McKenzie brings insight and foresight to clients across more than 70 global offices. Their team of 13,000 people, including over 6,500 lawyers, works alongside their clients to drive growth that is both sustainable – and inclusive.

With a wealth of experience across all relevant areas of law, their lawyers help clients navigate through strategic and operational business challenges, working across borders to find simple, creative solutions in response to legal and commercial developments affecting their business. From luxury brands to high street fashion stores, from food and beverage companies to international hotel chains, they advise some of the largest consumer goods and retail companies worldwide – helping them respond to any challenge they face at every stage of the business cycle.

Reference

Deloitte and Sustainable Products Initiative (2022) Sustainability & Consumer Behaviour Survey, www2.deloitte.com/uk/en/pages/consumer-business/articles/sustainable-consumer.html (archived at https://perma.cc/5KEM-R2ES)

04

Sustainability and ESG in the luxury industry

In this chapter, we examine the difference between sustainability and ESG, discuss how companies need to adapt and innovate to be fit for the future and why luxury is best placed to lead the way.

The main overarching theme is that silos breed risk. The second – and one that should not generate despair – is that genuinely achieving sustainability is impossible. Sustainability is a journey, not a destination. It's like being human – you are never finished, but you can enjoy a journey of continuous improvement and learning.

Luxury has been 'fashionably' late to many parties – the digital party and now the sustainability, ESG disclosure and transparency one. Although the issue of sustainability is part of many luxury groups' narratives, it is not at a brand level. Perhaps because highlighting sustainability could dilute the perception of luxury itself. Sustainability is often associated with affordability and mass appeal.

Perhaps they did not want to talk too much about sustainability, because luxury brands often cultivate an image of exclusivity, craftsmanship and timeless elegance. 'I think luxury responded later to this than many other industries because they think that if they are talking too much about sustainability, they would dilute the message of luxury and leave their customers confused,' said Sylvain Guyoton, Chief Rating Officer at EcoVadis.

'Today the subject has become so important,' he continued, 'too important.'

Luxury brands may have sustainability initiatives or technologies that they prefer to keep private to maintain a competitive advantage as revealing all their sustainability efforts could make it easier for competitors to replicate their strategies. Or perhaps luxury brands might be cautious about discussing sustainability extensively because they want to avoid any perception of greenwashing.

All this is sheer speculation. Overall, the majority of luxury brands across all sectors invest significant resources in research and development, design and innovation and have made considerable capital investment in upgrading their factories, acquiring and developing their suppliers, upgrading their systems, innovating with white chemistry and rethinking materials and processes.

An example of this is Fendi's factory in Italy, featuring raised gardens that maintain the native flora and fauna, supports ecosystem management and blends the site into the landscape by restoring the existing hillside where the factory was previously built. Fendi is not alone in respecting nature. The Edrington Group, owner of the Macallan Whiskey brand, has upgraded its factory with cutting-edge modern technology and blended the new operation into the Scottish hills with a semi-subterranean set of buildings combining functionality, materials and nature tastefully disguised with the farmland above the river Spey.

Many luxury groups and brands have recognized the importance of sustainability and are actively integrating sustainable practices into their operations, product development and social practices. They understand that addressing sustainability is crucial for meeting evolving consumer expectations and ensuring long-term business success.

Above all, the subject has become so important that it can't be ignored anymore. Patou, for example, is a small luxury brand owned by the LVMH Group, which is the first to disclose (without being legally required to) the materials that they use in their products and their environmental impact.

The question is how this information is going to be used to optimize their business to sustainability, as knowledge and disclosure are not the only solution to achieve a net positive future.

Is this information going to inform their innovation strategy? Is it going to be used to rethink the way businesses are working with their suppliers in order to lower their environmental impact? Would they co-innovate and co-invest with their suppliers to help create efficiencies? How are they going to enhance their social good? Are businesses going to produce less products, fewer products, fewer collections and build fewer hotels? Or change their business model? Or perhaps open-source their knowledge and processes to achieve net positive outcomes benefiting people and our planet so others can learn?

To be fair, I would like to pause and celebrate Patou's bold leadership, as although the questions are valid to be asked, the first step of every journey is always the hardest and it takes courage to be one of the first.

People love luxury, what it represents, how it makes them feel and what other people think about them if they are wearing it, using it, driving it, staying in it or going to it – but the new luxury consumers need a little more: they need to know that the company stands for something bigger than themselves and the product/places they stay/drinks they chose to represent their values.

The climate crisis is one of the most critical challenges facing humanity today and we will only make a difference if every business and every individual, within a business or not, plays their part in building a sustainable future. Every organization needs to act to deliver change – which requires clear and realizable targets, strong measurement, transparent reporting and a change of mindset, and therefore organization culture.

What does sustainability mean? The term was first coined in 1987 by Gro Harlem Brundtland, twice prime minister of Norway, as 'meeting the needs of the present without compromising the ability of future generations to meet their own needs' (United Nations Brundtland Commission, 1987). Today there are 152 developing countries with a population of over 6.77 billion people, according to the IMF (2023). To put this in perspective, this is around 85.49 per cent of the world's population. In order to achieve sustainable development in the Global South it is crucial to balance social inclusion, better quality of life for more people, environmental protection and sustainable economic growth.

The relationship between the Global North and Global South in terms of sustainability is complex and multifaceted as the Global North has historically been the primary contributor to global environmental challenges such as climate change, resource depletion and pollution as it has higher levels of industrialization, consumption and greenhouse gas emissions. This historical responsibility means that the Global North has a greater obligation to address environmental issues and support sustainable development efforts in the Global South.

The developed world or Global North often possesses advanced technologies, scientific expertise and knowledge of sustainable practices. Transferring these technologies and sharing knowledge with the developing world or Global South can help accelerate sustainable development efforts. This transfer can enhance energy efficiency, promote renewable energy sources, improve agricultural practices and support sustainable urban planning in developing countries.

This is why it is so important that companies and their suppliers work collaboratively, as businesses are nimbler than governments to help affect change on the ground. Collaborative efforts can include sharing best practices, joint research and development, policy coordination, as well as co-investing in order to upgrade factories, buildings, waste streams, etc. This type of collaboration can lead to more just, effective and equitable solutions to global sustainability challenges, both social and environmental. But this begs two questions:

1 Where can you find the best collaboration partners?
2 Who will finance the partnership?

There are many, many companies out there – some of them highlighted throughout the book – born with sustainable thinking in their DNA, developing IP and with great energetic teams to help them grow; however, they don't have the financial muscle to scale up. Just like in the early days of the internet back in the year 2000, there are many great partnerships out there that can help you advance the status quo – you just need to find them.

I truly believe that luxury can lead the way, by using its influence and aspirational position to promote sustainable consumption and production patterns in the developed world, such as reducing waste, adopting circular economy principles, and supporting ethical and sustainable supply chains. Luxury can have positive effects on the aspirations of the Global South as well. Where I come from, the developing world also has unique contributions to make by preserving and restoring biodiversity, protecting traditional knowledge and practices, and adopting innovative approaches to sustainability challenges.

Achieving global sustainability requires a collective effort that recognizes the interdependence and shared responsibilities between the Global North and Global South. The challenge is vast and a lot more complex than what I just described; however, the outcomes that the luxury industry can drive, coupled with Hollywood, the hospitality and music industries, are unparalleled.

ESG (Environmental, Social, and Governance) is a framework used to assess how a company or investment impacts the world, giving insights into how a company's practices and operations impacts nature and society and its own governance structures. Evaluating ESG factors helps investors and stakeholders with their sustainability performance and with the potential impact on their financial performance.

Sustainability, on the other hand, focuses on ensuring that present actions do not compromise the ability of future generations to meet their needs. It involves a fine balance of managing sustainable economic growth, environmental stewardship and social wellbeing.

Reporting in compliance with CSRD requires businesses to account for double materiality, which means they will need to report on how organizations are impacted by environmental and social factors (outside in) and how the organization delivers net positive outcomes in society and nature (inside out). Double materiality emerged due to growing pressures from governments, investors and the general public to better address the role of a company delivering positive outcomes to nature and society.

'While sustainability is a broad concept that includes ESG, it also includes other goals such as resource conservation, energy efficiency and waste reduction. It's very common to confuse the two concepts because sustainability is often only considered from an environmental point of view,' explained Claudia Lazzari, ESG Officer at independent private equity firm Mindful Capital Partners. 'Greenhouse gas emissions, carbon footprint, climate change impacts, and overall energy management are part of this and are certainly the most important issues that investors assess, but it is also about responsible business practices and supply chain, fair wages, health and safety issues, and prioritizing diversity, equity and inclusion initiatives.'

To make this really easy:

Sustainability is the heart of the business.

ESG is the goals and metrics of the business

and sustainable innovation creates long-term value and futureproof organizations.

Whether you are a micro, small, medium or a listed company, there are so many benefits to using an ESG framework to understand your impacts and create holistic transitional plans to drive positive outcomes, contributing to both value creation and responsible business behaviours.

ESG can be a tick-box exercise if you wish, but it can also be a really good roadmap to help you identify the actions that you will need, in line with resource allocation, to achieve your long-term goals and targets. Utilizing an ESG framework will enable you to stay ahead of potential risks and adapt your strategies accordingly to address environmental and social challenges that could impact your operations, reputation and long-term sustainability. Furthermore, it can help you mitigate potential disruptions in your operations and financial performance, stay ahead of future regulations and minimize the risk of penalties, legal issues and reputational damage.

It is worth mentioning that as environmental issues vary from sector to sector, social issues remain pretty much the same across the industry and across sectors, with only a few minor variances: employee safety, working conditions, social dialogues, lack of employability measures, human rights and modern slavery are in most supply chains whether luxury or not.

This framework focuses on how a company manages its decision-making and interacts with all its stakeholders, whereas sustainability looks at how those decisions impact the world and communities that the company operates in. Under its three sections – Environment, Social and Governance – are grouped a wider cluster of drivers. Figure 4.1 should help to visualize this point.

The E of ESG

ESG frameworks have played a significant role in driving attention and action toward sustainability and responsible business practices. Although ESG has a wonderful ring to it, in my view, GES (Governance, Environmental and Social) perhaps makes more sense as the governance of the business ensures that the standards always apply in an accurate and transparent way and the company acts with absolute integrity and is accountable to all its stakeholders including its shareholders.

Identifying climate risks enables proactive measures to minimize and/or mitigate potential negative environmental impacts as they can have significant effects on operations, profitability and the long-term viability of the business.

The following is a short list of a company's potential climate risks:

- Physical risks are the direct consequences of climate-related events such as extreme weather events (e.g. hurricanes, floods, wildfires), rising sea levels, heat waves and changing precipitation patterns. These can lead to property damage and increase operational costs causing business disruptions. Transitional risks are normally associated with policy and regulatory changes, shifts in consumer preferences, technological advancements and market fluctuations in transitioning the business to a climate economy.

- Reputational risks are a reality in an era where companies that are perceived as not addressing climate change or contributing to

FIGURE 4.1 The ESG Framework

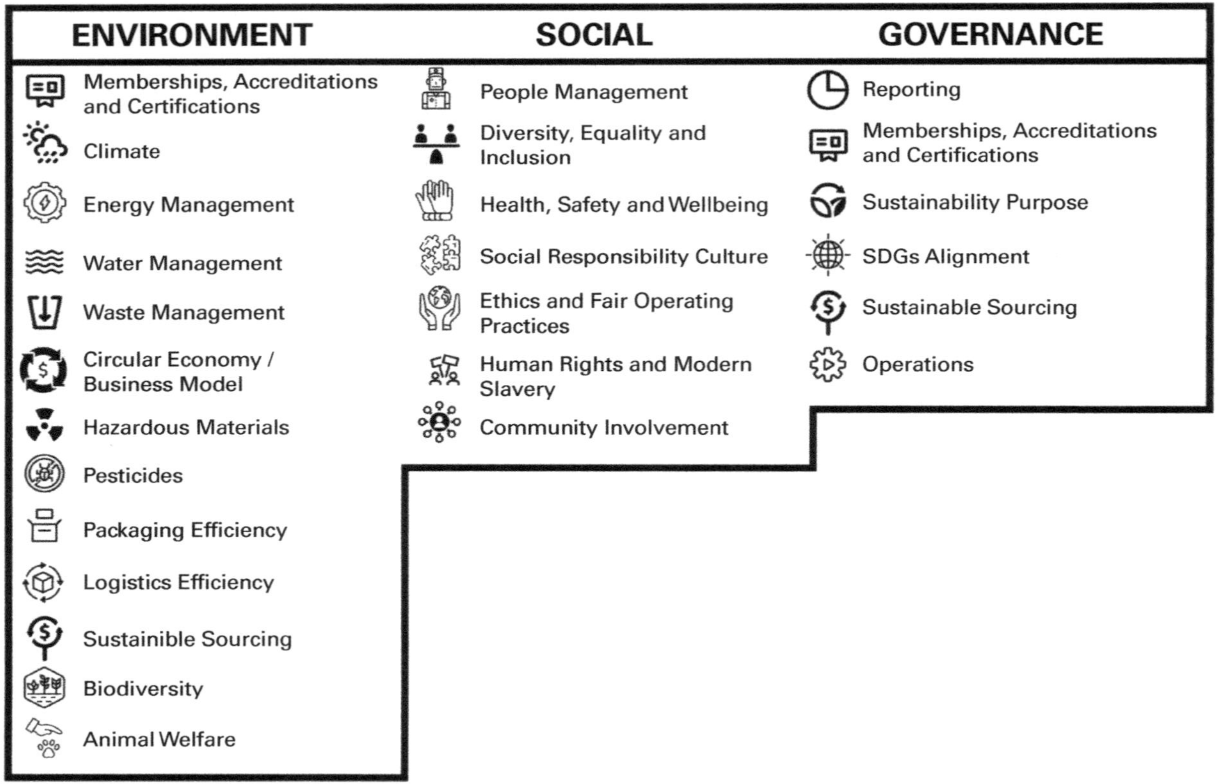

ENVIRONMENT	SOCIAL	GOVERNANCE
Memberships, Accreditations and Certifications	People Management	Reporting
Climate	Diversity, Equality and Inclusion	Memberships, Accreditations and Certifications
Energy Management	Health, Safety and Wellbeing	Sustainability Purpose
Water Management	Social Responsibility Culture	SDGs Alignment
Waste Management	Ethics and Fair Operating Practices	Sustainable Sourcing
Circular Economy / Business Model	Human Rights and Modern Slavery	Operations
Hazardous Materials	Community Involvement	
Pesticides		
Packaging Efficiency		
Logistics Efficiency		
Sustainible Sourcing		
Biodiversity		
Animal Welfare		

(Positive Luxury (2022)

environmental degradation can be cancelled, losing consumer trust and damaging the company's or brand reputation.

- New policies and regulations are being developed and updated by most governments, especially the USA and the European Union (see Chapter 9), with China following close behind, and leading in certain areas. To that effect companies may face legal challenges such as lawsuits for inadequate disclosure of climate-related risks or failure to address environmental harm not just from consumers but also from their suppliers' employees.

- Climate change has disrupted supply chains causing changes in agricultural productivity, water scarcity and increased resource constraints, making it more challenging for companies to have consistent quality in their raw materials, manufacturing and price. Perhaps one day even the luxury companies won't be able to source natural resources at scale due to cost and availability.

- Environmental and social impacts are interconnected and interrelated. Take air, water pollution, toxic chemical exposure and climate change for example. They will directly impact human health and quality of life. If these risks are foreseen, companies can take the appropriate actions to safeguard public health.

Climate risks can have significant financial implications for companies as they can result in increased costs for insurance, repairs and operational changes, as well as decreased asset values. Investors and financial institutions are increasingly incorporating climate-related risks into their investment decisions, and companies that are not adequately addressing climate risks may face difficulties in accessing capital or securing favourable financing terms.

In the last few years, there has been an exponential rise in the number of claims for climate-related damages, whether floods or fires or any other issues, which has left insurance companies not being able to renew existing policies or charging astronomical fees to do so.

This is not just for business but also has affected individuals all over the world. Insurance companies are now increasingly incorporating ESG factors into their risk assessment and underwriting practices. Some insurers are offering products that incentivize and reward environmentally responsible practices. Insurance costs should not be ignored when you are thinking about long-term business decisions.

The S of ESG

The social dimension of ESG refers to the company's performance and practices related to its people. This encompasses a wide range of considerations, including how a company manages relationships with its employees, suppliers, customers, communities and other stakeholders that involve the human touch.

Employee relations include factors such as fair and safe working conditions, equal opportunities, diversity, equality and inclusion, employee engagement, training and development programmes, mental health and many more.

Attracting and retaining talent is at stake across all industries, especially the travel, hospitality and service industries. Gen Z and young Millennials really want to work for companies that have sustainability as a core value and live it every day. In 2023 Paul Polman, former CEO of Unilever, outlined in his Net Positive Employee Barometer that there is an ambition gap. Even though many employees are aware that companies are taking some steps to address environmental and societal problems, approximately two out of three in each country say current efforts by businesses do not go far enough (68 per cent in the UK, 62 per cent in the US).

Many employees believe CEOs and senior leaders don't care about these issues. Almost half of UK employees (45 per cent) and over a third of US employees (39 per cent) believe these leaders are driven only by their own gain. Three-quarters say a company should take responsibility for its impact, not just on its employees and stakeholders, but on the wider world (77 per cent UK, 78 per cent US). Business, Polman argues, is sleepwalking into an era of conscious quitting.

Nearly half of employees say they would consider resigning from their job if the values of the company did not align with their own values (45 per cent UK, 51 per cent US). In fact, a third say they already have resigned from a position for this reason (35 per cent in both the UK and US). This number rises significantly among Gen Z and Millennial employees (48 per cent UK, 44 per cent US).

'There is clearly a pool of talent, energy and purpose that business leaders can tap into, trust, motivate and make them believe they can make a difference,' Polman told me. 'When we asked what is preventing employees from personally taking action to address environmental and societal issues, more than a quarter of Gen Z and Millennial employees say they don't know where to start [28 per cent UK, 28 per cent US], and many said they don't consider it part of their job [8 per cent UK, 34 per cent US], though clearly many would like it to be.'

'Companies need to show greater ambition, offer better communication and give agency to young people and proactively enrol them in the needed change plans. Although this may not sit comfortably with CEOs and the leadership team, this openness is the only way to give employees confidence that their company is taking action', said Polman.

Another aspect of the S of ESG is supply chain management and sustainable procurement – a company nowadays can't solely have a commitment to respecting and upholding human rights. Both within its operations and throughout its supply chain, it is necessary to ensure that periodic action is taken to ensure that there are no infringements in this area. This includes responsible sourcing, supplier diversity, equality and inclusion, labour standards, labour rights, child labour, forced labour and freedom of association.

As we have seen on the environmental side, considering how a company engages with local communities and supports their development, through initiatives such as community investment, volunteering and stakeholder engagement is necessary in order to help develop your suppliers and the communities where they operate.

And of course, protecting the interests of your customers, including product safety, data privacy, customer satisfaction and responsible marketing practices, is imperative.

Fflur Roberts, Head of Luxury for Euromonitor International, reinforced Polman's findings. She said her company has found that luxury goods businesses are under increasing pressure from consumers, employees, investors and regulators to improve their ESG practices. According to Euromonitor's latest Voice of the Industry: Sustainability Survey (2022a), only a third of experts surveyed in 2022 reported that their company prioritizes ESG when planning and updating their strategies, because of resources and budgets. Still today, people don't really conceptualize climate as the severe risk that it actually is.

Another survey carried out by Euromonitor International (2022b) stated that, while 41 per cent of professionals in 2022 say that their company has an ESG-dedicated team that plans, articulates and communicates their goals, vision and strategies related to ESG issues, only 14 per cent are currently publishing ESG-specific reports. Looking across the different industries, at 12 per cent, apparel and personal accessories (which includes luxury) sit in the middle of the list of those publishing ESG reports, while travel with 11 per cent sits just below that.

While environmental concerns are rising, a lack of coherent international legislation means only a third of fashion companies link sustainability investments to new regulations. Luxury companies are feeling the pressure to act, yet very few have a net zero strategy in place. The disconnect between long-term sustainable goals and efforts to achieve them could trigger consumer dissatisfaction, bad press and the boycotting of brands that are failing to reach consumer expectation.

The social dimension of ESG recognizes the importance of business activities on society. Companies today will also need to prioritize their social responsibility and their contributions in addressing societal challenges, such as inequality, access to healthcare and education, keeping traditional craftsmanship and contributing positively to the wellbeing, both physical and mental, of individuals and communities.

A good example of this is Dior, which is committed to sustaining support to the countries where the brand goes to collaborate with. The Dior Fall 2023 show, which took place on 30 March in Mumbai, paid tribute to this heritage and demonstrated a strong and lasting commitment to the Chanakya School of Craft, in favour of Indian women. A groundbreaking two-year partnership was formed with the House to train 200 Indian women from underprivileged backgrounds, as well as artisans who would like to increase their autonomy and skills. In a country where embroidery is essentially reserved for men, the objective is to help women in a very concrete way to acquire financial autonomy. An artisan from the Vermont atelier trained a teacher from the Chanakya School of Craft so this initiative could continue, and furthermore continued collaboration and exchanges between Paris and Mumbai have been organized to deepen these trainings during two-month sessions, said Chantal Gaemperle, Group Executive Vice President Human Resources & Synergies at LVMH.

The G of ESG

The G of ESG is perhaps where we should have started, as it shines a spotlight on the systems and processes through which an organization is managed, such as the establishment of structures, policies and procedures to ensure accountability, transparency and effective decision-making.

The governance framework is typically led by the board of directors which has the responsibility to oversee the organization's activities, set its strategic direction and ensure its long-term success as board members are accountable to shareholders, stakeholders and the broader public.

The governance practices and principles set by the board cascade down to the leadership team affecting all members in the organization. In order to have effective governance the company needs clear lines of accountability, robust risk management processes, ethical standards and a commitment to compliance with laws and regulations and plans to go beyond.

The governance of the company is supported by the development and implementation of policies and procedures that guide the conduct of individuals and the organization as a whole.

Good governance ensures effective decision-making, accountability, transparency, responsible management, establishing internal controls and mechanisms to monitor and mitigate risks, ensure compliance with laws and regulations, and safeguard assets. It also considers the interests of stakeholders, including shareholders, employees, customers, suppliers, society at large and now nature.

Engaging stakeholders can help ensure that the organization's actions align with their expectations and needs. Nowadays this includes clear commitment to transparency, which involves providing timely and accurate information to stakeholders about the organization's performance, strategy and decision-making processes. Transparent reporting helps build trust and accountability across all stakeholder groups.

Why? Because people need consistent actions, fulfilment of commitments, acting with integrity, admitting mistakes, demonstrating leadership, knowledge and skills to establish credibility, reliability and ultimately foster trust.

People in your organization are interested in learning about nature, diversity, supply chains; in fact what they care about is how to be part of the solution. What is your ESG blind spot that your employees can shine a light on and support you with?

The board

We will start by looking at a company board, its ESG governance mechanism and its capabilities to oversee, enable and support that governance. ESG does not arrive in isolation. Companies are facing political and economic uncertainty, market volatility and recession, regulatory changes at the speed of light, a fast-moving technology landscape including AI, increasing cybersecurity issues, the demand for transparency, investor activism and media scrutiny.

The first and most fundamental question a company must ask is also the most brutal – Do you have the right board?

Is the composition of the board fit to achieve a strategic balance of relevant skills, experiences and backgrounds? Does it have the right structure to build a culture, ensure the right team dynamics and a fluid relationship between the exec and non-exec teams? Can the board assign accountability for ESG to both the exec and non-exec teams?

It's key to have a diverse board, aligned with the overarching purpose of the organization with the right level of skills and experience to help shape, challenge and direct the change that is needed. Professionally, I see too many businesses spending time and money relearning old lessons.

A socially and professionally diverse board brings different perspectives. Another important factor to consider is how long a person sits on the board. This varies by country, but it is usually three terms of three years – which, at nine years, is way too long. In this environment, three years is a lifetime. A healthy board needs to think of a reshuffle every three to four years as a maximum. Think how different the world is today from just five years ago.

Building a high-performing, effective board is the result of thoughtful onboarding and evaluation, strong and committed leadership as well as good boardroom culture and dynamics.

Figure 4.2 offers a process checklist, making it easy for companies to monitor suggestions and disclosures, accomplishments and milestones. It will help you to understand what skills your board needs and how you rank them – the spaces at the bottom are for you to fill in what is important to your organization.

The shadow board

A growing trend in organizations is to have a shadow board – these types of boards are normally made up of a group of non-executive employees, mostly Gen Z or young Millennials, who are appointed to provide feedback and advice to the company's actual board. The shadow board is intended to represent the views and perspectives of employees, who may have a different perspective than the company's formal directors or executive team.

The objective of the shadow board is to provide input on key strategic decisions and business initiatives, or feedback on financial reports, sustainability and risk management strategies.

FIGURE 4.2 What skills does your board need?

Competence	Why?	Ranking
Industry experience	Important to understand the industry and sector nuances	
Sector experience		
Understanding of their fiduciary duties		
Governance skills and understanding of the legislative environment		
Empathy – listening skills and emotional intelligence		
Positive future-thinking skills		
ESG and risk management		
AI and Web 3		
Financial literacy		
Sustainable finance literacy		
Strategic thinking		
Biodiversity		
Animal welfare		

While the shadow board does not have formal decision-making authority, their insights and perspectives can be valuable in helping the actual board of directors make more informed decisions that take into account the interests and concerns of all stakeholders, including employees. In this way, the shadow board can help to promote greater transparency, accountability and employee engagement within the company.

The leadership team

Today's world comes with complexities and challenges that require a different style of leadership, especially if you are leading an organization with ESG and sustainability at its centre. The new leadership style requires adaptability and agility in order to quickly respond and adjust to shifting and evolving market conditions. It requires a collaborative and inclusive mindset, fostering a culture of collaboration, trust and mutual respect, valuing the collective intelligence of the company.

THE TOP FIVE QUALITIES OF A MODERN LEADER ARE THE ABILITY TO:

- Understand the balance between being a mission driven business and profit
- Clearly articulate a vision
- Align stakeholders, employees, investors, customers and ultimately product and processes to the core mission and vision
- Create transparency in communication and reporting that makes everyone feel involved and engaged with the successful outcome, as well as any bumps along the way
- Develop a new leadership style – inclusive and empathic – be open to new ideas, seek feedback, encourage a culture of learning and innovation

When considering if you fit into this style of leadership ask yourself: does your organization conduct employee surveys asking for anonymous feedback of the leadership team in order to detect any blind spots? How open is your organization to criticism? How willing is your organization to answer questions whoever poses them and be accountable?

This new style of leadership is based on actions not words, and is characterized by a shift in mindset from command-and-control structures to more collaborative and empowering approaches.

It recognizes the importance of human-centred leadership, social and environmentally aware decision-making and a focus on long-term sustainable outcomes as well as sustainable economic growth. Embracing this modern leadership is well-suited to address the challenges of a rapidly changing and interconnected world, fostering innovation, resilience and sustainable economic growth.

In summary, the way a company needs to approach doing business involves an attitude that starts at the top and permeates throughout the organization – allowing for feedback in the opposite direction. Good governance practices contribute to a healthy business and a healthy bottom line.

A stable culture

The most innovative businesses today, from start-ups, scale-ups to established organizations, have incorporated sustainability principles within their mission, vision and values.

A strong sustainability culture can make an organization thrive in every possible way. The key is to ensure that this remains constant and consistent as they scale up their operations and if the business is already of a sizable scale that it is translated from country to country. Sustainability is not just about setting targets, it can act as a unifier, that North Star that builds consensus and alignment, getting everybody working together for the greater good of the company, its people and nature.

Why don't I call it purpose, you may ask? In my view, purpose lost its purpose. There are many companies that have a purpose on paper, but not all follow it up with action. 'Purpose' has been so overused and the weight that it once carried is no longer there. This is why I like to call it 'The Mission', because it is about a brand or a company making a stand for a single key topic.

Brands are loved by many people around the world, and this gives them a really important voice to drive change. Having that voice brings a responsibility for those brands in order to create long-term value – social, economic and environmental.

In this context, on top of that wider sustainability lens that we already talked about, a brand's mission is their quest to go beyond impact and have positive outcomes in more targeted and specific areas where they have the opportunity and the credibility to do so.

The culture of the organization is not just about having a sound and inspiring mission and values on paper but about how people interact with one another, how the leadership behaves towards all the people of the organization and its suppliers and how they can drive the organization towards sustainable economic growth – meaning growing the top and bottom line without depleting natural resources. The business opportunity of doing so is unparalleled. It is hard to talk about growth without acknowledging the concept of de-growth. We must recognize that companies are bound, under the current economic model, to prioritize economic growth, which is not a bad goal to have if it is reframed as sustainable economic growth – and this does not mean let's make more stuff.

Growth plays to macro-economic stability, enabling increased living standards, protecting and creating jobs and increasing tax revenues. It is possible for businesses to 'do well' economically by 'doing good' for society and nature and this should not be a cause of tension; positive economic outcomes are a must if we want the sustainability agenda to thrive, this is why innovation is important. As Nicholas Ind writes in *Beyond Branding*

(2003): 'As businesses grow in power, so does their accountability.' They acquire larger roles that put them at the centre of our social and natural worlds. They can use this power for good by restoring our world and enhancing people's lives.

We are living through a transitional decade, and for that transition to be a success, we need to understand time and patience are of the essence, as change does not happen in a straight line. We are all navigating uncharted waters in unprecedented times.

Sustainability goals can range from mundane small everyday objectives, such as implementing a new travel policy or changing all paper to FSC to re-evaluating your business model, on-shoring your supply chain and rethinking your product mix, including diversification of your offering – for example, digital fashion as well as omnichannel retail, whether ESG goals are quantitative forms of evaluation that companies use to measure and report progress. Innovation, accountability, transparency and traceability are what sit at the intersection between sustainability and ESG. When people talk about sustainability, their minds can wander off to the world of carbon reductions, forever chemicals, waste management, water and energy consumption, plastic, modern slavery and a whole list of topics. But sustainability is more than that.

It is a complex topic, and you're looking to pull many different levers all at the same time to bring about positive outcomes for your business as well as wider societal and environmental change.

FIGURE 4.3 Your mission is your North Star

The power of brands on a mission

Marketing and communications are at the heart of brand and reputation building. Marketers can play a key role in enabling people to make more conscious choices and unlock the commercial value of sustainability. Up to now the sustainability departments have not leaned into marketing and communication, or their agencies, for that matter, but we need their help to influence behaviours.

The Reimagining Way is a simple methodology to help companies – brands and suppliers – to answer the difficult questions, such as:

- How can my business make people's lives better?
- How can my business drive positive outcomes to nature?

This criterion can be applied to any brand and/or supplier as this is becoming a licence to operate. The space for companies being less bad is becoming narrower and narrower. This is the time where companies will need to demonstrate why they are positively good, which is driven by legislation and partly by consumers and investors.

In order to succeed in the quest of 'doing well' by 'doing good' brands need to grow or build their innovation strategy.

The Reimagining Way helps companies build a sustainability culture to deliver net positive outcomes instead of just focusing on bettering their impacts (moving from less bad to being positively good).

In this way companies will be able to unlock the value of their sustainability investment, differentiate from their peers/competitors and truly capture the minds and hearts of all stakeholders including consumers and employees.

How to do this? By aligning your mission, vision and values with your sustainability and product strategies in a consistent and cohesive way which will enable your business to remain relevant and build a legacy. This is how companies will be able to differentiate themselves, as every company's mission is unique to them and therefore their story.

Parfums Christian Dior's commitment to leave beauty as a legacy

The luxury industry has an immense responsibility and opportunity to make desirability marry with greater positive outcomes to better nature and our world and empower societies. Parfums Christian Dior have defined their

FIGURE 4.4 The Reimagining Way methodology 2023

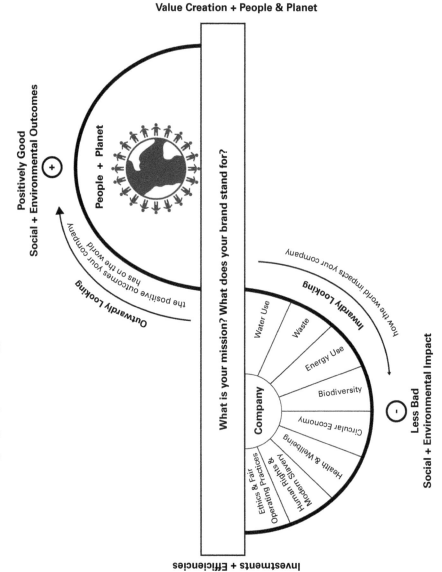

Value Creation + People & Planet

Positively Good
Social + Environmental Outcomes

+

People + Planet

Outwardly Looking
the positive outcomes your company
has on the world

What is your mission? What does your brand stand for?

Inwardly Looking
how the world impacts your company

Water Use

Waste

Energy Use

Biodiversity

Circular Economy

Company

Health & Wellbeing

Modern Slavery

Human Rights &

Ethics & Fair
Operating Practices

Less Bad
Social + Environmental Impact

−

Investments + Efficiencies

collective mission: to leave Beauty as a Legacy. Beyond words, this is about commitments and tangible actions. To give you a little bit of history, the Maison has been creating beauty products since 1947, from fragrances such as Miss Dior and J'Adore to make-up and skincare. While they offer a luxurious aesthetic experience, they also pay special attention to the quality of the materials they use combining the benefits of nature, sustainability and science, while making products that have a negative climate and biodiversity footprint, which they work rather hard to reduce.

I had the pleasure of interviewing Isabelle Sultan, Chief Sustainability Officer at Parfums Christian Dior. Isabelle has an unbeatable passion and knowledge when it comes to agriculture and sustainability – she has a quiet confidence in her words which is backed by her wealth of experience of over 20 years working at Danone.

'In the field of biodiversity, we are transitioning to organic and/or regenerative flower farming in the 42 gardens and partner gardens around the world that are generating our signature natural origin ingredients,' she said. '70 per cent of these gardens are already adopting organic practices. The challenge is to go beyond organic practices that are a great lever to preserve biodiversity into regenerative practices that will help restore and bring back more carbon into the soils, more biodiversity, and more resilience. We are members of UEBT (Union for Ethical Biotrade) a non-profit organization that promotes sourcing with respect for a world in which all people and biodiversity thrive. We are committed to having these gardens and partner gardens UEBT certified by 2026,' Isabelle explained.

She concluded, 'We are also gradually transitioning the sourcing of the alcohol we use for our fragrances, which is made from beetroot, to regenerative cultivation practices starting with a shift of the equivalent of 45 per cent of our volumes in 2023. This is only possible with our partners and the committed farmers they work with in the North of France notably. In the field of climate, we have a very bold science-based commitment to reduce our full scope carbon emissions by 46 per cent between 2019 and 2030, which means acting at every step of our value chain.'

They are investing in eco-design from their packaging to their points of sales and their formulations. And more broadly it is about the positive role they are playing in culture, standing for a more progressive society.

Just like their parent company, LVMH, Parfums Christian Dior believe that luxury exists at the intersection of creativity and nature. Studies show that over 50 per cent of the global economic value created worldwide is linked to services provided by nature (World Economic Forum, 2020).

The House of Dior is fully aware of its dependence on nature: more than 80 per cent of the ingredients used in its fragrance, skincare and make-up lines come from natural origins. The link between the House and flowers is notably very strong as they are at the core of the perfume scent and active ingredients. According to the IUCN (International Union for Conservation of Nature) red list of endangered species, flowers are becoming extinct at twice the rate of insects, three times the rate of birds and 1.5 times the rate of mammals.

Dior understands that their supply chains will be affected unless they protect them, cultivating them in a regenerative way within their upstream supply chain, in the cradle of perfume Grasse for instance but also in the rest of the world. Also, beyond their direct supply chain, they are helping to reintroduce flowers into agricultural ecosystems so they can drive healthy soils, healthy biodiversity and better resilience for communities.

Isabelle and the Dior team are working with Hectar, the greatest agricultural campus dedicated to regenerative cultivation established at the gates of Paris and with WWF, to model a way to achieve their mission to protect the plants and soils that produce the flowers.

Isabelle is one person, and her team alone is rather small in comparison with the multiple challenges ahead. When I asked her how she will achieve this she said, 'We are upskilling 100 per cent of the teams to understand the global climate and biodiversity challenge and act in their day-to-day jobs.'

The path to a sustainable future is challenging. But it is a journey in which we can all contribute, to seed change, to advocate, to take action. Now. This is the Reimagining Way.

From ambition to action

An established company that has an ambition to be sustainable requires to effectively innovate and reshape every aspect of the organization – the board, the leadership, the products, systems, operations, legal, finance, compliance, supply chains, HRD and innovation – but it also needs to look outwards to change its relationship with partners, suppliers and ultimately their tribe.

As Einstein famously said, 'Insanity is doing the same thing over and over and expecting different results' (quoted in Wilczek, 2015). If you make different choices, you will certainly have a different result. If you tweak the edges rather than innovate, you are unlikely to affect the overall outcome.

To go through this transition will require a strong sustainability/regenerative culture within the organization and at every touch point in the business and along its supply chains – including its relationship with suppliers. The place to start is at the top. A C-suite and executive leadership actively engaged to the point that their bonus and compensation depend on their sustainability innovation and ESG deliverables, which need to be on par with the overall economic objectives of the organization. The second phase is to extend this structure for compensation across the entire organization and manage its execution.

A company needs to ensure that all senior leaders are responsible for developing, communicating and activating ESG and sustainability strategies in their day-to-day job, not leaving this to the head of sustainability. If senior leaders do this, they can achieve a sustainability mindset enabling them to run the business while transforming it to deliver value to a wide range of stakeholders, including shareholders.

A lot of luxury companies are privately owned, owned by a charitable trust or a foundation or listed but with strong family involvement in shareholding and voting rights.

Companies today have to reshape their executive board with new roles such as Chief Sustainability Innovation Officer, Chief Sustainability Officer or Chief Culture Officer to reflect the importance of brand perception beyond their product or service.

There is still a lot of work to be done in addressing gender mix and racial diversity. There is also a lack of meaningful representation from ESG and sustainability practitioners who can help execs to align their budget and resources to create a meaningful and achievable transitional plan. And there is also a lot of work to be done to understand exactly why the company exists.

What is refreshing is that in a rather short space of time companies have moved from commitment to action and from transparency to accountability – making real change tangible.

Back in 2002 I built one of the first sustainability consultancies in the UK. We scaled up to work in China, USA and Europe then sold it to a global communications group to reach a global scale. What I've learned is that showing people how to fish is the best way to transform businesses at pace and scale.

The Reimagining Way methodology has been co-created with business and academia to inspire companies to build a sustainability innovation culture in order to deliver net positive outcomes and deliver value to all stakeholders and nature – instead of just focusing on impact.

The best way to explain this in the old way of 'carrots and sticks' – on the left are the environmental, social and governance (ESG) topics that impact the business, and soon will need to be reported and measured mandated by law. This is the language of stick which requires investment to drive efficiency and reduce cost.

On the right-hand side is the language of carrots, which is the thought that companies can rally behind in order to deliver a positive impact in the world. This needs to be part of your mission, your innovation and product strategy and your communications. This is how companies will be able to differentiate themself, as every company is unique.

If you must, fear change but do it anyway

I had the pleasure of interviewing John Kotter, Professor of Leadership, Emeritus, at Harvard Business School and author and founder of Kotter International. John Kotter has been an inspiration to me and many generations in business leadership and change management. I had the good fortune to study under his leadership and reached out to him for advice. He teaches that deciding where we are going requires an understanding of where we came from. The structures we put in place had a purpose, and only by truly understanding the original purpose can we decide if they are fit for the future.

The modern organization was invented in the late 19th century as part of the Industrial Revolution. It was invented to bring people together to use new technologies to make new products and services much, much cheaper and much more reliable. New forms of transport – trains and steamships – meant that these products could be introduced to a larger market. The organization's purpose was mainly stability and efficiency, so management was created to keep things under control.

'The average modern organization now in 2023 is still very management centric – but the founding principle of that management is still keeping things under control efficiently and reliably,' he explained. 'This, of course, is very different from changing things.'

Kotter shared with me that management may see change as an existential threat. Middle management in particular have been trained all of their careers to keep things under control. When they're presented with the idea of changing the structure or the practice of their organization, their habits, mindsets and built-in instincts are to resist.

'The name of the game is getting some people that matter to start doing things in a new way that fits with what you're trying to achieve,' he suggests. 'Get some results that unequivocally show that this was done better. Communicate that out and celebrate it. Start building a movement. At a certain point, you'll get some mindset changes, including some of that middle management group. Not a lot, but some. And then eventually, you create a new culture around this. You get sustainable change.' This has never happened before, except when it did.

Sustainability, innovation and ESG touch every single department within an organization, as climate and social compliance changes affect production, procurement, R&D, logistics, finance, marketing, HRD, etc – it is essential that knowledge does not live within a person or a department, instead it should travel fast and wide across every individual in the business.

This is why you need reimaginers in the organization – these team members are a mix of high-profile charismatic leaders as well as management and junior-level individuals hungry for learning and growth. Good knowledge and stewardship are essential for success to ensure that people in the organization bridge the knowledge gap and ensure that this knowledge spreads within the organization.

How can you ensure that the reimaginers succeed? A senior member of the team needs to be on board with the programme and encourage it, which means allowing the time and providing resources to ensure that the programme is successful.

Reimaginers will have access to sources and the right data to ensure that they can back their narrative with facts and resources to ensure that they make the programme engaging but, most importantly, to gain top-down support to ensure that they can engage with everybody and drive meaningful change.

Professor Kotter then drew a simple diagram (Figure 4.5) for me and said, it's simple, you see? Reimaginers are of the essence if you want to build a 21st-century business, he commented.

People don't realize the order of magnitude of change to transition an organization, Kotter said, but this is like the Industrial Revolution: change is in the air, and, although uncertain, accelerating.

FIGURE 4.5 How do you achieve change? Hand-drawing by Harvard Professor Kotter

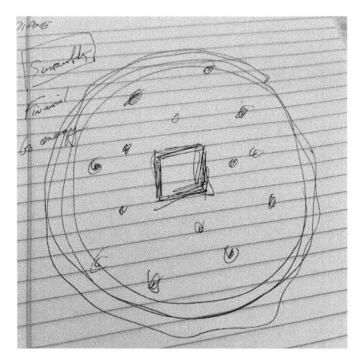

The Kotter eight-step approach to change management

1 Create a Sense of Urgency: Leaders should effectively communicate the need for change, highlighting the risks of maintaining the status quo and creating a sense of urgency among their teams.

2 Build a Guiding Coalition: To drive change, it is crucial to assemble a diverse and influential group of individuals who can act as a reimaginer. This coalition should have the necessary skills, credibility and authority to lead the change effort.

3 Clarity: Having an inspiring vision for the future is essential, however a vision coupled with a clear sense of mission and a roadmap for achieving the desired outcome is the perfect recipe for success.

4 Communicate the Vision: Effective and consistent communication is vital to ensure that the vision, mission and strategy are understood and embraced by all stakeholders. Leaders should consistently and clearly communicate their vision, explaining the rationale behind the changes and addressing any concerns or resistance.

5 Empower Broad-Based Action: To implement change successfully, Kotter emphasizes the importance of empowering employees at all levels. This involves removing obstacles, encouraging innovative thinking and fostering a culture of ownership and accountability.

6 Generate Short-Term Wins: Celebrating early and tangible wins helps maintain momentum and build confidence in the change effort. Identifying and achieving quick victories demonstrate the effectiveness of the change initiatives and motivate employees to continue their efforts.

7 Consolidate Gains and Produce More Change: After achieving initial wins, it is essential to avoid complacency and continue driving the change forward. Leaders should use the momentum generated to tackle more significant challenges and make the necessary adjustments to achieve the long-term vision.

8 Anchor the Change in Culture: To make change sustainable, it must be embedded in the organization's culture. Kotter emphasizes the need to ensure that the changes become the new norm by aligning the systems, processes and behaviours with the desired culture.

Kotter and Martin Townsend, Director at the Centre of Excellence for Sustainability, British Standards Institute (BSI) are aligned in the belief that you need to take people along a journey of hearts and minds so that there is a true understanding of the need to innovate both from a brand perspective and what it represents, but also how a sustainability innovation makes for a more resilient business, as well as being good for the planet.

Such a shift at a corporate level will often come through an enterprise awareness programme helping to bring everyone up the learning curve and the important role that they can all play. As the conversation on what makes a truly sustainable business is not standing still, such a programme needs to continue to evolve, sparking new ideas with new knowledge and innovation to help a company reduce cost, ensure brand values and keep a competitive advantage.

Townsend also agrees that the most successful cases in his experience drive change as it is good for business, and not one that is based on financial incentives alone. 'A single lens approach to driving change won't embed change in the culture of the business,' he explained.

The key is to continue to be inquisitive about the opportunities and possibilities and innovate. In companies of all sizes and complexities, change now is inevitable, those that don't adapt and innovate won't be around in the coming years.

What will happen after 2030, 2040 and 2050 when organizations achieve their objectives? Stopping and patting yourself on the back is not an option, instead organizations must shift their focus towards promoting regenerative behaviours, actively restoring and replenishing our ecosystems, embracing circular economy principles and fostering practices that prioritize the well-being of both the environment and society.

The narrative of net zero is getting organizations caught in the illusion that net zero is the end game. Net zero is a step on the journey, and actually, some of the biggest challenges will come after we achieve net zero. This is the same with each of the 25 drivers of ESG. Organizations are fundamentally in a transition to reimagine their business models, products and what legacy they are leaving that betters everybody. Inaction has a high price tag, including not being in business anymore. Sustainability innovation should be the organization's North Star, not something that is negotiable. The health of our society and planet depends on it.

Break the silos

There are many correlations and parallels between the digital and sustainability transformations of the business world. The digitalization of businesses unfolded over time through a combination of technological advancements, organizational strategies and evolving market dynamics.

A deeper integration of digital technologies, processes and strategies into business operations was an easy decision to make in order to drive efficiency, innovation, customer experience and overall business performance.

Businesses moved into building capacity across all the different parts of the organization to embed technological capabilities – this actually evolved into digitalization and the data that drives real insights into the organization, which have the capacity to drive efficiencies and bottom-line sustainable growth.

We are in a transitional decade, and there are still a lot of tools that have not yet been invented or tested at scale. But, like the old IT teams, the sustainability and innovation teams should position themselves as a business partner, building capacity to help every individual in the business to skill up.

The desire to be sustainable typically originates from the top, but change comes from everywhere, especially in small and growth businesses. Organizations that lean into sustainability innovation and put processes in place to integrate sustainability practices into all departments will also bring diverse perspectives and opportunities for growth.

Sustainability and innovation needs to be on the CEO-level agenda. It really needs to be driven by the key decision makers of a company. But the most important thing is that you incorporate sustainability and innovation on a measurement/action level at every step of the value chain,' said Dr Richard Federowski, Partner in Roland Berger's Consumer Goods & Retail team. 'If you just implement it as a strategic goal and you only establish a sustainability department, it is not enough. To succeed you should incorporate sustainability and innovation into the value chain, into your business model at all organizational levels. The pain point is to overcome operational resistances and make sustainability affordable and an all organizational effort.'

Interdepartmental collaborations and touchpoints are essential. The move towards digitalization has played a significant role in breaking the sustainability silo by facilitating collaboration, knowledge sharing and integration of sustainability innovation practice.

'If all business stakeholders understand what the journey ahead will entail, and what will be required of them and their teams, it will be so much easier to get the job done. We need great marketing, communications and sourcing colleagues with the skills and understanding of the sustainability agenda, not a bigger sustainability department,' said Judith Batchelar, OBE, Board of Trustees Accounting for Sustainability.

Here are some practical tips on how to do it

1 Assess your ESG, digital capabilities and sustainability and innovation practices. Identify areas where sustainability goals align with digitalization opportunities. This assessment will help you understand the existing strengths, weaknesses and gaps.

2 Clearly define your sustainability and ESG objectives and outcomes prioritizing initiatives that will have the most significant impact on your business and align them with your overall strategy.

3 Appoint a cross-functional team that includes representatives from all departments, establish clear roles, responsibilities and communication channels for efficient coordination.

4 Identify areas where sustainability and digitalization can reinforce each other. For example, leveraging digital technologies for energy management,

supply chain optimization, data-driven sustainability reporting or customer engagement can enhance sustainability efforts. Look for opportunities to use digital tools to monitor, measure and communicate sustainability performance.

5   Assess your digital infrastructure and invest in the necessary technologies, systems and tools to support sustainability initiatives. This may include adopting cloud computing, data analytics platforms, IoT devices or sustainability management software. Ensure that your digital infrastructure supports data collection, analysis and reporting on sustainability metrics.

6   Establish a centralized data management process to collect, store and analyse sustainability related data. Use digital analytics tools to gain insights into resource consumption, carbon emissions, supply chain impacts and other relevant sustainability indicators, in order to inform better decision-making and track progress towards your sustainability goals.

7   Build capacity by providing training and awareness programmes to promote a culture of sustainability literacy. Empower employees to contribute ideas and participate in sustainability initiatives encouraging a sense of ownership and collaboration across departments.

8   Establish mechanisms to monitor and report progress on sustainability integration by developing key performance indicators (KPIs) that measure progress and the impact on sustainability goals.

9   Sustainability integration is an ongoing process. Continuously evaluating and refining your sustainability strategy, market trends and stakeholder feedback will create a culture of continuous improvement and innovation. Sustainability is not a one size fits all, it is different for every business because every business affects the planet and its people in a different way.

How does your business affect society and nature?

References

Euromonitor International (2022a) Passport Voice of the Industry: Sustainability Survey

Euromonitor International (2022b) Passport Voice of the Consumer; Sustainability Survey

Euromonitor International (2022c) Passport Voice of the Consumer: Lifestyles Survey

IMF (2023) cited in WorldData.info, Developing Countries, www.worlddata.info/developing-countries.php#:~:text=A%20further%20downgrade%20takes%20place,proportion%20of%20the%20world%27s%20population (archived at https://perma.cc/Y5JW-PA6D)

Ind, N (2003) *Beyond Branding: How the new values of transparency and integrity are changing the world of brands*, London and Sterling: Kogan Page

Polman, P (2023) 2023 Net Positive Employee Barometer. From quiet quitting to conscious quitting, February, www.paulpolman.com/wp-content/uploads/2023/02/MC_Paul-Polman_Net-Positive-Employee-Barometer_Final_web.pdf (archived at https://perma.cc/KS8G-4W9L)

United Nations Brundtland Commission (1987) Sustainability, www.un.org/en/academic-impact/sustainability#:~:text=In%201987%2C%20the%20United%20Nations,development%20needs%2C%20but%20with%20the (archived at https://perma.cc/868G-V7U4)

Wilczek, F (2015) Einstein's Parable of Quantum Insanity, *Scientific American*, 23 September, www.scientificamerican.com/article/einstein-s-parable-of-quantum-insanity/ (archived at https://perma.cc/6JLL-6RB9)

World Economic Forum (2020) New Nature Economy Report II, www3.weforum.org/docs/WEF_The_Future_Of_Nature_And_Business_2020.pdf (archived at https://perma.cc/H7ZH-D7NK)

05

Changing the luxury model

Luxury does not mean expensive, for the sake of it. In fact, luxury and sustainability are two sides of the same coin – why? Because the principles of sustainability and luxury are very much aligned. Both embrace innovation and a long-term perspective.

Luxury products are often designed to last, focusing on durability, high-quality craftsmanship, attention to detail and superior materials. This emphasis on quality resonates with the sustainability principle of favouring durable, well-made products that have a longer lifespan. By investing in luxury items that are built to last, people can buy less and buy better.

Similarly, sustainability advocates to conserve resources for future generations, advocating for practices that reduce environmental impact and promote social wellbeing in the long run. Additionally, there is a growing awareness of the environmental impact of luxury products, leading to the adoption of eco-friendly manufacturing processes, transparency and the use of renewable and more innovative materials.

Luxury products are often associated with exclusivity and rarity, leveraging this concept by producing limited quantities of goods, using unique or eco-friendly materials, and implementing innovative design approaches. This approach aligns with sustainability principles as it discourages mass production, reduces waste and encourages the appreciation of quality over quantity – furthermore, you would probably never throw away luxury items, you would repair, sell and/or gift them.

The principles of sustainability and luxury converge in the concept of conscious consumption. People are increasingly seeking products that align with their values and have a net positive social and environmental impact in the world. Although luxury is by no means perfect, they give people the option to buy products that are aesthetically pleasing, combining high-end quality with a mindful operation of the entire business from recruitment to product development enabling people to feel good about what they buy, differentiate themselves and stay relevant in an increasingly conscious market.

The luxury industry has seen stable growth for the last 40 years, give or take. Despite this, luxury businesses, like other businesses, have no choice but to think about changes to their operating model, processes and structure, and social and environmental sustainability goes hand in hand with these all.

In a fast-changing world riddled with uncertainty, any business setting targets and commitments without changing the way they 'always do things' is taking part in a meaningless exercise.

Any operating model and action plan needs to deliver on sustainability goals and ESG metrics, to effectively manage risk, have a resilient business, reduce operating costs, gain better returns and/or effect change. Businesses could lean into exploring different models to future proof their businesses.

For example:

1   Embrace Brand as a Service (Baas). Subscription models provide access to products or services for a recurring fee. This is not just exclusive to Spotify or Netflix, these types of models are also applicable to other sectors such as hospitality. For example, the Sea Containers London hotel launched its first subscription service offering their regular guest overnight stays, gym access and a truck for their personal storage, with monthly rates starting from £1,550 p/m (approx. $1,920). Glossybox is one of the beauty industry darlings where you can subscribe to receive five new beauty products each month.

2   Sharing economic models enable people or businesses to share resources. These platforms facilitate peer-to-peer transactions and provide access to underutilised assets, promoting resource efficiency and flexibility – such as private jet companies.

3   On-demand models provide immediate access to products or services whenever needed. Companies like Deliveroo offer on-demand delivery services, while platforms like Upwork and Freelancer connect businesses with freelance professionals for on-demand work.

4   Digital marketplaces connect buyers and sellers, facilitating transactions and interactions, like eBay or Gumtree.

5   Circular economy models focus on minimizing waste and maximizing resource efficiency. These types of models are great for luxury. The quality and craftsmanship lends itself well to embracing renting, re-setting, leasing,

repairing, reselling, etc, creating more sustainable consumption patterns. Some good examples include Treasury Collective or Reflaunt.

Fashion e-commerce company Farfetch, for example, operates on a market-place business model connecting the inventory from boutiques and brands, in stores and warehouses all around the world through technology, explained Stephanie Phair, Group President at Farfetch. 'Unlike how it was before, where brands had to produce specific products for one store, produce products for a different store and produce additional products for a third store, now Farfetch opens up the visibility of all the stock so that it can sell to a global audience. And so, the stock becomes much more efficient. So what's produced has a better chance of selling,' she said. 'Ultimately, it hopefully helps brands' merchandising plans in terms of not having to produce these pockets of stock that then go unsold and turn into waste.'

Where luxury should excel is when talking about people rather than consumers. People are more than just consumers. They are the media, employees, partners, sons and daughters, but above all they are citizens.

The younger generations don't like to be referred to as 'consumers'. Neither do I, and I suspect you don't consider yourself to be part of that group. Do you?

The power of individuals to choose is an expanding concern for companies – not least because of the increasing power of employees to choose in a market with more jobs than people and a growing flexing of their power to disrupt, create or destroy consensus as well as the power to destabilize.

Luxury cannot easily be defined – and it does not automatically come with a high price tag. It means different things to different people, and even in the luxury industry, the definition of luxury is changing. For health-conscious Zoomers, organic or premium food is considered a luxury, they prefer the supplements, snacks or smoothies that they see on TikTok over fashion. These foods are a status symbol and are used to communicate belonging to a specific cohort. The luxury market is witnessing growth in previously stalling or outdated market segments: for example, traditional silverware and crystal are dusted off and back on the table.

This represents a shift – instead of keeping special pieces for occasions, it is about elevating every day to spark joy in little things and have an emotional bond between the objects, the user and the memories that connect them. Living in the moment is something that this generation has done very well, and perhaps should not be frowned upon but occasionally embraced.

This performative kind of consumption is to Gen Z what logos and SUVs were to previous generations. It is a way to affirm status that is more subtle and based on lore as a currency. How do you demonstrate status in a world where everything is visible, and you can have everything within a minute's notice? Perhaps it is about having the memories, the appreciation of past times and previous lives of the product. Zoomers are savvy and emotion-led collectors. They seek unique pieces, whether clothing or tableware, not just for aesthetic value but to elevate everyday moments and romanticize the mundane, as simple things make them feel special.

The younger consumers who have been deprived of many life-affirming experiences are adopting a hedonistic mindset to life. They defy convenience and quick fixes, creating an opportunity for products and experiences that deliver a maximalist joyful feeling.

The new luxury

Luxury today is about experiences and how that experience makes you feel. It is something that ignites desire and leaves you wanting more.

'The pattern of luxury is changing. About 10 years ago, my prediction was, that there would be a creative renaissance in 2025. But looking at it, I think the pandemic has impacted this. We are now in 2023, and we are seeing flickers of new ideas, new creative approaches and some interesting radical thinking starting to emerge. It obviously takes time to come through in a broader way, but I do believe we're at the beginning of a new wave of something, maybe a movement of sorts,' said Linda Hewson, former Group Creative Director of Selfridges.

When you think about creating desire as a brand, you are thinking about the power to imagine tomorrow. The ability to anticipate problems and find solutions before others – this is how luxury leads the way.

Luxury is like a dance with paradoxes. Time and history on one hand, modernity and relevancy on the other. This is how luxury can move fast when it comes to change in some cases, but move slowly, perfectly controlled in others.

Luxury as an industry is about exceptional products and/or experiences, well crafted, well made, with great quality and with people and the planet embedded from the creative process to retail and after care. And when we talk about the luxury industry, I don't just mean fashion and beauty. We are discussing a multi-billion-dollar transversal industry with a number of adjacent industries – including travel and hospitality, leather goods, watches, cars and experiences.

Today luxury is diversifying to new business models and new sectors. In a strategy of embracing luxury as a broader lifestyle.

Giorgio Armani was one of the first fashion houses to enter the gastronomy business in 1998 and already has around 20 locations worldwide; at the beginning of this century they launched Armani/Casa, their first dedicated home store in Milan, after a year and with great success they expanded to New York and Los Angeles. A decade ago Armani partnered with Emaar Properties and opened their first hotel in Dubai and is now expanding in the MEA region. Kering invested in new technologies and services for the next generation of luxury buyers – some of their investments are luxury handbag subscription rental service COCOON, resale platform Vestiaire Collective and NTWRK live video shopping – whilst the Prada Group entered the homeware market and is testing the waters in the gastronomy space by opening a temporary Prada Caffè in the high-end department store Harrods in London in 2023.

Likewise, LVMH is at the forefront of moving into the broader luxury lifestyle segment: Dior and Louis Vuitton both run their own branded restaurants and cafés, and the Bulgari hotel brand, launched in 2001, now operates a collection of seven resorts around the world – each offering a unique immersive experience into the luxury world of the respective brand.

The luxury giant also invested in the historic Parisian department store La Samaritaine, transforming it into a shopping, dining and cultural experience featuring exclusive food and drink concepts as well as art installations, which reopened in June 2021. Moreover, it operates the Jardin d'Acclimatation, France's oldest leisure park. Inaugurated in 1860 by Napoléon III, the park was completely renovated in 2018 and offers 42 attractions and 18 hectares of walking trails to almost 2 million visitors.

The term luxury – just like the term purpose – is overused, and it has had, at times, negative connotations in some parts of the globe.

Luxury as an industry, regardless of the sector, has a unique opportunity to reposition itself by being more inclusive, more democratic, more mindful and more intentional in leaving the world and its people in a better place.

'In today's world, where everything changes so fast, we perhaps need to look back over our history, to a time where there was a slower pace of life, where there was time to craft products, to develop people, to transfer skills, and to leave something for future generations really mattered,' said Dame Polly Courtice, DBE, LVO, Emeritus Director and Senior Ambassador, Cambridge Institute for Sustainability Leadership. 'Now, where measuring our impact is becoming increasingly required (and rightly so), perhaps we can also spend a little time looking back over history to consider what sort of long-term outcomes we are seeking to achieve, and whether we really have developed the right mindset to do so.'

On one hand, brands will need to provide full transparency about their broader impacts to deserve being trusted and, on the other, brands need to simplify their narratives so that people can engage. The question for businesses is how their brands and marketing activities play a part in this agenda in order to stay relevant in a rapidly changing world. I believe in conscious choices and conscious opportunities to make a positive difference to the world, and it will open opportunities for the business to flourish.

Putting people at the centre of what you do will provide better long-term value for all shareholders including nature. In every corner of our planet, the reality of the climate crisis is hitting home, the world is becoming a hostile place for animals, including humans, our oceans and plant species to survive. Brands are seeding in fertile ground as people have become more conscious of our natural world.

And talking about fertile ground, it makes me focus on nature as support is mounting for grassroots movements to assign nature legal rights. By acknowledging nature as a stakeholder, companies would need to consider nature when developing and deploying their business plans and resources. Nature Positive Trust is a non-profit organization that provides a simple way for organizations whose products or services are inspired by nature to pledge a small percentage of their turnover as a royalty for using 'nature's property'. The money is deployed to conserve, replenish and restore our natural worlds and/or oceans.

What is striking is that the entrepreneurial and intrapreneurial mindset is very much alive in the luxury houses, and its leaders have a good balance between rational business objectives on one hand and a sparkle of intuition with the sensitivity of art, creativity and culture on the other.

Most good leaders have the ability to disrupt as well as understand how to navigate the turbulent waters of transition and modernity – the external pressures and expectations from customers, employees, investors and media expect luxury to act as a guardian of our planet, and society.

Great expectations

Leigh Pezzicara, Vice President, Sustainability at skincare brand La Prairie, explained that in the past, it was difficult for people to see how sustainability and luxury go hand in hand.

Today people recognize they are – or should be – the same thing. Whilst she extends the argument across all industries, Pezzicara believes this is especially true for luxury goods and experiences.

The higher the quality and the price point, the greater the consumer expectations. 'People believe in authentic brands, and authentic brands stay true to their DNA and values,' she explained. 'That means that with new leadership, the sustainability focus does not slow down or go away. In fact, the absolute opposite.'

'We are lucky to have a CEO advocating for sustainability. But perhaps even more importantly, sustainability is truly at the heart of our culture and values, and this is what ultimately will stand the test of time.'

Consumers believe that sustainability should be inherently integrated, she comments. In the past few years, aspirational brands have disrupted the sector with different interpretations of luxury products and services – all open to experiential approaches, whether that be pre-loved, repair services or any other innovative business models.

At the same time, industry demographics are changing. Millennials and Generation Z accounted for 72 per cent of the global luxury market in 2022 (Lin, 2022) and were responsible for all luxury market growth in that year (D'Arpizio et al, 2023). Moreover, according to the latest Bain & Company-Altagamma Luxury Study, spending by Generation Z and the even younger Generation Alpha will grow three times as fast as that of the other generations by 2030, making up a third of the market (D'Arpizio et al, 2023).

According to Fflur Roberts, Head of Luxury at Euromonitor, luxury and fashion companies are increasingly using sustainable business practices as a marketing strategy to improve their reputation, gain competitive advantage and create profitable business opportunities.

'Whilst sustainable products, waste and sourcing remain top of the agenda for luxury and fashion companies, a shift towards a more diverse and inclusive world has been very notable, with more companies addressing social mobility and looking at more affordable luxury and new hiring practices,' she said.

'Today's consumers have been re-evaluating what is important to them and are making more mindful consumption and life choices based on new-found values. For luxury and fashion businesses, this means putting value creation at the forefront of innovation and communication and seeking to work with talent coming from non-traditional backgrounds.'

Digital business models, second-hand buying and selling, group buying, re-commerce and buy now, pay later (BNPL) have grown rapidly over the last decade in response to unstable economic conditions, environmental concerns and technological advancements. Brands such as Salvatore Ferragamo and Emporio Armani are amongst those offering BNPL, Breitling Watches offer zero interest finance and Vestiaire Collective offers Wear Now Pay Later and you can split your payment in instalments up to 12 months.

There has been a significant increase in the percentage of digital natives who are choosing to buy or sell pre-loved items, swap, repair or rent instead of buying since 2019, according to Euromonitor's Voice of the Consumer: Lifestyles Survey, Roberts pointed out.

'The fact that this period of economic uncertainty is set against the back-drop of rising trends such as mindful consumption will likely drive further fundamental shifts in how people shop, and it is notable to see how the industry is responding.'

Kering, for example, has increased its stake in luxury resale website Vestiaire Collective and luxury handbag rental platform COCOON, while US grocery giant Walmart has partnered with ThredUp to improve its fashion offering. Even in China, where pre-worn clothing was once considered bad luck, younger people are embracing more sustainable consumption patterns and have been increasingly turning to second-hand platforms like Idle Fish, Paipai.com or Treasury Collective.

The latter is the brainchild of Haley Lieberman and Adam Shulman, who have a long-standing love for vintage and artisanal goods and have spent years searching for the most special and meaningful items to add to their collections.

They found that the process of discovering and curating these treasures could often be isolating and disconnected from a larger community. So they set out to create a platform that brings together like-minded collectors and treasure hunters, allowing them to discover, curate and share their finds with a supportive and passionate community. It's a lesson for business.

If traditional luxury brands want to stay relevant, they should be part of a virtuous circle.

Luxury is about creating desire. Enchanting through high quality products, crafted with exceptional savoir faire. The people, the artisans are fundamental. Human capital is at the heart of performance and success according to Chantal Gaemperle, Group Executive Vice President Human Resources & Synergies at LVMH:

> An engaged and happy workforce at all levels makes the difference. Offering them the right working culture where they feel empowered is one of the keys to retain and develop people, a key to success.
>
> Very often the solution, the idea comes from within. What is important in our culture is to push boundaries, strive for inventing tomorrow, cultivate best practices, respect the DNA of the brand but disrupt enough to develop creative solutions before others so you can lead the way. Helping people grow and help them achieve their personal goals is the key to retaining talent.
>
> It is true that luxury used to be associated with opulence and waste and an air of exclusivity, but Covid has given birth to a positive luxury, a more respectful and considered type of luxury closer to the French Art de Vivre philosophy (art of living), a combination of exquisite aesthetics, attention to detail and life-enhancing and joyful experiences.

Changing the luxury operating model to help change the world

The business model across luxury, from fashion to beauty, from jewellery including watches to premium drinks and from hospitality to experiences, has been set up to optimize cost. Complex supply chains are becoming increasingly difficult to control as most of the impact within most organizations lies in the supply chain, with the exception of the hotel industry, where the impact on property management is significant.

The business model needed today for businesses, whether luxury or not, is to optimize for sustainability.

Most companies may have done a carbon assessment, but they have not yet done it from an ESG perspective and that means doing so in a holistic and organized way, where at the end of the year or three-year period, organizations can measure their outcomes.

Some of the outcomes that a company can expect are, for example, the improvement of its reputation among investors, and other stakeholders, leading to increased trust and loyalty; saving costs as companies will reduce waste, optimize resource use and streamline operations; and lastly, the investment in R&D will help with the launch of new products and services that meet sustainability goals and could discover new revenue streams.

Overall, companies that prioritize and optimize sustainability can experience a range of outcomes, both positive and negative. While there may be costs and challenges associated with sustainable business practices, the long-term benefits of sustainability can outweigh the short-term costs and result in a more resilient and successful business over time.

Another thing to watch out for when choosing partners to help assess carbon emissions and the ESG baseline is to take into account that most companies are modelling their businesses on 'proxy data' – estimates, assumptions and secondary data – and that is a huge problem to start with and gets worse when businesses are forced to commit to targets.

Let's say that you don't understand what's behind the measures that you are setting targets against, so what are you actually going to reduce? From where exactly?

Let's make this easy. I have a passion for running – once upon a time my favourite distance was a marathon, but now, mostly due to overused knees, I'm a forced fan of 10 km... So, let's imagine I said I was going to improve my 10 km time by two minutes, but I didn't actually know what my 10 km time was. How do I know what improvement I will have to do, right? How do I know what it means to improve? How much effort will I have to put in? Do I have to do other training to condition my body to be race fit? What would it take? How long would it take?

Perhaps I would base my improvement on an estimate of how the average runner would improve. But I'm not like the average runner – I'm 5 ft 2", under 48 kg and I'm conditioned to run long distances. (No judgement please.)

That's the approach many companies are taking. Some companies are promising to double their growth and halve their ESG negative impact. How is that going to work?

This is a good framework that will help you cut your CO_2 footprint, and/or any other impacts, such water, waste, etc.

Sometimes reduction ambitions are not based on reality. The question that companies should be asking themselves is how will they reduce their impacts if they keep doing the same things in the same way that they always have done it? Is growth based on price increase? If not there is definitely a need for innovation.

How are they going to cut their footprint in half if they make more stuff and in the same way that they always have done? Is their growth just based on price increases?

FIGURE 5.1 Reimagining impacts reduction

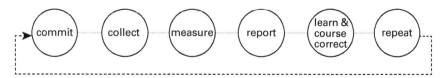

Some of these ambitions are not based on reality. We are setting ourselves and the next generations up for failure if we don't set the cornerstones for the evolution of the business in the future. That does not mean just doing the right thing from an ethical perspective, I'm also talking about setting the business up for success from a financial standpoint – and this is not just the next CEO's problem but the one after that too... and ultimately it is about the legacy of the company, its reputation, its longevity.

The other big elephant in the room is suppliers... when companies change suppliers every quarter or so, it's very difficult to get commitment. If the business is growing, it is hard to keep the same suppliers unless they grow too. Every time that the product is updated or upgraded, whether adding new styles, new bottles, or new blends, companies will need different people with different skillsets.

How is your organization set up to adapt to change if, in the not-so-distant future, customers drive demand so hard that the designer dictating preferences may flip, and the future of fashion is on-demand or made to measure?

The way brands 'show up' in the world is becoming incredibly important. How are organizations going to address the inequality and intersectionality issues? How are they going to optimize for sustainability? How will they transform their mindset and heartset to address people as citizens instead of consumers?

The pressure is mounting for all companies, not just luxury ones. Boards and leadership teams are actively listening, because people, whether inside or outside organizations, are looking for innovative brands that resonate with their values, and nowadays people won't hesitate to cancel brands.

One thing to take in account is that there are many nuances to these issues, such as regional differences and blurry lines between reality and perception. Talking with Dina Khalifa, Senior Research Associate at Cambridge University on luxury and sustainability, she shared that there has been a lot of research undertaken on these topics. One of the research questions was: Do you think luxury brands should play a role in tackling inequalities and what are consumer attitudes towards luxury brands' initiatives to become more inclusive?

The initial findings show that consumers in general hold negative attitudes towards luxury and don't believe that luxury brands could be inclusive. This sentiment is particularly strong among consumers from lower socioeconomic backgrounds, which is not surprising, and also more among those who do not buy luxury than those who do, which is again not surprising. This is consistent with previous research which shows what we call 'the clean luxury fallacy': those who buy luxury think luxury is clean because it's so expensive and they paid so much that it means it's doing everything right.

As the negative sentiment towards luxury comes mainly from those who do not buy luxury, it is crucial to make the industry inclusive. The most important way to achieve this is to first look at workers' rights, pay and the supply chain within the company, and then also look at what comes after that – racial and gender diversity. What is astonishing today is that very few luxury houses have racial diversity at a leadership level, however the gender gap is better than it was before, said Khalifa.

Technology is an enabler from a communications perspective as well as from a supply chain standpoint, as it connects the downstream and upstream of businesses providing transparency.

When you think about people in their role as employees, they are as important as your investors and/or your customers – they are the 'quiet disruptors' inside the house. They are the ones giving the wider world the early warning signs either way for organizations as they share with their friends or post on social media if they see any inconsistencies and/or discrepancies.

The network effect of the workforce is huge, and they are the ones who will make a real difference to a company's reputation. The golden rule is that there must be consistency between what a company says and does every day and everywhere. There could be hurdles not exclusive to luxury brands but for any business setting ambitious targets and pursuing seemingly unattainable goals, unless a substantial investment is made in the value chain.

'For businesses that have been around for a long period of time, that can be quite painful,' warns Tom Beagent, Partner, sustainability at PwC. 'Priorities and incentives within an organization typically deliver on existing drivers of perceived value, so when you bring sustainability into that mix, you've got to hardwire it into the existing structures, decision-making processes and incentives,' he explained. 'It's very easy to set a target. You just have to say I'm going to do this; the hard yards are actually delivering on the promise by making sure that every decision across the business is not only driving towards better financial performance but is also, at the same time, delivering on the sustainability targets.'

Creative destruction or creative collaboration?

One of the ways that we will see a paradigm change is when new players come to the market with new innovations, different and/or better aesthetics and a different narrative.

Does anyone remember Nokia? It's the perfect example of creative destruction, a term that Joseph Schumpeter coined in his landmark book *Capitalism, Socialism, and Democracy*. His argument is simple: in the early 20th century, the incremental improvements to horse and buggy transport were incredibly valuable, and he recognized that innovation would make it even more valuable.

With the introduction of Ford's Model T in 1908, however, there was no improvement they could make that could rival Model T. Horses couldn't match horsepower.

Interestingly, we have a distortion of the pure creative destruction model when it comes to electric vehicles, proving how regulation and innovation can sometimes operate hand in hand. It's safe to say that the creative minds behind social media could not have predicted either the Arab Spring or the controversy over election manipulation.

The purpose of creative destruction is to transform the market for the better, and improve people's standards of living by helping improve productivity by examining norms within an industry and identifying the inefficiencies holding back that industry's growth.

Collaboration can be an important driver. Businesses collaborating with their suppliers can better optimize the technology they use for their products and develop entirely new product lines or business models. The best outcome is when every person within an organization has improved their standard of living.

Indeed, adversarial relationships take on a 'me-first' mindset, looking to undercut business partners or customers. This hinders entrepreneurship and holds back innovation. A collaborative approach will lead to a true win-win for companies, making businesses more cost-efficient and better able to compete.

When Darwin talked about survival of the fittest, he meant that in a competitive environment, the individuals or organisms that are most well-adapted or fit for their environment are more likely to survive and reproduce, passing on their advantageous traits to future generations not the strongest or the fastest.

CASE STUDY

Tesla and the complication of disruption

The Tesla disruption model is counterintuitive. The classic disruptor – exemplified by the steel mini mill – enters a market with large incumbent businesses producing good quality products with bloated systems.

The nimble disruptor produces a cheaper product that is just good enough, forces the incumbents to abandon the bottom end of the market and then improves quality until the old guard cannot compete.

Tesla entered the market with an expensive, high-quality product. It had been supported by US government money from the US Defense Advanced Research Projects Agency (DARPA) and it was competing with high-end vehicles on a values and innovation pitch.

Tesla created a gadget on wheels. It is more like a phone than a car. The way it operates, the way it's made, the way it's distributed, how the maintenance works and how the customer experiences the relationship are all unlike other cars. Tesla cars communicate with the Tesla network, and although they can't connect with each other yet, they all connect indirectly through that network.

The data produced has huge potential. Even so, Tesla's rise has been supported by regulations to remove fossil fuel cars from the roads in the world's three biggest car markets – China, the US and the EU. Regulation has increased the market.

And so, whilst from the outside, Tesla appears to operate in isolation, in fact it is collaborating with governments for funding and to increase the size of its market. It is disrupting fossil fuel engines but not doing so alone. The Tesla is closer to the railways than the Model T.

Hirsch (2015)

The new old new models

People are savvier than ever when it comes to sustainability. They know that the infringement of workers' rights, scarcity of natural resources and water are not concepts – they are a reality. 'Putting sustainability at the heart of your strategy is not an option, it's a necessity,' said Marie-Claire Daveu, Chief Sustainability and Institutional Affairs Officer at Kering.

People are expecting companies in all sectors to move on these topics, but how if companies that are truly doing it don't communicate?

What we can learn from luxury is the ability to sell an aspiration, a positive narrative and a dream that, somehow, everybody buys into – consciously or not.

Historically, luxury brands told very little about themselves. Chanel, only a few years back, voluntarily published their financial data for the first time as they were never required to do so. The brands in the sector, from hotels to jewellery to fashion, that shared more than expected reaped the benefits.

In 2024 we can confidently state that the industry moved from small, family-owned companies with hand-made products towards multi-billion-dollar businesses.

Legislation in the EU nudges all companies, luxury or not, to disclose how and where their products are made – this is called Extended Producer Responsibility. It is now a compliance matter that companies are embracing, but people expect a lot more than compliance from luxury.

Who is truly excited about the Recommended Dietary Allowance (RDA) values of a sandwich or the ingredients on the back of cosmetics bottles? We have seen the food industry disclose RDAs for years, but companies still make the headlines for bad practise.

Let me give you a few examples to illustrate my point: in 2022, 130 people in Slovenia fell sick from a salmonella outbreak caused by steak sold by a single company (Food Safety News, 2023a); Nestlé was forced to close a factory after an E. coli outbreak in its frozen pizzas killed two children (Food Safety News, 2023b); and Norwegian authorities discovered listeriosis in five people from a single brand of smoked salmon across 2022 (Whitworth, 2023). More than 500 people from Finland, the United Kingdom, the Netherlands, France, Germany, Denmark and Portugal suffered from shigellosis – which delivers a week of diarrhoea, fever and stomach cramps – from a handful of hotels in Cape Verde (Food Safety News, 2023c).

These are just a few examples. The RDAs didn't help as they are just one part of the story, just like the Extended Producer Responsibility.

I had the pleasure of speaking with Marie-Claire Daveu, Chief Sustainability and Institutional Affairs Officer of Kering. Marie-Claire is a force of nature, a combination of grace, femininity and brilliance, and she steered the group towards taking bold actions and claiming a leadership position since the start of her tenure.

We need a company-wide approach if sustainability is to avoid the same fate. 'A company has to bake sustainability into the strategy, and the governance of the organization makes sure that the targets set are met,' said Daveu. 'The governance starts at the Board, and it trickles down to the top management – everybody needs to be involved.'

The rules

The investment community is showing it understands that companies need to be more responsible and more sustainable. As a result, the governance of businesses is also changing. As Leigh Pezzicara, Vice President, Sustainability at La Prairie said, 'Presently when there are investor days, the kind of questions that they bring to the table around sustainability are exponentially more sophisticated and greater in numbers.'

Luxury is in a privileged position because its products have inherent qualities that their mass counterparts don't have. Quality, durability, craftsmanship, asset-class status and brand equity are just some of the attributes that enable luxury brands to produce their product and monetize it many, many times over. Extending the product lifetime not only has environmental benefits but also creates greater incentive for the preservation of skills that contribute to the continuity of craftsmanship and cultural heritage. For example, a vintage Patek Philippe will always hold or increase its value over time in some instances. An old TV, not so much.

However, the main issues have not changed – overconsumption, inefficient production, human rights – all the classic 'stuff'. Thankfully industries are getting regulated, which will accelerate that compliance baseline and allow for comparison, but it won't solve all our problems. Although legislation is there in some industries, it is a well-known fact that it is most economical to pay fines than make changes. I'm sure that I'm not alone in thinking that this type of practice needs to stop and personal accountability need to take over.

The time for accuracy is here to stay. If a t-shirt is 100 per cent organic cotton, the cuffs cannot contain elastin. 2025 – the mid-point before the 2030 sustainable development goal commitments will be honoured – will be the first reality check for those companies that put targets and commitments out there without any real plan of how to meet them. Will you meet your targets? The second reality checkpoint will be in 2030.

Companies have made or will be nudged to make commitments that will be difficult to deliver unless all primary and secondary data is collected and analysed. Companies such as Positive Luxury help companies collect all their ESG data in one place, providing a gap analysis of the risks to help companies to transition their business taking in account the trade-off that companies will have to face.

Companies hiding behind certifications and/or prioritizing single issues, failing to address the transition systematically and then prioritizing their material issues will be financially worse off and with the same feeling of playing an endless game of Whac-A-Mole. It is not an oxymoron or an ambition to be sustainable and profitable, it is a reality that companies can achieve with the right team, board support, tools and investment in innovation and adaptation.

CASE STUDY
The Macallan

The Macallan distillery in Scotland was established in 1824, and since then, has been recognized as the world's leading single malt whisky.

Since its founding by Alexander Reid, a barley farmer and schoolteacher, the company has been a leading brand not just because of its amazing craftsmanship, quality and taste, but also for its long-standing care for our planet and its people.

In 1926 Janet Isabella Harbinson, the owner of the business, crafted what became the most valuable bottle of wine or spirit ever sold at auction – The Macallan 1926.

By doing the right thing for herself and the community, she made history for all the people that have joined The Macallan ever since. The company works on the principle that doing the right thing involves having the long term in mind, which underpins every decision.

The company has always accepted that the right path is not always the easiest and that they will not achieve all that they want on their own. And these principles run throughout the organization – starting at the top.

I met with Igor Boyadjian, managing director of The Macallan and member of the Edrington Executive Committee. He is softly spoken, but you can see the energy and passion in his eyes when he talks about this job.

When I asked him what had changed since Covid, he paused, looked me in the eye and thought for a while before replying. 'I've learned a lot about what resilience is first-hand, and that's an understatement,' he began. 'We had to switch overnight into survival mode. That was a good opportunity to step back and really reflect on what's happening out there, thinking harder about the right thing to do in the long term. That's for the business and beyond the business, for people and beyond our people.'

'As a good corporate citizen, we had to ask – what are the big decisions and the big choices we need to make to operate and change… because at that point we all realized how fragile we are.' Speaking for a company where the product is directly affected by the seasons and the weather, this fragility was perhaps already more obvious than it was to many. 'But we tend to have short memories as humans,' he said with a wry grin.

'Now is a good time to act before we start forgetting what just happened. So, it's something we can leverage to our advantage to operate change. Saying "let's keep doing what we used to do" is not going to work for anyone'. Beyond the immediate crisis management, Igor and his team embraced the new challenges and the new normal, redefining the right thing to do from the sustainability roadmap to the growth framework. 'It's acting with a lot more transparency as well, which I think is part of the new norm – and not necessarily only for consumers but for all our stakeholders,' he explained.

'Let's be open, blunt and honest about progress and the elements that we are trying to implement as well as that what we're implementing is slightly shifting the growth framework towards longer-term KPIs.' It is important to engage with employees and suppliers at all levels. 'We have frameworks in place to help everybody understand their role and how they can all contribute to the success of the company and its sustainability in every possible sense – social, economic and environmental,' Boyadjian explained.

The Macallan's teams are focused and incentivized to make the best decisions for the long run. 'We know where we're going and what we have to do to get there but we are very mindful of the steps that we need to take now in order to get to that midpoint,' Boyadjian continued.

Objectives were aligned with budget cycles and resources to ensure that every year, the business makes incremental positive steps towards its 2030 goals. 'Of course, a crisis will happen – especially in the times that we live in – however, we are ready to course correct when needed.'

According to him, a sustainable organization still needs to deliver profits to fund the transition, invest in the growth of its people, in their development and in ensuring they support them with the cost of living as well as helping its suppliers to develop and grow sustainably.

Nobody needs luxury. It's more a desire, a dream, the pleasure of owning a luxury good or experiencing luxury. This is why there is no better incentive than doing the right thing. This responsibility towards our people, this mindset of duty and care, gives you the right to operate in the luxury industry. It's about quality over quantity, enjoyment and sharing, which ultimately translates into better value and better values.

These are the mindset and heartset shifts that we need globally. Focusing on doing the right thing, looking after your people, and delivering a great quality product and a great brand instead of chasing short-term profits as your main objective will eventually translate into more value in the long term, he is convinced.

According to Boyadjian, one problem is that a lot of listed companies have the pressure of quarterly results. 'The cycles are so fast that it does not always allow them to have the time to do the right thing and to make the right decisions for the long term,' he said.

'Of course, we can't ignore growth, otherwise we won't have businesses. Regardless of the sector, luxury brands have the duty of legacy as the custodians of that brand. They have to maintain heritage, craft and people. As a leader of a luxury brand, your role is to leave the brand in a better state than when you found it.'

Boyadjian said. 'We have very diverse teams and we need to embrace differences throughout the business.' Leadership in the business has a compensation package linked to sustainability KPIs. Those financial incentives are about making the right decisions for the teams, suppliers and the business – 'this is what we call sustainability,' the managing director explained. 'It's almost obvious to highlight the importance of having incentives that are directly linked to every function of the business. Implementing sustainability is everybody's responsibility.'

Figure 5.2 shows the social and environmental sustainability vision for The Macallan. Everyone in the organization knows what the vision is.

Furthermore, everybody, from the CEO to the suppliers, believes that they can deliver that vision and explain the role they play in delivering those three words.

Marie-Claire Daveu at Kering agrees. She is confident that Kering's success is due to having that conviction and clarity from the top. With clarity, it's easier to do complex things, creativity flows from the creative team and down into the brand execution team reviewing and balancing sustainability, insight and marketing capability.

What is the reason behind the success of The Macallan?

The success of The Macallan's sustainability strategy is down to the idea of it being part of everyone's 'day job'. The company has sustainability champions in each area aligned to meet 2025, 2030 and 2050 targets. Sustainability is ingrained in the minds of those throughout the whole organization. 'We have six generations working at The Macallan,' Boyadjian said. There are diverse teams and these can be embraced to capture diversity of thought and ideas where everybody in the business is inspired to look for improvements.

The company is working closely with their suppliers to align with those who share the same values, beliefs and urgency to leave the world a better place. Success

FIGURE 5.2 The Macallan Vision, Purpose and Mission

Vision
Crafted Without
Compromise

Purpose

Doing the right thing with long-term in
mind for our single malt whisky and our
global social and environmental legacy.

Placing social and environmental responsibility
at the heart of everything we do.

Decision-making guided by a belief that the right path
isn't always the easiest path.

Guiding us to make the right decisions now to shape a rich
and diverse social and environmental future for us tomorrow.

Mission

Knowing we cannot achieve all that we want on our own.
Hernessing innovations, collaborations and the exchange of
experience and knowledge to acheive our goals.

Driving visible positive change.

Demanding more of ourselves because of our capability to lead and inspire others.
Evolving as leaders by sharing our progress openly.

Establishing a legacy of positive action built on innovation, collaboration and creative
problem solving.

comes down to shared values in the way that every component of a product is delivered.

In the case of The Macallan, it's about 'craft without compromise' when creating everything from a cask to a piece of packaging.

Kering has the same vision when it comes to working with suppliers. Once a year, they gather all suppliers together, share what the objectives are for that year and how those fit within the overall plan.

They make clear that each one of them plays a pivotal role for the company to be successful. Kering and The Macallan both understand that sustainability and innovation are not a cost but an investment. When there is a business case for doing things better, they don't wait for their budget cycle. They present a business case and get things done – why wait to do the right thing? The determination of a

FIGURE 5.3 How to deliver a cohesive and coherent sustainability strategy – The Macallan

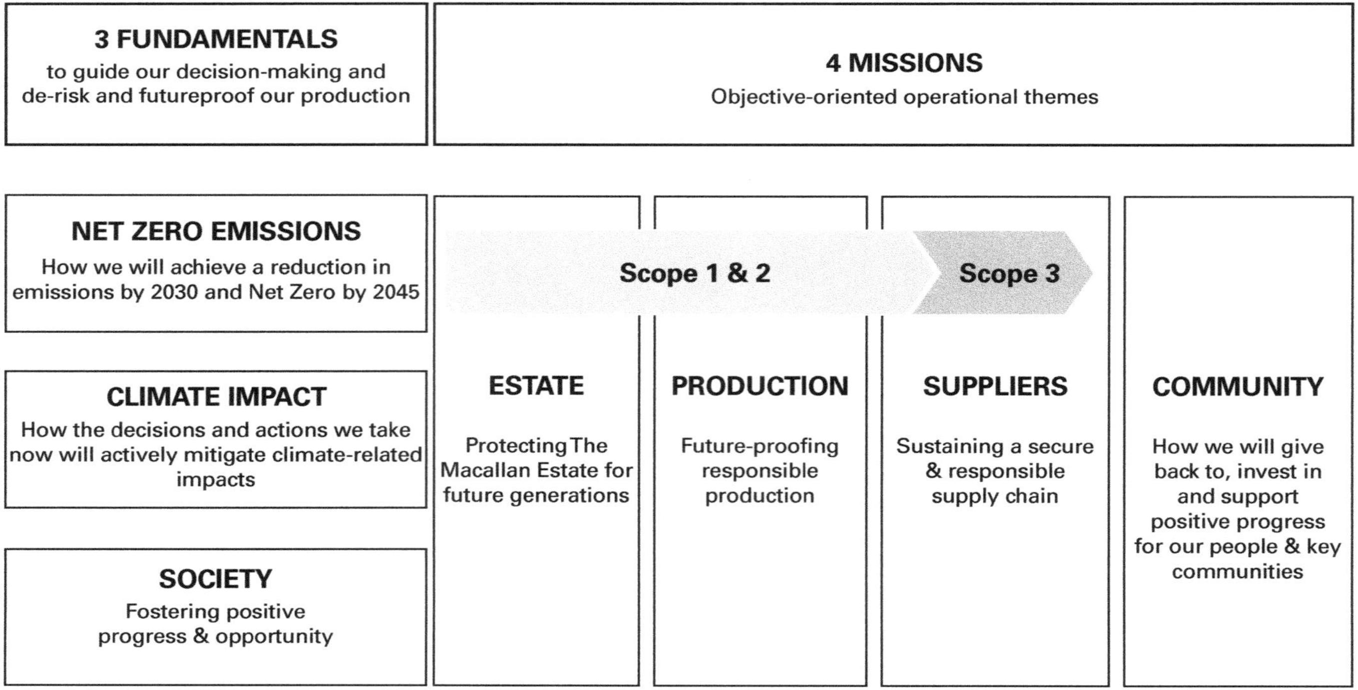

3 FUNDAMENTALS

to guide our decision-making and de-risk and futureproof our production

4 MISSIONS

Objective-oriented operational themes

NET ZERO EMISSIONS

How we will achieve a reduction in emissions by 2030 and Net Zero by 2045

Scope 1 & 2

Scope 3

ESTATE

Protecting The Macallan Estate for future generations

PRODUCTION

Future-proofing responsible production

SUPPLIERS

Sustaining a secure & responsible supply chain

COMMUNITY

How we will give back to, invest in and support positive progress for our people & key communities

CLIMATE IMPACT

How the decisions and actions we take now will actively mitigate climate-related impacts

SOCIETY

Fostering positive progress & opportunity

company and its board to deliver to the mission consistently is what makes a company successful. When you have a clear vision, the appropriate processes, innovation capabilities, a quality product, and storytelling mastery, why not take action? Compelling narratives backed by facts build trust and inspire people to join the journey.

The Macallan strategy at a glance

Elizabeth McMillan is the driving force behind their strategy and implementation. Elizabeth said, 'Introducing the updated strategy in 2021 has been both very rewarding and motivating. It has given us a future-fit framework that allows us to focus on the big priorities, breaking them down from stretching goals into clearly defined 12 month actionable workstreams. We know that this is a journey and change won't happen overnight but with the new framework now in place everyone can see the part that they play in the bigger picture.'

Tables 5.1 offers some tools that you may find useful to organize your thoughts, track deliverables and successfully transition your business between phases or through different planning horizons as part of your strategy change cycle.

The process of strategy transition will guide you to stay focused on your budget and closer to your goals.

Do remember that this is a living document, as the context keeps changing and you need to keep updating it.

These are some of the questions that you need to ask yourself and your teams to ensure that you are on track:

- Are you in line with the vision and values of your company?
- Do the areas that you are focusing on represent the things that you need to achieve?
- Do you have the right team and the right governance?
- Have legislation and/or risks changed? Do you need to course correct and/or re-prioritize? Do you still need this? (This is a tough one as some projects may be on the way, some of them may not have started – and even if you are passionate about them, you must know when to postpone or remove them from your plan. 'No' is a full sentence and a rather powerful one.)
- Do you need to add anything?

TABLE 5.1 Vineyard example – How to set up a strategy transitional plan and evaluation

Topic	Goal	2025 aims	12-month objectives	Lead	Current Status	Deliver by
Climate impact	Develop a mitigation and adaptation plan to prepare and respond to climate change impact on our Estate	Protect enhance and monitor Estate biodiversity and wildlife habitats	Produce, cost and schedule a plan for habitat and landscape conservation	Catherine Smith	Project, and costs agreed. Ecological audit completed by 1/23. Recommendations on communication to other teams, ongoing monitoring	April 23

The disintermediation solution

Vertical integration or disintermediation is a model that works well for luxury as in the last 10 years luxury brands have bought or are in the process of buying a lot of their specialist suppliers.

Vertical integration enables better margins, transparency and faster speed to market. This is not only happening across the value chain, but we have also seen businesses cutting out intermediaries and going direct to consumers (DTC).

For over two decades, hotels and airlines have led the way on this trend, and now jewellery, beauty and fashion are following suit.

In the fast fashion world, Zara's success is partially due to its vertically integrated model that allows the company to not only produce goods fast but also at low cost. Going forward, they will face raw material challenges from quality, consistency and price, just like everybody else.

Luxury's take on disintermediation goes from the farm/field all the way to their retail operations. Since 2012, Richemont, Hermès, Chanel and LVMH have been strategically investing in the management and control of their supply chains. LVMH acquired a majority stake in Loro Piana, a brand known for herding its own Andean vicuñas, in northern Argentina. Loro Piana serves not only as a consumer brand but also as a supplier of fabrics to both LVMH's own brands and some of the most renowned luxury brands worldwide. The same tendency is evident in the world of cosmetics. Chanel grows jasmine and roses near Grasse to create a lot of their scents. The company was so concerned about maintaining the quality of its raw materials that it built extraction machines right in the middle of the rose fields to avoid any damage due to the flowers being bruised in transport. They bought the fields a few years back.

To date, Chanel has invested over a billion dollars in the acquisition of over 40 of their suppliers, including Italian knitwear Paima, and has set up 19M, a beautiful building in the centre of Paris where they can be all housed together.

Disintermediation is not a trend but a business strategy. For example, the beauty brand Irene Forte Skin Care has always had traceability from farm to bottle. Most of her ingredients come from her own organic farm in Sicily and neighbouring areas in the Trentino region.

In summary, leaders across companies of varying sizes are currently navigating an unprecedented and intricate blend of volatile circumstances. To effectively adapt to this ever-evolving landscape, the key lies in maintaining flexibility in the execution of strategies, fostering innovation and placing a high priority on ESG considerations. This approach will empower companies to drive sales on demand while reducing waste and excess stock.

The circular economy, aka the re-world
(renting, repair, refiling, reset)

Today, the sentiment of circular goods or pre-love is covetable and exciting, in fact I would go as far as saying that old stock is a goldmine.

A few examples of this are Coachtopia from Coach, a community of designers that reimaged the future of accessories because they believe the future of fashion is circular, and Julie Pelipas' Better, a platform that helps big brands give deadstock garments new life. Most of our environmental footprint comes from extraction and production of raw materials, according to Daveu, Chief Sustainability and Institutional Affairs Officer at Kering. By leaning into circular business models, companies can mitigate this. Here are some examples.

CASE STUDY
Heat.io

Consumers are not the only people interested in sustainability. Investment funds and angel investors know that fashion must start to get more sustainable. Circular businesses, especially in fashion, are taking a lot of momentum from both investors and consumers.

One young business that has been rather successful at disrupting the traditional luxury business was backed by LVMH Luxury Ventures and the Hermès family very early on.

Heat.io revolutionizes the off-price space, and it's a favourite of Gen Z. This concept is a dream for Gen Zs as it is highly Instagrammable and perfect for creating content. It has helped Heat build a community, with viewers evolving into customers, flooding the brand's socials with user-generated content.

They curate their offering by working with over 80 luxury brands based on the consumer's style profile.

Consumers buy a box, but have no idea what it's inside. They get an SMS alert when a new drop is available, they select the size, and the mystery box will be dispatched. If they don't like it and/or if it does not fit, they can return it.

CEO and Founder Joe Wilkinson's background lies in his personal shopping and styling for celebrities, YouTubers, gamers and footballers. He spent a lot of time in multi-brand retailers buying clothes on behalf of other people. Instead of just shopping for clothes, he started building relationships with the stores.

As he was styling, he became aware of the issue around surplus products – not those that go on sale but those left over. This was good stock from brands that didn't want it to be discounted because they didn't want to damage the brand equity.

In the past, these brands had three options:

- The grey market – the sale of the goods by unauthorized dealers

- Take it back and try to sell it through

- Destroy the product – which is, let's face it, the worst

Heat.io created the mystery box to solve this. They put two or three items inside, and the customer will get more value than the price they pay for the box.

This created a solution for brands to move their overstock by getting it to the hands of Gen Z customers, not at a discount or in an outlet, so people don't get used to that habit. Wilkinson argues that young people don't care about the latest season, preferring to think about fashion in a seasonless way. They mix and match pre-loved items with older seasons or historic designs. Indeed, as fashion is becoming an asset class in some countries, some older items have more value than new ones.

Today, people buy a Hermès bag and can resell it for double in a year's time. When Wilkinson started Heat.io, he sent many mystery boxes to former clients – Youtubers and gamers who would film the 'unboxing'. The average age of Heat.io's clientele is 18 to 24 years old, and the average value of a box is £500. The mystery box is a vehicle to buy something good and durable, wear and resell it if they don't want to wear it any longer.

The elephant in the room – consumption

The issue with consumption is that we overdo it. Caroline Brown is the former Managing Director of Closed Loop Partners, a company started by Ron Gonen in 2014 to invest in developing solutions for the development of the circular economy across multiple stages of companies.

Closed Loop invests as early as pre-seed and seed venture. 'Everything we invest in must be something that is helping to further the development of a circular economy and to move our economic model from a linear system,' Brown told me. 'This is an economic model that keeps materials in play

TABLE 5.2 Example – Progress tracking of material topics

Priority	Topic	Progress report	Risks	Budgets	Resources
1 (needs action, planning or delivery within 3 months)	Net zero	Delivery has been agreed with the business, it's been set a target and a baseline and transitional plans delivery date is on schedule	All risks internalized, and understood and are in line with mitigation actions	Budgets are set and there is less 5% tolerance expected at completion	A cross-functional team has been ensembled
3 (within a year / 18 months)	Biodiversity	Progress is behind transitional plans, however, steps have been identified to course correct	Ongoing monitoring is required. Risks and issues exist, however next steps, owners and dates coupled with mitigation actions are agreed	Between 5% to 10% tolerance expected on a baseline budget. Ongoing monitoring required	A cross-functional team has been ensembled. May need external expertise to deliver
2 (within 6 months)	DE&I	Progress is behind plan and no transitional plan has been crafted nor has budget allocation and/or baseline	Significant material risk and/or issues with delivery have been identified resulting in a non-delivery and no clear actions to address	Greater than 10%–15% tolerance expected to be completed on the original approved budget. Need to agree next steps and a budget increase	Needs additional/ different internal resources. May need external expertise to deliver

continuously rather than a model with a waste pathway. In a circular pathway, the product is made, the product is used and the product is returned to the beginning of that system either through recycling, resale or recapture of materials so that it can be continuously reused.'

Sustainability, innovation, circularity and transparency are the main changes that she has seen today. Younger generations expect to be able to look under the hood of the products and companies that they're engaging with. This desire did not exist before, and technology enables this type of visibility.

'I personally don't understand the fear of transparency,' Brown said with a smile. 'If you start by being honest with yourself, you have the opportunity to have a clear view into your supply chain challenges whether they are material challenges, environmental challenges, or fair labour challenges.'

A culture of transparency followed by the technological development of transparency tools, followed by a complete breakdown and disruption of supply chains – the combination of those three accelerated a new paradigm. Add the voice of the new consumer and the pressure from the capital markets, light the blue touch paper and retire.

But, of course, transparency and accountability are not the same thing. Many companies display the list of their suppliers on their website – that is indeed transparency. But how many of those suppliers are good? As Sylvie Benard, former Environmental Director of LVMH, explained, that is accountability.

Transparency serves as the initial crucial step toward instigating any form of change, as you cannot effectively alter or improve something that remains hidden or unmeasured. This holds true for companies seeking to modify their behaviour, people making informed choices and capital markets comprehending the ESG impact of their portfolios.

The sector has increasingly drawn the attention of investors, regardless of whether it has historically been their focus. This heightened interest has significantly increased the available capital. However, recent years have also exposed the industry to greater transparency, revealing substantial profit losses during the Covid-19 pandemic, a lack of resilience in supply chains, evolving consumer attitudes and regulatory challenges. All these factors signal significant transformations within the industry, necessitating the development of fresh systems, technologies, business models, materials, innovation and mindsets.

What are the new capabilities and culture required for companies to remain relevant?

References

BankMyCell (2023) Number of iPhone users in the world/USA (2023), www. bankmycell.com/blog/number-of-iphone-users#section-2 (archived at https:// perma.cc/RZ45-KRC4)

D'Arpizio et al (2023) Renaissance in uncertainty: Luxury builds on its rebound, Report, Bain & Company, 17 January, www.bain.com/insights/renaissance-in-uncertainty-luxury-builds-on-its-rebound/ (archived at https://perma.cc/7H6V-2QRG)

Food Safety News (2023a) Salmonella outbreak solved with 130 sick; steak tartare blamed, 27 January, www.foodsafetynews.com/2023/01/salmonella-outbreak-solved-with-130-sick-steak-tartare-blamed/ (archived at https://perma.cc/ RER2-AAAE)

Food Safety News (2023b) Nestlé to close factory in France linked to deadly E. coli outbreak, 31 March, www.foodsafetynews.com/2023/03/nestle-to-close-factory-in-france-linked-to-deadly-e-coli-outbreak/ (archived at https://perma.cc/ E7UN-UDG3)

Food Safety News (2023c) Sweden was also affected by illnesses linked to Cape Verde, 3 January, www.foodsafetynews.com/2023/01/sweden-also-affected-by-illnesses-linked-to-cape-verde/ (archived at https://perma.cc/6JAC-YX3N)

Hirsch, J (2015) Elon Musk's growing empire is fueled by $4.9 billion in government subsidies, *Los Angeles Time*, 30 May, www.latimes.com/business/ la-fi-hy-musk-subsidies-20150531-story.html (archived at https://perma.cc/ LH83-9H6C)

Lin, S B (2022) Gen Z and millennials are driving growth in the luxury-goods market, study shows, Business Insider, 17 November, www.businessinsider.com/ gen-z-millennials-buying-driving-luxury-market-bain-study-2022-11?r=US& IR=T (archived at https://perma.cc/9VYR-R3ZC)

Whitworth, J (2023) Sampling issues found at producer linked to Listeria outbreak, *Food Safety News*, 16 March, www.foodsafetynews.com/2023/03/sampling-issues-found-at-producer-linked-to-listeria-outbreak/ (archived at https://perma. cc/C7M7-L5W6)

06

Mindsets: What they are and why they're needed in order to shape or change towards a sustainability culture

In this chapter, we will explore mindsets and heartsets, what they are, why they are important and how they influence corporate culture.

The two main problems that people face are either economic or existential. We are insatiable, always wanting more, and afraid of scarcity and starvation. We want more food, more clothes, more holidays, more time, more sex, more power, more land, while at the same time saving as much of our own energy as possible, forgetting that our world has limited resources.

Are we wired that way? Right at the heart of our brains is an area known as the striatum. It coordinates our planning, our decision-making and our motivation. This is a critical part of the reward system in our brain. It receives dopamine signals, the feel-good chemical, which helps regulate our motivation by giving us pleasure when we make the 'right' choices – to eat, to have sex, to do what it takes to stay alive and reproduce. As a result, it plays a key role in learning and forming habits. We get a dopamine hit when we satisfy a need or a want – and it is why we always want more, whether buying something to wear, to eat or to watch at one click.

Because this system helps us learn, it can of course be trained and retrained. We can help our brains to want enough or less and be rewarded for it. The stimulus for this can be social – for example society frowning on smoking indoors – or personal – the desire to lose weight for a special day so heading to the gym and feeling good about it. It can come from choosing a train journey instead of flying because we are helping our children have a future. To change our thinking, we need structure and support.

Let's look at the following example: if you want to run a marathon, you need a systemic approach, consistency and training.

First of all, you must set your goal. Do you want to finish the race in a certain time? If this is your goal, you need to be clear about what is possible given your 10 km time or your marathon time and then plan accordingly. If your goal is to improve your personal best time (in which case you already know what that specific time is), it's simply a matter of setting your training schedule, following it and achieving your target. Or if it's simply about finishing the race, then you need to make sure you're fit enough to do that. Depending on what your goal is, you will need to have a different approach to achieve it. The second step is what I call your secret weapon. It's always a good idea to go to the doctor and make sure your body can take the challenge, especially if you have any pre-existing health conditions. Then it's about creating a training plan to stick to, and that's a combination of running, rest days, gradual mileage increases and my absolute favourite, cross-training at the gym. If you do that, you can avoid injury and have an excellent race.

This is the same when you aim for a net positive organization – it is a journey of continuous improvement, innovation, adaptation and collaboration. It is a holistic approach that considers environmental, social and economic factors in order to create long-term value for all stakeholders and nature while enhancing the wellbeing of society. This is not a feel good, thoughtless, made-up expression, this is what the most successful organizations are working on today to keep being relevant in the future.

This is where mindset, heartset and culture come into play. It is easier to run a marathon if you train with somebody, it is easier to lose weight if everybody in your household eats healthy. And it is easier to run a sustainable organization if everybody is thinking about it.

To shift mindsets, you need to have a good understanding of your own agency and surround yourself with people that encourage you to reach your full potential and that share your values. Convene them around you and develop trusted friendships and trusted partnerships, at a fundamental human level, inside and outside the organization. Creating a shared narrative and establishing a common language is key to finding alignment and consensus. Transformational leaders are key to shifting the systems.

Mindsets are personal frames of reference. Your mindset is different to mine and typically determines our rational and analytical thinking. It is derived from the way that we see life, process external stimuli, and our assumptions and expectations about the world and ourselves.

Heartset is closely related to our emotional and intuitive processes. It describes how you connect with your emotions and with others in a compassionate and empathetic way as well as cultivating positive emotions such as love, empathy, gratitude and joy. Heartset is an integral part of what is expected from leaders and executive teams today.

Culture, in a country or a company, is effectively a collective mindset. When groups of people gather with a shared sense of purpose, finding areas of agreement and a fertile ground for collaboration. The stronger the sense of shared purpose, the more powerful the culture becomes.

All of these arise from our beliefs, our subjective truths, that are intrinsically correlated with our upbringing, the things that we have been exposed to, our past successes, setbacks, drive, decision-making and self-determination. Our belief system impacts how we see our life, work and relationships. Altering our beliefs is often a formidable challenge, frequently accompanied by apprehension. Endeavours to reshape our convictions can evoke a sense of threat. Our abilities and potential are intricately intertwined with these very beliefs. Now, the intriguing question arises: how do mindsets and heartsets come into play, and can we truly modify them? Does it appear that individuals in leadership roles are particularly steadfast in their beliefs?

Mindsets

Our mindset influences the way we think, feel and respond to some situations. Understanding, encouraging and cultivating empowering mindsets will influence how people and organizations approach their goals, relationships and development and of course will influence and determine the quality of the outcomes.

Mindsets are sometimes mistaken for heuristics, as both help us distil complex world views into small digestible pieces of information, and play a huge role in determining how we adapt, understand and/or shift our point of view.

For instance, consider the belief that giving up drinking would be a challenging endeavour, and pursuing a marathon would jeopardize friendships due to the extensive time commitment required for training. In this simplistic illustration, to shift one's mindset, it's crucial to cultivate a genuine desire for training or a compelling reason to run the marathon, such as raising funds for a charity or proving personal capabilities. Success is more probable when beliefs align with actions.

For example, if you change out of your running clothes and head to the pub instead of dedicating the allocated time to training, your behaviour contradicts your stated beliefs. Similarly, if you're a smoker (behaviour) and genuinely wish to quit, you're more likely to succeed. Conversely, if you attempt to quit smoking solely due to external pressure or health recommendations, you may relapse because your personal conviction to quit was never firmly established, even if you're fully aware of the health risks associated with smoking (cognition).

This cognitive dissonance stems from our unconscious beliefs – something that we established as a fundamental truth a long time ago, perhaps in childhood, and now runs on 'autopilot' in the background.

As individuals, we are inclined to spot inconsistencies in what others are saying or doing and whether the inconsistency is real or perceived, people tend to either question, reflect, adjust, deconstruct and criticize. For example, it could be that a person talks a lot in order to cover a lack of knowledge or may be aggressive and not listen so that others feel they cannot point out any mistakes.

Why is this important?

Stanford Professor Carol Dweck popularized the idea of fixed vs growth mindsets when she published her book, *The New Psychology of Success*. She wrote that with a growth mindset, anything is possible, as one cultivates love for learning, willingness to take risks and a belief in the power of effort and persistence. Having a growth mindset enables people to see failure as a path to success and a way to unlock their full potential and navigate the challenges that lie ahead with a positive outlook. With a growth mindset, you never stop learning and growing (Dweck, 2007).

The characteristics of a fixed mindset include the ingrained belief that things cannot change, learn or evolve. Typically, people with fixed mindsets don't take risks because they fear failure, feel threatened by other people's success and hide their flaws as they don't think there is anything they can do to change them.

It is obvious which of the two mindsets you would like your leaders to have and be a key ingredient to your organization's collective culture.

The growth mindset is vital to any progressive organization, especially young ones. You need to foster experimentation, entrepreneurship and innovation to stay current. It is ok to not to get things right as long as you do it with integrity, learn and evolve.

One of the reasons it can be hard for an organization to change could be because the culture at the leadership level has more people with fixed mindsets than growth mindsets. If this is the case, it is less likely that there is an appetite for the organization to want to disrupt itself and/or innovate.

Mindsets are changeable if you are willing to defeat your cognitive distortion, which are the internal filters and biases that fuel our anxiety.

Exercise 1: Please replace a fixed mindset with growth mindset thoughts.

Exercise 2: Please continue writing a list of your fixed mindset statements vs your growth mindset ones, now with the focus of gaining or sharing your sustainability knowledge.

Rachael De Renzy Channer, who served 12 years in the British Army and is now the Global Head of Sustainability at global leadership advisory firm Egon Zehnder, has a profound sense of dedication to her duty to help others and to be of service. She is a classic example of someone with a growth and collaboration mindset. When you talk to Rachael, her narrative is positive, even if the topic is difficult. She chooses positive words and builds on topics rather than blocking them.

When she talks about her time in the army, her compassion for others stands out. She references the 'Serve to Lead' motto from her time at the Royal Military Academy Sandhurst and measures her success as a leader through wellbeing from both the physical and mental perspective.

TABLE 6.1 Fixed vs. growth mindsets

Fixed Mindset	Growth Mindset
This is too difficult	I'll give it a go
I may learn a thing or two	This is really useful to me
There is no point in trying, I'm so unhappy	
Continue the list with your fixed mindsets…	

TABLE 6.2 Sharing sustainability knowledge

Fixed Mindset	Growth Mindset
Continue the list with your fixed mindsets…	

We talked about the mindsets needed to build a 21st-century organization. She said, 'We're moving away from this legacy of the "superhuman CEO" who has the answer to everything and may not fully embody the values of the organization. We need to be more tolerant of failure – using it to learn and perhaps take imperfect action versus perfect inaction. We also need more empathic leadership.'

'Every person is an island, and nowadays, we can't assume that people are willing to tolerate passive aggressiveness or patronizing attitudes from their leaders. We need leaders with a balanced mindset and heartset, camaraderie, empathy and honesty are some of the character triads of 21st-century leaders that have not been central to businesses today.'

Rachael sees the role of CEO as an orchestrator. As somebody who leans into their board role as a steward and in their executive role to operationalize sustainability values into the culture of the organization, and always leads with values and beliefs.

In terms of culture, organizations can be similar to people in that a clash between belief and behaviour creates dissonance. That's why, in 2024, it is no longer possible to have a purpose statement if you have a big behavioural gap within the organization.

A behavioural gap – in fact, any kind of organizational dissonance, especially if it 'leaks' externally – is destructive from a reputational and employee morale perspective. It may lead to the risk of being 'cancelled' as a leader or as a company altogether.

This is why it is important to think about mindset from the very beginning of the journey at the recruitment process. You can start by understanding what you need and then recruit people with the right mindset and heartset, not just skills, education and/or experience.

This is important in all areas of the organization but especially important when you are recruiting the candidates that will succeed the current leadership. Learning, adapting and transforming is what successful organizations do and will need, especially in the next few years as the economy is in flux.

You may want diversity, sustainability and entrepreneurship, but you need to know that the diversity mindset, the sustainability mindset and an innovation mindset as potential disrupters are actually going to be welcomed and accepted in the culture of the organization.

If not, you will end up with a business where you spend all your time managing the tension between disruption and continuation, Rachael explained. 'Right now we have the Chief Sustainability Officer role, this "superhuman" person charged to solve all the sustainability problems in the organization, and integration is the real key. We need to break the sustainability silo to get all of the knowledge to flow freely throughout the organization because it's impossible that one team can do it all. Sustainability departments may grow, but without the right culture this can be to the detriment of the wider organizational knowledge and capacity to evolve the business and business model to incorporate the sustainability agenda.'

Identifying who has a growth mindset in the business is key, as without a small army of committed and enthusiastic growth mindset people, all of the things that we've described become very difficult to do.

In many organizations, over 40 per cent of their workforce have fixed mindsets, which is the mindset that does not accept challenges, accept the need to disrupt itself and the organization, and work as a system instead of a silo. It will be very difficult to change anything big or small – curiously, this is not linked to generations or level of seniority with the company.

The brain is neuroplastic, meaning nerve connections or networks, can continue to branch, grow, change and reorganize throughout our life with surprising results and unexpected consequences.

If we keep learning, experiencing and exploring, our brains will form new neural connections or mindsets at any point in life, and this will keep our brain young.

Did you know that London black cab drivers are required to learn 320 different routes through London before they gain their licence? Their hippocampus is larger than the average person's as they have to retain and use a huge amount of information.

Researchers at University College London are in the middle of a research programme to understand how the driver's route learning protects them against dementia.

Acquiring new ideas can happen at any time in life and the result can be anything from a new career to a stronger mind and this is valid for both fixed and growth mindset people. The more you learn and consciously choose to believe that you can change and grow over time, the happier you will feel in yourself.

Challenging your preconceptions isn't easy, but the results can be impressive.

Only by challenging your assumptions can you spot the mistakes in them and prevent those mistakes from damaging you. Think the unthinkable and you will be fine.

Professor Olivier Oullier, neuroscientist, founder and CEO of Inclusive Brains, encourages questioning any negative views you hold about yourself and the world around you and creating new narratives that are more self-serving.

Oullier believes that the kind of leadership we will practise depends on the mindset we hold. Our experiences, especially at work, are defined by micro-movements, he explained to me – eye contact, smiles or simply being there. As a result, your team is constantly perceiving signals from you about the company, about their work and about what you might think of them. Who a team's manager is and what kind of mindset they hold and project to others determines the kind of team, productivity and levels of satisfaction and wellness that the team will experience.

Oullier has studied how brainwaves synchronize when people physically interact with each other. Some of his most recent field research shows that if care is one of the mindsets of your leadership team, you will end up with a psychologically safe, high-performing work environment. People will show respect and empathy towards one another as some networks in the givers' and receivers' brains synchronize, facilitating interpersonal connection and shared purpose.

Unfortunately, in today's organizations, often as a result of the fallout from the pandemic and working remotely, we are brewing a scarcity mindset where we perceive everything to be limited – time, money and care.

When resources are perceived to be limited, fear and politics thrive, and people become anxious about their future.

The opposite approach is an abundant mindset. It feeds our confidence and people feel ready to explore and broaden their perspective. Whilst employees find space and inspiration to connect to their purpose and creativity, the organization becomes a better business as the focus is on finding opportunity and synergy creation.

Organizations with a growth mindset and heartset make better businesses.

This is an invitation to reimagine what your life and work could look like if we approach people, work and the world around us in a different way.

How would you change your approach to people and the world around you?

CASE STUDY
The winning mindsets

This is how Dan Carter, one of the greatest number 10s of international rugby and captain of the All Blacks, changed his mindset in the face of unlikely odds.

I had the pleasure of interviewing Dan Carter – a fly-half for the All Blacks. Dan is the world's highest point scorer in rugby union test matches and is viewed by many as the best fly-half in rugby history. I asked him to teach me the All Black Mindset Way...

'Controlling your mind is one of the hardest things for people to do,' he began. 'Your mind often plays games with you and looks for ways of escaping or ways of trying to find a shortcut. When things are challenging, it is the thing that tells you to stop or give up.

If you can control that, you can achieve anything you want. You can achieve things that you never thought you'd be able to achieve.'

These words echo in my head when it is sunny outside and I would rather play tennis than stay indoors writing... but back to Dan. 'All the rugby teams and players, we all train in similar ways on the training field or at the gym to try and be the best rugby players we can be,' he pointed out.

'We'd been the number one team in the world for three years, then we went to the 2007 Rugby World Cup in France and we got knocked out in the quarter-final. We were the worst-performing All-Black side in the history of world rugby events. It was catastrophic. We were extremely upset. But one learning that we got was that we weren't putting enough time into our mental strength. Why spend hours on the training field, hours in the gym each day and not spend any time on controlling your mind?' And now, the number one rule for the All Blacks is – never look at the scoreboard.

This is a sacred rule. Imagine there's 20 minutes to go and everyone starts looking at the scoreboard, the numbers are looking bad and the team thinks – oh no, we're going to lose.

'What if we don't win? All our fans in New Zealand, all 5 million of them, they're going to be upset. We have to win, right? We can't lose. Your mind is so focused on the outcome that you forget about what you need to do in order to win,' Dan explained. 'You need to focus on the process, the team, and that means that you will win.'

For the next four years leading into the next Rugby World Cup in New Zealand the All Blacks learned about mindset and being able to perform under pressure. They developed the courage to try new things, evolve their game and have the tools in place to control their minds. 'We learned all these new breathing techniques,' Dan said. 'We learned a lot about when we're under pressure, how our mind reacts and whether it wants to try and escape or just freezes or goes into a state of fight where you start arguing with the referee or disagreeing on certain decisions.'

This is what the All Blacks call the state of red. Any player's mind can go into a state of red. The key is the ability to get it back into a state of blue – a blue head is when you are thinking clearly. You're calm, you're very good in your decision-making. 'We spent four years working on our mental strength,' Dan continued. 'In the 2011

Rugby World Cup at home, we were in the final playing against France – the team that beat us in 2007 – and we were playing extremely well. But they were playing out of their skin. They were hitting us with all sorts of pressure. We had been put in these challenging situations in our training. We were able to think really calmly, our decision-making was very clear, we had great communication and because of the work we had been doing for the past four years, we actually wanted to live in these high-pressure situations because we knew that, in order to be successful, we had to be able to perform under pressure.'

It was the first time the All Blacks won a World Cup in 24 years and Dan made it sound so easy. To try to apply that to an organization, I asked him how the collective mindset works.

Everyone reacts differently and their minds work differently, he explained. 'We had to work out how to focus on yourself and how your mind works when you're put under pressure. It's one thing on the training field and another when thousands are at the stadium and millions are watching you on the TV. For me, it was always freezing. The position that I played in was #10, the decision-maker. I needed to be speaking and making all the decisions for the team, guiding them around the field, giving direction for the rest of the team to follow. One of the worst things I could do was freeze. I had to go externally out of my mind to get me back on task, to get me back in the moment. So, I'd whack myself on my leg and I'd remind myself – focus. What do I need to do right now, in this moment? Forget about the outcome, forget about the potential result, forget about the mistake that I just made, whatever it was that put me into this state of red.'

But in a team environment, players need to learn about what their teammates do and what state they go into. Dan knew that his teammate on his outside was likely to go into a state of fight. He'd be yelling at the referee, trying to aggressively tackle opponents. He wasn't thinking about the team. He was just in a state of real aggression.

'I'd talk to him, get him to focus on who's tackling him and how to get out of this state of fight, getting back to thinking clearly and back on task,' Dan explained. 'So it's about you initially but then it's the people beside you helping you to think clearly. The most important part of the art of winning is actually being able to control your mind and helping your teammates control their minds when they are put under pressure.'

Actions vs words

The first step in a winning mindset is to set goals and to have a purpose. You need to have certain values to live by but far too often, your mind or your team can focus on the outcome or the financial return that shareholders want and forget about the process.

To be successful, you must put a huge amount of focus on the process and bring your team into having that same focus. That ensures everyone is aligned. But there's no point in just telling people what to do all the time unless you're out there doing it yourself.

Sport is like business – you know what to do, but every day is different. When you go to work or when you step into the pitch, the next 80 minutes or eight hours is pure creativity.

For me, the best form of leadership is getting out there and showing and inspiring the people that look up to you through your actions on a consistent day-to-day basis. Far too often, you see people saying the right things and then acting in a different way.

That's not leadership. With your actions, you're inspiring and motivating the next generation as well your employees and the people that look up to you. It's important that you control the things that you can control – your output, what you're prepared to give, your communication.

Don't waste time on things that you'll never be able to control.

You must also expect the unexpected. That, Dan explained, is important. 'In the All Blacks, we'd meet as a team the day before the game and we would come up with three really bizarre things that might happen in the game tomorrow – we lose two players, they get red carded and they're out of the game. How are we going to react? We're going to slow the game down, we're going to try and go to more five-man line outs, that sort of thing. Or what if we're down by three points with five minutes to play? You can either take a penalty for three points, or you can kick to the corner and try and score a try to help you win.

It's highly unlikely that these situations will happen. But it prepares you for the unexpected. So when something out of the blue happens from the opposition or some decision made by the referee that's completely wrong your thinking is so much clearer.'

Dan stressed that rehearsing these scenarios helped them become aligned as a team. There was no point in having the captain do these sessions alone. Having the whole team work together sets up lines of communication and problem-solving attitudes.

I asked him about trust – something that you earn with consistent behaviour, by doing what you say you will... Today, trust is being eroded by doubt. He said trust is really important in a team environment.

Firstly, you need to focus on your job and your role because if you're constantly looking over your shoulder and making sure that everyone else in the team is doing what they're supposed to do, then you'll forget about your role and your responsibility. Focus on nailing your task and your role within the organization. If you trust your team to do the same, that gives beautiful synergy.

Dan gave the example of Richie McCaw, the All Blacks captain in France in 2007. 'He took all the responsibility on himself,' Dan explained. 'If there was a message to be told to the team, he'd be giving it. If there was something that needed to be dealt with involving the referee, he'd do it. If there was something that was happening within the team that he needed to talk to the coaches about, he'd be doing it. And because he was doing everything for the team, he wasn't playing well. He took on too much responsibility and didn't trust the people around him.'

The All Blacks had a senior players group and he turned to them for advice and support. He started playing better. He could focus more on what he needed to do to play well.

'When he was playing at his best and trusted the other leaders and the other players in the team, the easier it was for the rest of us to relax and play our best,' Dan recalled. And then he said something I hadn't expected, but which strikes to the heart of this book.

'When I walked off the field after my first game, I wasn't 100 per cent fulfilled,' he told me. 'I didn't want to just be an All Black that played 10 games or one or two seasons. I wanted to add to the legacy. I wanted to hand the jersey back in a better place than when I got it.'

He was part of building an all-inclusive culture in the team where everyone, no matter what background they came from, felt really valued.

'We had New Zealanders, Pacific Islanders from Fiji, Samoa and Tonga, we had a South African, an Australian and even a player from England. So we got one length of coloured string for each culture – Australia, yellow, Fiji, white – took all the different pieces of string and wound them together to make a really strong rope. We had that rope in our team room and the changing room. It would travel around everywhere with us because that was a show, a sign of unity. It didn't matter what shape or size you were, the culture you've come from, what religion, your culture, your sexuality – you're a rugby player so you're just welcomed with open arms.'

The sustainability mindset

Why is this relevant? The critical business lesson is that an organization's culture is a collection of individual mindsets that either work together or against each other.

A company's culture/mindset is learned from the leaders and passes through the organization, diffusing through every team. The leadership, the board and the people along every step of the supply chain to customer-facing staff are 'your team'. If you win, they win, if you lose, they lose – and, of course, vice versa.

In today's corporate world, conversely, there's a culture that if one wins, not everybody else wins. That is why sometimes you have people that are pulling in the opposite direction in your organization, sometimes in your own teams, creating dissonance.

For leaders to succeed in their endeavours, every person in the organization needs to have the same North Star, the same goals, the entire organization, whether there are five, 10 or 500,000 people, needs to be rooting for the leader's success – their success. This is the biggest pain point to successfully embedding sustainability into the company's strategy and into every business unit.

Effective leaders and managers invest time in getting to know each member of their team on a personal level. By doing so, they can assess each individual's emotional state and capacity on a given day, enabling them to determine the appropriate level of tasks or responsibilities to assign when the team members arrive in the morning.

My personal hero

Susannah Rodgers, MBE, a fellow Young Global Leader (YGL) and a Paralympic Gold and Bronze Medallist in butterfly-style swimming, has felt the sharpest possible end of this. 'When you are a swimmer in the final of an event, there are eight chances to win and you are dedicating four years of your life to, in my case, around 35 seconds of a race. When I used to turn up to training, and I was having a bad day, or was tired, it would affect my training and, if that was how I trained, how could I guarantee I would be ready for those 35 seconds? My coach could tell just by the way that I was moving in the water that I was tired, and he would change the entire set for the day because he knew what I could or couldn't do. He knew when he could push and when he should back down. That's the kind of skill you need as a coach or a leader because you must know your swimmer or your team as humans and really understand what drives their goals – approaching this in a holistic whole person way.'

You are your team's coach. If you are in a positive mindset, you will enhance the collective productivity at an organizational level. How you lead and the type of soft skills that you may have are crucial to get the best out of people nowadays.

The sustainability mindset is a combination of...

Fostering a sustainability mindset involves several essential steps. Collaboration is at the heart of this transformation. People generally lend their support when approached for assistance, both within and outside the organization. Equally crucial is accountability. It's perfectly acceptable not to possess all the answers initially, but it's imperative to demonstrate a willingness to find solutions, whether they come from within the organization or from external sources. Susannah (Susie) Rodgers openly shared in our interview that going through perceived failure helped her grow, teaching her the lessons and the processes she needed to reach her goal. 'I came in fourth place in London 2012,' she said. 'That is why I wanted to do better and win in Rio' and she did bring gold home.

Susie has won over 30 medals, 20 of which are gold. What inspires me about Susie is her fearless determination and belief, nothing is ever hard or difficult for her. If we go swimming together, a rare occasion due to my inability to keep up, I would sit at the edge of the pool complaining about the temperature whilst Susie takes her prosthetic arm and leg off, fearlessly and defiantly jumps into the (freezing) water, (shouts a few words of 'encouragement') and glides away with incredible freedom and grace.

FIGURE 6.1 The sustainability mindset

Growth Mindset

You will need to learn a lot of new skills and embrace change, and equally, you will need to share your skills and learning

+

Heartset

Requires empathy, inclusive behaviours and openness coupled with future thinking and innovation

Sustainability Mindset

A growth mindset has a lot to do with being brave and bold. If you have the conviction, and a plan, you have to try. If at some point one has to change the plan or evolve it, that is part of the journey. If the business has the resilience, being honest is the best policy, and you will keep your employees motivated by saying 'sorry we don't have all the answers yet, but we will work on them together as together we will get there faster', and more often than not people will be right behind you and pull the weight.

If people feel that they are trusted and that management is being transparent with them, then there is that circle of trust within the company that will make people stay because they feel that they can change things and that they have an impact. It's about giving people autonomy and trusting them.

When transforming the organization to a sustainability mindset, it is important to understand the dominant mindset already in the organization which will help you find a made-to-measure approach. Find examples as proof points that transcend the intellectual and emotional nature of messaging.

What overarching mindsets impact your organization's culture?

Growth?
Fixed?
Collaborative?

Please fill in any other mindsets that come to mind.

How do your team and/or the board react when you give difficult feedback?

What have been your biggest setbacks?

What did you learn from them?

Product before profit

Culture impacts how people are managed based on their beliefs and values. A meaningful way to affect an organization's culture is to influence employees' individual mindsets and beliefs, which is done through training and managing the skills gap. The more you know, the better you feel about yourself. As you evolve and learn your mindset changes.

On 3 April 1973, Marty Cooper placed the first call from a mobile cell phone while working at Motorola. Do you remember that phone? Heavy was an understatement. 40 years later, we can't imagine life without a smartphone. We find out what time our next train is, read the weather forecast, speak with our friends and colleagues, research facts and information or spend 15 minutes a day scrolling through endless videos of dogs, cats and animals, any animals – or maybe that is just me!

Nowadays, a simple USB-C charger has more computing power than NASA had at its disposal when the Apollo mission landed on the moon. This is the result of how we solve problems. In 2001, Steve Jobs created the iPod and iTunes with a specific objective in mind – selling more Macintosh hardware.

Apple was always about the hardware and the software was the enabler to sell hardware. Steve Jobs saw a legitimate means of creating something that would enable better sales of Macintosh and subsequently of the iPod. 'Steve had a large vinyl collection, the question that was put to him was, how would you like to have all of the tunes on your vinyls on one device so that you could then access all your music when you wanted? He got it immediately,' said Joe O'Sullivan, a former Apple operations executive, who worked under Tim Cook and the late Steve Jobs. Ten months later, the iPod was born.

In addition to having a device with all his music on it, Steve Jobs has also solved the music piracy issue. 'We believe that 80 per cent of the people stealing stuff don't want to be, there's just no legal alternative,' Jobs told *Esquire* in 2003, the day after he launched iTunes. 'So we said, "Let's create a legal alternative to this." Everybody wins. Music companies win. The artists win. Apple wins. And the user wins, because he gets better service and doesn't have to be a thief' (Jobs, cited in Langer, 2003).

While trying to prevent piracy, Jobs set up the founding technology that led him to launch the first iPhone, which at the time was not equipped to download apps from third parties. Jobs learned quickly that individuality was at the cost of having a closed wall garden, and that was not a sustainable solution – that is why the next generation iPhone was born open.

'Simplicity is the ultimate sophistication,' declared Apple in its first marketing brochure (Isaacson, 2011). Jobs came up with a simple idea: let's get rid of the on/off button. The phone would gradually shut down if it wasn't being used but turned on again when reengaged. But his innovation didn't stop there. He asked himself 'what happens if you think of a great idea six months from now?', introducing the iPhone in 2007 (Jobs, 2007). And so, the iPhone became all about the apps. His vision was that everyone could own an iPhone, which, at first glance, may appear similar, but in reality, each iPhone would be profoundly distinct, reflecting the individuality of its owner.

Jobs' passion was to build an enduring company where people were motivated to make great, innovative products. 'Everything else was secondary. Sure, it was great to make a profit, because that was what allowed you to make great products. But the products, not the profits, were the motivation. Sculley [former Apple CEO John Sculley, who ran the company from 1983 to 1993] flipped these priorities to where the goal was to make money. It's a subtle difference, but it ends up meaning everything - the people you hire, who gets promoted, what you discuss in meetings,' Jobs told Walter Isaacson (2011), whose biography about him was an instant bestseller after the Apple CEO's death in October 2011.

The same is true with sustainability – it is about building the apps, opening it up to collaboration and building innovative products that enable people to live better lives. After all, Apple is one of the top five most successful companies in the world with an operating profit of over $122 billion pre-tax income in 2022 (Statista, 2023).

Solving today's problems can create incredible opportunities for now and in the future. In 2023 we have more data points than ever before about how climate change affects industries, countries and individuals, but none of this data seems to be translated into meaningful actions. Why?

We need a new approach – the Apple approach to disrupting the world at large. Could the luxury industry, Hollywood, the entertainment and hospitality industries lead the way by creating 'new aspirational lifestyles' models of what is cool or good? Could we create new habits that can disrupt the status quo? Could we create innovation consortiums to create the world that we would like our children to live in? There are many benefits of being analytical that tend to ignore the holistic perspective and interconnectedness to one another, and there are also endless opportunities to innovate and change this crisis into an opportunity for yourself and society at large.

Extractive vs. regenerative mindsets

A 'regenerative' mindset sees the world as an ecosystem built around connections. As the environmental scientist John Muir wrote in his 1911 book *My First Summer in the Sierra*: 'When we try to pick out anything by itself, we find it hitched to everything else in the Universe.'

Unfortunately, the human world currently chooses competition and individualism and the extractive mindset, where profits are based on taking as much of a finite resource as possible faster than anyone else and selling it for as much as possible.

Seth Godin, formerly Yahoo's president of direct marketing and author of *Permission Marketing: Turning strangers into friends and friends into customers*, once asked a legendary American music promoter called Bill Graham why he charged so little for tickets for a Bruce Springsteen tour since the tour sold out so quickly. He suggested Graham increase the price to $100 a seat – which, back in the 1980s, was an enormous sum.

'I could do that,' Graham replied. 'But the thing is, I'm here all year round, and my kids only have a limited budget to spend on concerts. If I charged that much for one concert, they wouldn't be able to come to the other shows I book...' (Godin, 2015).

Our economy is like the touring industry – we could think like Bill Graham and set out to ensure that our customers keep returning forever as our prices are set with longevity and community in mind. Instead, we are charging as much as we can for every ticket and not thinking about next year's tours or the year after that or if our grandchildren will be able to afford to see a rock concert at all.

Over the next 30 years, we need to move from an extractive mindset to a regenerative one. This type of mindset is about creating and nurturing new types of systems that can be sustained and restored, fostering collaborative and inclusive approaches that promote equity, justice and wellbeing for all stakeholders including nature.

This is an imperative today, but we should be mindful that it will take time. Having a regenerative mindset doesn't mean that we need to sacrifice profits. In fact, as Bill Graham's argument shows, the opposite is true. It means profits for the long term – a plus for the bottom line, a plus for people and a plus for nature.

Speaking with Carole Collet, Professor in Design for Sustainable Futures at Central Saint Martins and Director of Maison/0, the Central Saint Martins-LVMH creative platform for regenerative luxury, she explained the problem designers face with changing mindsets. 'Up until recently, designers have had an extractive mindset in relation to the natural world,' she explained. 'We easily forget the consequences of our material sourcing when we solely focus on their creative potential. To make a piece of wooden furniture, we cut a tree. To make a shirt with conventional cotton agriculture, we incentivize the destruction of our soils and biodiversity. For too long we have looked at the natural world as an endless bank account of resources that we can keep taking from.'

This is changing today. 'We are beginning to understand the limits and consequences of this approach. Instead of using nature as a resource for design and production, we can think of design as a means to restore ecosystems. With regenerative design, we can literally flip the creative process and design a product that can help restore an ecosystem.' We also need to reimagine how we educate designers. 'One of the focuses of Maison/0 is to develop a disruptive creative curriculum and we have launched a new MA Regenerative design course in 2022 at Central Saint Martins to do just that. We have integrated an ecologist and an anthropologist alongside a designer in the academic team to ensure our students understand how to design for nature, not just with nature.'

Regenerative design aims to work with or mimic natural ecosystems. It uses systems thinking to create resilience and integrate the needs of society coupled with a thriving natural world.

Businesses have an incredible opportunity to break the silos and really answer the questions that the younger generations have been asking themselves – how can I be part of the solution? The biggest pain point that we have today is that we roughly know what the carbon footprint of a product is, and we have tools that enable us to track the ingredients and composition of products – but what corporations have not yet done is connect the data to the people and think about how they can replenish the natural world and add value to individuals and our society.

The next step is to marry cognitive data with emotional content on how an individual can engage and connect with the meaning of the data. This must not be a feeling of helplessness or hopelessness but a sort of euphoria, knowing you are being useful and feeling good about actions and decisions taken – or, of course, the anticipation of doing so. Climate change has a slow feedback loop and people have short attention spans and almost no patience. Finding the joy in anticipation should not be hard. As children, we instinctively understand the delight in waiting for a birthday or a holiday. Getting there, as the saying has it, is half the fun.

Humans delight in craft, in making, in pleasing each other and dreaming of good things to come. There's a link between one's emotions, actions and the stimulus that we received from our external environment. When we overcome cognitive dissonance, we will start feeling what's at stake and how one unintentionally participates in and/or contributes to unsustainable practices, like overuse of electric usage or buy and throw away culture.

We are wise to use what's available to us without damaging the environment to which things might return. It is something we have known for centuries. To pick one obvious example – the Aesop's fable 'The Goose that Laid the Golden Eggs', written over 2,500 years ago. There is a similar story in Buddhist texts written sometime before Aesop. It is, in other words, a very old and very well-known story.

A couple is given a goose that lays one golden egg every single day. After some time, they become convinced that the goose has a great lump of gold in its belly. They kill it and cut it open, only to find it has the same internal organs as any other goose. What it means for them is that they will have no more golden eggs. This is a story we seem to have forgotten. Eight billion people and counting, we're depleting the world at an unprecedented rate. We are cutting into our goose with brutal indifference. We need to invent a better method to produce and consume. In today's world, organizations will need to think hard and fast about how to achieve true transformation creating value along the way for all stakeholders.

The key question is – how can organizations empower individuals so that this is a joint mindset and a shared culture? This is especially important when thinking about Gen Z because of their willingness to get involved and help solve environmental and social problems. Can nature teach us to create a sustainability mindset? Is our creativity or our resilience or both combined our key for survival?

When speaking with Stephanie Phair, Group President at Farfetch and a fellow Argentine, she said that 'Big changes do not happen all at once, they happen as a succession of small stimuli and decisions that eventually bring you to a different destination.'

She believes transformations will only be successful if you tie them into your business and to the financial goals of your business. 'We took a long hard look at the Farfetch mission,' she explained to me. 'We are the largest destination for luxury fashion, but we're also a technology provider for the luxury industry and we're a platform. And so we really wanted to play on that platform approach. We need a dual approach. We need to become more sustainable, but we also want to use our platform, our audience, our technology, our global reach, our ability to have impact and be the platform for the good for the industry. We've had very good feedback over the years that our sustainability strategy is very aligned to our business strategy, to our mission and it is a way that we can progress sustainability from a business point of view.'

Companies today have the capacity to understand their areas of impact from an ESG perspective. However, what companies don't have is one single place where they can quantify their impact and understand their outcome, analyse their risks and opportunities and be able to have easily digestible insights for better decision-making. If companies foster a transformative mindset, not limited to individuals within the organization but also cultivating relationships with communities and peers to drive positive change and innovation, it would be easier for people to have a collaborative approach to ESG and sustainability. By embracing a transformative mindset, individuals and organizations can adopt different behaviours and think about things with a more open mindset because they see the entire picture of the whole organization instead of part of it and, in this way, play a role in reimagining the future to be more equitable and regenerative.

To further the sustainability mindset within organizations we need to improve our language skills, said Christian Toennesen, Group Sustainability Director at Selfridges Group. 'Sustainability started out with all these movements,' he said. 'It started out as separate things and now it has become the thing itself.'

Sustainability teams need to learn procurement, marketing, operations language and legal; finance, sourcing and production teams need to learn the sustainability language. We need to be blending or integrating these two sides of the business – sustainability with every other function and encouraging people to be comfortable with the discomfort of not knowing all the answers.

How do we think differently? 'In order to operate in the complexity of this century we have to do some inner work,' Scharmer (2009) wrote in *Theory U: Leading from the future as it emerges*. So how can we use this?

In my view, we have fallen short as a movement to connect the sustainability vision and mindset to individuals and their role, driving meaningful change and fostering a collective commitment to sustainability and innovation.

When communicating with your teams, employ vivid and descriptive language to help them picture the direct and indirect impacts of their work. Showcase instances where their efforts have made a tangible difference. Embrace and celebrate their ideas and suggestions for improvement. By doing so, individuals and organizations can gain a clear understanding of the significance of their contributions. Equally, finding the right way to tell your company's story is key for success. People gravitate towards stories because they are a fundamental aspect of human culture. Across the world, children are narrated bedtime tales to provide them comfort and ease them into sleep. Climate change, undoubtedly, possesses all the elements of a compelling narrative. We initially failed to heed its warnings, grappled to find solutions, but now we have the opportunity to collectively rewrite our future. We can collaborate and innovate in order to find the solutions needed for a more harmonious world and, ultimately, live happily ever after in harmony with nature.

I'm an optimist, believing in our capacity to drive change within ourselves, our businesses and the prevailing norms. Legislative measures are propelling this transformation, compelling companies to foster innovation and adapt. There is a growing demand for a reimagined world from people, and technology plays a pivotal role both downstream and upstream in addressing these challenges, benefiting both consumers and manufacturers. For the vast majority of companies, these changes should have been previously managed in other aspects of their operations. Reflecting on the late 1990s and early 2000s, industries previously untouched by digitalization exhibited reluctance before ultimately embracing it.

Similar to how the digital team was once siloed, the sustainability team faces a similar situation today. With time, the luxury industry had to undergo internal digitalization. It became evident that digital is not a separate entity but an integral part of every aspect of the business. Digitalization became ingrained in the mindset, and companies began hiring digital natives. I believe a similar parallel will unfold with sustainability within businesses, as mentioned earlier.

Sustainability will be part of every function of a business and embedded in everything that teams do. Just like with the adoption of the iPod and the iPhone, the people will buy into a sustainable lifestyle. This mass adoption and inflection point hasn't happened yet, but I do believe that technology is an enabler to fast track us to mass change.

Carole Collet at Central Saint Martin's recalls the moment when the digital world converged with her own. She had to familiarize herself with tasks like sending emails and downloading files, vividly recalling the divide between those who were tech-savvy and those who were not:

> We found ourselves in a position where we had to completely redefine our work processes and seamlessly integrate digital tools into our daily routines. This shift was both real and rapid. Now, we urgently require a similar transformation in the field of design, one where we infuse deep ecological knowledge into the

creative process. This ensures that our designs are geared towards restoring the health of our planet.

Let's embark on a journey to reimagine our world. A world where we're conscientious about our energy consumption, where we protect and maintain the cleanliness of our water bodies, free from plastic and sewage contamination.

Let's reimagine a world where we assume responsibility for ourselves and extend respect to those who differ in appearance or thought. A world characterized by increased tolerance, generosity and patience. The truth is, our world can be different if we have the courage to reimagine it, if we dare to think differently, to aspire to different things.

And remember, it's perfectly fine if you don't get everything right on the first try. Embrace failure as a stepping stone for personal growth. In life, every experience is either a victory or a lesson.

What steps can a company take?

- Ensure that your mission captures the minds and hearts of everybody in your organization. In order to deliver your mission goals it is important that all goals, targets and incentives link back to it.

- Although it may not be possible to create a mission statement that resonates with every single person in the organization, fostering inclusivity and focusing on shared goals, values and visions of the future are good starting points. Success looks like everybody in the organization embodying the mission through their actions and behaviours. The best way to achieve this is to consistently incorporate it into performance evaluations, goal-setting processes and decision-making frameworks.

- Assessing your company's current ESG and sustainability practices is the first step to identifying areas where improvements can be made, such as energy consumption, waste management, supply chain practices, diversity and inclusion initiatives, employee wellbeing, ethical governance and many more. It is only by understanding how good or bad you are that you can set meaningful, clear and measurable sustainability goals, aligning with your business and sustainability strategies. For example, you may aim to reduce greenhouse gas emissions, increase diversity in leadership positions or be nature positive by regenerating and rewilding the areas where your raw materials grow. Integrating sustainability into your overall business strategy is a must, as, in this way, you can ensure that environmental and social topics are taken into consideration and integrated into decision-making processes, including product development, resource allocation and market positioning. This helps make sustainability an integral part of your organization's mission and DNA.

- Develop an ESG framework that outlines the key metrics and indicators to track and report on. This framework should cover environmental impact (e.g. reducing your water consumption), social impact (e.g. employee wellbeing, community engagement) and governance practices (e.g. board diversity, ethical guidelines). Aligning these metrics with recognized standards and frameworks, such as the Global Reporting Initiative (GRI) or Sustainability Accounting Standards Board (SASB), TCFD, etc will make your business a lot more resilient.

- Involve all your stakeholders – employees, customers, suppliers and investors – in the sustainability journey, fostering a sense of ownership, enabling you to address the priorities of your different stakeholders in an engaging and efficient way.

- Implement concrete initiatives and practices that support sustainability and ESG goals. Develop action plans, allocate resources – financial and human – and assign responsibilities to drive implementation.

- Regularly monitor and measure your organization's progress towards sustainability goals and ESG metrics by collecting and analysing sustainability and ESG data, assessing performance and identifying the areas for improvement will enable to set processes to achieve transparent reporting, demonstrating your commitment and progress and outcomes.

- Sustainability is an ongoing journey. Staying adaptable and responsive to emerging sustainability issues and stakeholder expectations is key to ensuring organization resilience and sustainable economic growth.

Broaden the dialogue

Being sustainable has a long feedback loop and consumers can lose heart. What the sustainability movement has fallen short of is that the messaging of sustainability does not offer instant gratification for the good deeds – neither physically nor emotionally – and that is not how we are wired, we need short feedback loops to keep people interested.

There is still a say-do gap barrier when it comes to adopting sustainable solutions. The main drivers for people to buy are design, functionality, comfort, convenience, etc; sustainability attributes come second regardless of what they say. Ultimately, it's all about the product or the service.

With the global cost-of-living crisis escalating, it's crucial for individuals who are hesitant to opt for sustainable purchases due to cost considerations to grasp why certain products come with a higher price tag (Boston Consulting Group, 2022). For instance, everyday cleaning products that exclude harmful substances like chloroform tend to be pricier. The same holds true for products with reduced packaging or lower volume due to concentration. Although people might not vocalize it, there's a common perception that they're paying the same or even more for less.

Perhaps, companies need to adopt more innovative strategies to communicate why sustainable choices are pricier and what these alternatives entail. Additionally, considering setting the green choice as the default option could encourage more sustainable consumption habits.

Are you open to changing your mindset and finding out how you can move your organization to greatness?

Exercise:

- What would I like to change about me or my work?
- Where would I start?
- What steps will I take?
- What would the outcome look like?

References

Boston Consulting Group (2022) Consumers are the key to taking green mainstream, 13 September, www.bcg.com/publications/2022/consumers-are-the-key-to-taking-sustainable-products-mainstream (archived at https://perma.cc/9FK3-NBQH)

Dweck, C S (2007) *Mindset: The new psychology of success*, Ballantine Books (reprint edn)

Godin, S (2015) Overcoming the extraction mindset, *Seth's Blog*, 12 June, https://seths.blog/2015/06/overcoming-the-extraction-mindset/ (archived at https://perma.cc/SYD9-KXRG)

Isaacson, W (2011) *Steve Jobs: A biography*, New York, Simon & Schuster

Jobs (2007) cited in Schroter, J (2011) Steve Jobs introduces iPhone in 2007,
    YouTube,www.youtube.com/watch?v=MnrJzXM7a6o (archived at https://
    perma.cc/7MMR-JGU8)

Langer, A (2003) Is Steve Jobs the god of music?, *Esquire*, July (published online
    10 September 2014), www.esquire.com/news-politics/a11177/steve-jobs-esquire-
    interview-0703/ (archived at https://perma.cc/KT4T-R7B6)

Muir, J (1911) *My First Summer in the Sierra*, The Riverside Press Cambridge,
    Houghton Mifflin Company, Boston and New York

Scharmer, C (2009) *Theory U: Learning from the future as it emerges*, Berrett-
    Koehler, San Francisco

Statista (2023) Leading companies in the world in 2022*, by pre-tax income,
    Statista, 15 March, www.statista.com/statistics/269857/most-profitable-
    companies-worldwide/ (archived at https://perma.cc/SQ4U-L9EH)

07

Creating a climate for change

Culture is what you do when nobody's watching.

Culture is something that one learns and transmits from person to person, and it evolves and changes over time.

Organizational culture is shaped by its leadership, mission, values, industry and employees, and it plays a pivotal role in how the organization operates and performs and how it is experienced by others including customers, suppliers and investors.

A strong organizational culture fosters a sense of pride amongst its stakeholders, promotes positive behaviours and outcomes such as innovation, collaboration and customer satisfaction and, more often than not, offers a fertile ground for a sustainability innovation culture to flourish.

As we have seen in the Macallan case study, mission-driven for-profit companies share their missions with all stakeholders in the organization – from the board and leadership teams to all employees, customers, investors and suppliers. Their mission is embedded in everything that they do – product, communications, advertising – and it is not just about turning a profit. When people connect with a company's mission, everybody wins, and in a highly legislated world this will be the differentiator.

Employees have job satisfaction and pride, companies are more resilient and profitable, and the outcomes that they create make communities and biodiversity better overall. What is not to like?

I had the pleasure of interviewing the team at leading international management consultancy Oliver Wyman – Keith McCambridge, Partner and Head of Organizational Effectiveness Europe, and Laure Charpentier, Principal in the Retail and Consumer Goods Practice in Paris. Both were very open and knowledgeable. McCambridge said that 'Organizational drivers shape your attitudes, your beliefs, your values and your mindset.'

McCambridge gave the following example. 'If somebody is rewarded in an organization for personal achievement and individual delivery of key performance indicators, then their attitudes and their beliefs are going to be focused on satisfying that requirement. If I am paid based on what I deliver, not what the person next to me is going to deliver, then my mindset will be focusing on my activity. Those mindsets then subsequently inform behaviours. If I need to focus on my activity, the behaviour I will show is likely to be selfish, insular, and predominantly focused on those KPIs. I'm not going to be selfless. Those behaviours then ultimately give an organization the culture that it deserves. So drivers lead to mindsets, mindsets inform behaviours, behaviours deliver the culture that you deserve.'

Culture either enables performance or disables performance

Unless your organization is continuously conscious about how these drivers are affecting mindsets and behaviours, culture becomes obsolete and starts to hamper your ability to progress. Having a well-defined vision of excellence and a clear destination in mind is absolutely essential as the starting point for any journey.

Organizations and their teams need to be really clear about their mission, what service they offer and what their reason is for existing. 'The luxury industry is no different,' says Laure Charpentier. 'Nowadays, people, especially the younger generations, want to be part of something that they believe in. Typically, they only will spend two to five years working for the same company, and they want to make that tenure count.'

However, this extends beyond just employees; I'm referring to all stakeholders. Investors now anticipate the highest returns achieved in an ethical manner, with a focus on how a company positively influences the environment, communities, and society as a whole.

I spoke to John Elkington, a pioneer in sustainability, who said, 'It is genuinely shocking how, even today, sustainability and business strategy often do not go hand in hand. Top teams in large organizations risk missing brewing disruptions with the potential to collapse their business models – and, ultimately, impact us all. When such moments come, they often follow what Hemingway called a "gradually, then suddenly" trajectory. One moment everything's fine; the next your future is shot. Maybe AI will help top teams pivot in record time, but don't count on it. More likely, you'll discover that better prepared and perhaps more innovative competitors – including people you've never heard of – are eating your lunch.'

Since the beginning of the decade we have lived through a period of unprecedented uncertainty around the world. Firstly Covid-19 and then the Ukrainian conflict left most countries around the globe forced into behaviour change when it came to sustainability, mainly because of the cost-of-living crisis, and when a behaviour is practised for long enough it becomes ingrained in the culture. Is the cost-of-living crisis what will make us more mindful of the resources we use?

Only time will tell. What I do know is that unlike in 2012, even with recession risks looming, businesses, the financial markets and governments are not taking climate or sustainability topics off the agenda, in fact they are leaning into sustainability innovation in order to face the energy and water crisis and deal with supply chain disruption. All stakeholders understand that sustainability innovation is a business opportunity.

The most forward-thinking companies are investing in sustainability and innovation in order to enhance their bottom line and mitigate future price crunches in raw materials, water and energy. What we have learned from previous downturns is that companies with strong sustainability strategies and ESG metrics are more resilient than the ones that have approached sustainability as a tick-box exercise.

Cultivating a sustainability innovation mindset and, consequently, fostering a corresponding culture is paramount for a company to maintain a comprehensive and unified approach. This approach helps the business navigate through challenging times by prioritizing what truly matters. It is absolutely overwhelming the amount of work that all companies have to do in order to report on environmental, social & governance (ESG) issues, however, rather than cutting these short the best-placed companies are the ones that will identify the issues that are most material to them. You will need to map your own journeys to sustainability depending on your ambition, culture and growth appetite. The stronger your culture, capabilities, process and sustainable business practises, the more competitive advantage and success your business will enjoy.

The good news is that you can anticipate inflexion points before they emerge and, although there are no signs of the luxury industry slowing down in the short term, this inflexion point is on the horizon. And while luxury has been one of the most resilient industries for over 40 years, there is no guarantee that this will remain the same in the next 40 years. In order to stay relevant, companies need to innovate in order to remain relevant in the lives of their customers. Something that luxury has done really well up to now.

The CSIO and CIO

Creating a climate for change is not a one-time event but an ongoing process. In the last 10 years or so we have seen the Chief Sustainability Officer (CSO) gaining momentum within companies, building their sustainability teams, and building internal capacity. In today's landscape, we observe the Chief Sustainability Officer collaborating closely not only with the Chief Sustainability Innovation Officer but also extending their influence across all facets of the organization. The expectations regarding what a CSO can deliver to the organization have soared. They are now required to possess a comprehensive understanding of sustainability, alongside proficiency in various domains such as business strategy, organizational management, legislative compliance, risk assessment and material issues. This blend of technical and business acumen must be complemented by a high level of emotional intelligence to inspire trust in the process and encourage individuals to embrace change. Furthermore, CSOs must excel at articulating outcomes in an engaging manner to a diverse range of stakeholders, from investors and the board to employee. This role is becoming a lot more central within organizations in response to the existential challenges of business, including capital allocation for the prioritization of capital investments and innovation.

Adaptation and innovation are two words that resonate in every department of most organizations, including the boardroom, as we are in a period of great economic and social uncertainty. Nowadays the CSO and the CSIO share that responsibility. Pre-pandemic, the role of the CSO was mainly about managing reputational risks and creating a feel-good factor about the organization, and innovation was in the hands of R&D. Today there is a clear need for these roles to exist at the same level and they ought to work collaboratively. That is why the most avant-garde organization have a CSO and a CSIO.

Sustainability and sustainability innovation are not just about doing the right thing but leading companies through a transition. For that very reason, CSOs and CSIO are now being invited to the leadership team, involved in co-creating company strategies and in the case of the CSO integrating ESG metrics throughout the organization. In today's companies where you have different generations working in the same place it is imperative to have a strong corporate culture with sustainability at the heart of it. In other words, the role of the CSO is moving from a silo to a transversal role in the organization, enabling the CSO to interact across all functions of the business including in investors meetings. Meanwhile, the CSIO is focusing on the transition of the business by innovating collaboratively with internal and external partners.

These roles are strategic roles for the business, focusing the organization on what matters most in order to deliver stakeholder value.

Companies have been complacent in recent years; however, a tsunami of legislation and directives are popping up on both sides of the Atlantic and companies are now paying a lot more attention to the trade-offs and conflicts that exist between stakeholder interests and ESG topics as financing the green transition is key to staying relevant in the not-too distant future. For example, hotels will talk about brand purpose rather than fair pay and modern slavery.

A lot of companies today produce what is called a materiality matrix to identify the critical ESG topics, but the reality is that a lot of companies are not differentiating what creates value vs ethical concerns or between strategic opportunities and risk mitigation, resulting on a 'everything is material' mapping, without remediation plans in place as it is unrealistic for companies to solve all their material issues at the same time without a prioritization list. This is particularly relevant as the newly created reporting standards will come into play from this year (2024), enabling investors to make like-for-like comparisons between companies in the same sector. The reality is that investors are now engaging in sustainability topics, specifically on how companies are making progress, because in turn their portfolios are also being questioned.

Nowadays, the Chief Sustainability Officer has a significant presence in investor meetings, often alongside the CEO and CFO. This shift in dynamics often involves the CSO reporting to the CFO and other high-ranking executives. This move places the CSO's role on the executive floor, ensuring that sustainability efforts are intricately tied to the company's core objectives, with a focus on long-term value creation.

Furthermore, a notable transformation is the CSO's collaboration with a cadre of 'technical' experts who specialize in various critical areas such as carbon and biodiversity accounting, human rights and modern slavery.

However, it's essential to underscore that success isn't solely reliant on technical expertise. It also hinges on fostering collaboration across business units and functions where sustainability and innovation play a pivotal role in creating business resilience, and ultimately sustainable economic growth.

There is a growing recognition among companies that it's essential to incorporate ESG targets into executive and leadership compensation, including roles like the CEO, CFO and CSO. However, it's worth noting that many of these targets primarily focus on risk mitigation, such as carbon reductions, water efficiencies, diversity, equity, and inclusion (DE&I), rather than being linked to innovation and adaptation of the business, which hold greater significance for the long-term sustainability of the organization.

What is encouraging to see is that in a very relatively short space of time, we're talking about the 'acting' instead of the 'committing', which in my view is phenomenal progress.

But a step change is required as we companies are still trying to understand how they realistically affect and how to measure it. It is possible to hold a stakeholder forum and share the journey of a product, but the million-dollar question is – what has changed and what will change at a micro-planetary and societal level, if anything?

The real challenges are about to come, pushed by new legislation and disclosure obligations, including double materiality and the reporting of comparable sets of metrics.

The outcomes that companies will need to deliver are multi-year projects. It won't be possible to start and finish this in one budget cycle, so the expectation of growth will also need to change, at least from an accounting perspective, as this new mindset will enforce long-term thinking. Companies will need to start investing their capital to produce societal and ecological outcomes that can take years to mature to be sufficiently meaningful. We are about to enter a new sustainability cycle, and this is your opportunity to choose your partners for the journey and establish how will you embrace innovation in order to be successful.

The main challenge for luxury will be tuning into their luxury consumers, as they have not started that dialogue. On the surface, the luxury consumer is not interested in sustainability but in purchasing that particular brand they love. Scratch a little deeper, and that same consumer is interested in sustainability in other aspects of their life, for example conserving energy or water, driving an EV and buying healthy food – although sometimes they are not healthy in their habits.

How can luxury brands tune into their audiences?

Natural diamonds, leather and opulent packaging are not attributes that are perceived as valuable by many people anymore, especially the younger generations. It is true that the desire for a brand starts in the digital space, but then what? How are you going to move from 'see' and 'want' to 'buy' and 'keep'? The main pain point for brands nowadays is to form meaningful and long-lasting connections with their audience, especially in the digital world.

Sustainability innovation is the new frontier. Having an innovative approach to new products, services and sectors coupled with business model development is key to unlocking customer value and new revenue streams.

What is truly compelling to people today is what the brand stands for and says about them.

Is it time to reimagine the way companies sell luxury?

Luxury brands serve as a powerful magnet that draws in individuals who share a special connection with a particular aspect of the brand, whether it is their aesthetics, their narrative, their values or their products or services themselves. These individuals can be seen as a community in a stricter or looser sense of the word depending on the brand.

The pain point for brands today is that they are renting communities on other people's platforms and are completely dependent on algorithms.

In the beginning stages of social media, a brand may enjoy a strong and natural reach to its followership. However, as the platform continues to mature, the organic reach of the brand will inevitably decline. Consequently, the brand will constantly face the task of investing in nurturing 'their' community, lured by the implicit promise of being able to communicate with their social followers.

With the increased dominance of just a few platforms, increased privacy regulations and events such as the iOS 14.5 update in mid-2021, brands are waking up to the fact that those platforms have become gatekeepers between them and their audience that had originally committed to engaging directly with the brand.

In August 2023, the average organic reach of Facebook pages was 2.31 per cent (SocialStatus, 2023). Let me put this differently – more than 97 per cent of followers do not get the content they subscribed to.

'People want to belong to a group that shapes the future of what they wear, watch, own or rent. The more involved they are, the stronger their emotional relationship is with a brand. Tuning into your audience is crucial for luxury brands to understand and engage with your target market effectively. The successful brands of the future will own their community relationship as the lines between brands, consumers, and influencers have become blurred, allowing everyone to participate in creating value for brands and for themselves,' said Roy Bernheim, Co-Founder of Decommerce.xyz.

This newfound closeness enables brands to gain a deep understanding of what their community truly cares about on a personal level. By communicating directly with their audience, brands can establish a genuine connection that fosters loyalty and trust. Luxury brands stand to benefit greatly from this approach.

Decommerce.xyz is a community software for brands to build a community in their websites or landing pages. I asked Roy how he moved from founding a menswear company to building community software. 'I knew you were going to ask me this,' he said smiling. 'We realized this when we built our community-led menswear brand TBô Clothing from 0 to 300,000 customers. We involve our customer community in several different areas of the business, including product co-creation'.

'Understanding what our customers wanted was key to reducing waste – by only producing what they needed – and driving brand equity. It seemed odd to us that we were experiencing rapid sales growth and were producing more professional content yet were getting ever lower engagement on and organic traffic from social media platforms, that is why we built Decommerce. Our beliefs are rooted in radical collaboration, this is why we decided to white label and share it with others as it creates a harmonious partnership where brands and their customers work together to craft an exceptional experience that resonates deeply with their shared values and aspirations. We never looked back,' said Roy.

When you have a strong culture, this is easy to do as brands know what they stand for, and when you do, it is easy to bring it to life visually and experientially and create a strong emotional bond people feel, so they can remember. This is not marketing, it has to be genuine to be credible, said João Paulo Testa – aka JP – creative director at London-based advertising agency AMV BBDO. 'From my perspective, brands can connect with their relevant audiences by understanding the power of knowledge and storytelling. When you have a story to tell, people stop, listen and engage. A story creates a sense of belonging, creates meaningful cross-cultural connections. You can make the reader, viewer and listener part of the story, and that is even more powerful. What has changed in modern luxury is that brands are adding a little mystery and anticipation to the stories – for example, unexpected collaborations with artists, musicians or other brands from a different sector or positioning. This triggers curiosity, discovery, desirability and then belonging.'

He continued by saying that people today expect luxury to behave sustainably; it is the being that matters, it is the way they manifest, not so much what they say. Everybody can look cool, but being cool is different.

It is the same with sustainability – it must be real across every touchpoint, every product and every activation. Let's take Rimowa, for example, a German brand proud of its well-made aluminium suitcases. Their advertising is pristine, showcasing the product at the centre of their campaigns. This time, the company just launched a campaign called 'A lifetime of memories' to highlight the fact that they have a lifetime guarantee. The campaign encourages people to think about their luggage as a travel companion, with their scratches, stickers, dents and dirt from the road. The bag is not perfect, but still beautiful. The advertising, you would say, goes against all the principles of design, beauty and the luxury market, but it doesn't, it makes you connect with it. There's also a story to tell from a sustainability point of view. 'This suitcase will last you forever, which is the very reason why you may want to buy another one,' said Testa.

JP has been rather generous with his time, so I asked him one last question: How can we succeed in changing the climate narrative? He smiled and said, 'When you understand that we are the problem, this conscience wakes you up and it becomes easy to find solutions. Every small action counts. Every small thing you do inspires people to emulate you, and you become a voice, the voice turns into a statement, the statement becomes a behaviour and just like that, you become a reimaginer that can truly change the narrative and the world forever.'

The reimaginers

John Kotter put it beautifully: change could come from anywhere in the organization as there are always people – active or not – that are questioning the status quo.

Reimaginers are generationless. They actively work to create positive and meaningful change. They are motivated to make a difference, improving the world around them. They are lateral thinking, creative and, as Solitaire Townsend (2023) put it in her latest book, *The Solutionists*.

Creating change is often a long and challenging journey, where you will face obstacles, setbacks and criticism – but the scars in the journey are valuable learning in striving to create sustainable and systemic solutions.

Reimaginers are not dreamers or theorists; they are action-oriented, with a growth mindset. They actively look for opportunities to make an impact, whether through direct interventions or advocacy, to drive positive change in addressing the pressing challenges of our time.

The luxury industry is full of reimaginers across all sectors, and all of them offer lessons. For example:

- Leo Rongone, CEO of Bottega Veneta, launched the programme 'Certificate of Craft' guaranteeing repairs and made the bold move of quitting social media.

- Francesca Ragazzi, Head of Editorial Content at *Vogue* Italia. Under her leadership, the magazine featured for the first time a paralympic athlete.

- Nina Marenzi, founder and director of The Sustainable Angle: Future Fabrics Expo. Nina started to raise awareness of the impact of materials and the need for innovation 14 years ago.

- Stefania Lazzaroni, General Manager Altagamma, Helen Brocklebank CEO Walpole, UK, Caroline Rush, CEO British Fashion Council, Bénédicte Epinay, President and CEO Comité Colbert France, Carlo Capasa, CEO Camera Nazionale della Moda Italiana's (Italy's Chamber of Fashion), and Steven Kolb, CEO Council of Fashion Designers of America (CFDA) for protecting, promoting and developing the luxury industry in the UK, Europe and the USA.

- Claire Bergkamp, COO of not-for-profit Textile Exchange, is on a mission to inspire brands to use certified sustainable fabrics, and eliminate virgin plastics from their supply chains.

- Rene Macdonald, founder and Creative Director of Lisou. Rene's collections have only a few pieces of the most exquisite silk hand-printed in-house.

- Rafael Mich and Carlos Couturier, co-founders of Grupo Habita, a Mexican hotel group that celebrates Mexican beauty, culture and entrepreneurship, have been innovating in this space for many years. They have recently opened the Theri Hotel Terrestre in Oaxaca, Mexico generating 100 per cent of its energy from solar power, showing that it is possible to be 100 per cent off the grid in the hospitality business.

- Hedda Felin, CEO of Hurtigruten Norway, a cruise company working to sail their first zero emission cruise by 2030. Although this is six years away, the company is working to improve the sustainability of all their existing cruises.

- Iris Van der Veken, Executive Director at Watch & Jewellery Initiative 2030, is leading the watch and jewellery industry to reimagine themselves.

- Leah Wood, Scott Wimsett, Bell Jacobs and Helen Taylor, climate advocates, using their public profile for raising awareness of climate change and social justice.

- Patrick Goddard, President of Brightline, the first privately owned and operated passenger rail system in the USA. The trains will connect from Orlando International Airport to Miami in just three hours, a route that is normally travelled by car or flown. The train journey will be at the intersection of hospitality and transportation, giving passengers a one-of-a-kind experience.

- Christopher J Nassetta, President and CEO at Hilton. His vision was simple, to make Hilton the icon that it once was and he leaned into excellence in hospitality, and he succeeded. As the national chair of the USA Travel Association, he strives to use the innovative strategies that served him well at Hilton, to create unforgettable end-to-end experiences when travelling in the USA, making the USA once again a travel destination.

- Storm Keating, television producer/director, businesswoman and mother. Storm uses her voice to support sustainable businesses and raise awareness of social and environmental causes around the world.

- Patricia Sancho, founder and CEO of Le Petit Planet, one of the first platforms for re-commerce for kids.

- Arizona Muse, a fashion model, climate and social justice activist and founder of Dirt Charity. Arizona has dedicated her life to actioning systemic change along the fashion supply chain, starting with how our clothes are grown.

- Tina Bhojwani, founder of AERA NYC, a certified vegan and Butterfly Marked shoe company, using innovative materials that are 50 per cent bio-based and 50 per cent synthetic. The shoes are artisan made in Veneto, Italy.

- Tiffanie Drake, journalist, environmental activist and author of *The Rule of Five*. Sustainability storytelling at its finest, Tiffanie help generations of people to reimagine their relationship with fashion.

- Claire Colleti, Environment and Sustainability Manager at Dior, Eva Alexandridis, founder of 111 Skin, and Lisa Franklin, founder of Lisa Franklin skin care sustainability, leading their organizations towards a journey of continuous improvement.

- Samantha Chapman, Global Head of Marketing and Sustainability at Stephen Webster, Anu Huhtisaari, Head of Sustainability Garrard, Celine Herweijer, Head of Sustainability HSBC, Karen Pflug, Chief Sustainability Officer Ikea, Nancy Mahon, Chief Sustainability Officer Estee Lauder, and Rebecca Marmot, Chief Sustainability Officer Unilever are all inspiring women championing the sustainability transformation.

- Gemma Mortensen, co-creator of New Constellations and co-founder of an organization that helps people imagine and create a better future by taking people through an immersive journey to transform their life.

- John Hackett, founder of Arena Flowers, the first florist that uses their Flowers' waste to create their packaging.

- Jamie Gill, founder of The Outside Perspective, a not-for-profit for people of colour, aimed at increasing representation within operational roles in the fashion and luxury industries.

- Valerie Keller, co-founder of Imagine, has extensive expertise in building transformational leadership communities and was, alongside Paul Polman and the Kering team, a key player in setting up The Fashion Pact launched at the G7.

- Charlie Beasley is a consultant at Egon Zehnder with a focus on reputation, governance and regulation. A key part of his work has been helping both Egon Zehnder and the clients and candidates he works with to reimagine how they think about diverse identity and life experience and the leadership strengths they bring.

- Hamish Scott, Development Director, Positive Luxury. Hamish made a step change in his career from the Royal Opera House to sustainability and has inspired the luxury industry to reimagine processes, materials, guest experiences, putting environment and social change as part of their strategies.

- Livia Firth, co-founder and Creative Director of Eco-Age has been challenging fast-fashion since 2010, when the term was still in its infancy. Livia is the executive producer of *The True Cost* documentary and has been a campaigner against human rights abuse.

- Rachael Johnson, Head of Risk Management and Corporate Governance Policy and Insights, The Association of Chartered Certified Accountants (ACCA), for her leadership on risk management and governance and for translating the complex language of risk and governance into a language that is easily understood by anyone.

- Samata Pattinson is a fashion entrepreneur, best known for her work as CEO of Suzy Amis Cameron's Red Carpet Green Dress, which showcases sustainable fashion on the red carpet every year at the Oscars as part of its activities.

- Leigh Barrett is Chief Sustainability Officer at the Marbella Club. Leigh transformed the business and managed in 24 months to integrate sustainability into the business strategy and all the functions, both front and back of the house.

- Mei Chen is General Manager and Head of Lifestyle & Luxury at the Alibaba Group. Mei has been growing exponentially Alibaba's second-hand platform marketplace to contribute in a positive way to climate actions, embracing sustainability, digital transformation and the pursuit of net zero emissions.

- Zulu Ghevriya, CEO Smiling Rocks, an innovative lab grown diamond companies that couples environmental responsibly with social good.

- Carmen Busquets, a fellow Latin American from Venezuela. Carmen is a philanthropist and investor who champions fashion-tech and women equality. She was the co-founder and founding investor in Net-a-Porter.

- Mabel van Oranje is a fellow Young Global Leader, serial entrepreneur for social change and founder of Girls not Brides and VOW – Mabel's mission is to end child marriage.

The list, fortunately, is vast. In every corner of the world, there are ordinary people doing extraordinary things. Igniting conversations, taking action, innovating, making introductions, collaborating, providing the funding or the platform and making things happen for good.

The luxury narrative is a juxtaposition of their heritage and/or the approach of reimagining that heritage in modern times, desirability, order and simplicity told in a multi-sensorial, aesthetically beautiful way.

Linda Hewson, former Creative Director of Selfridges, said, 'At Selfridges, we put creativity right at the centre of the business and used it as a driving force, at the time it was a bold thing to do. The creative team took inspiration from a wide net including art, fashion, philosophy, music, news and contemporary dance. I feel proud that we created this platform or engine of conversation and transformation – the Selfridges platform, where we talked about meaningful issues in an approachable, engaging and sometimes playful way, issues such as over fishing, ocean plastic, body image, gender equality and mental health, we turned these issues into experiences that customers could participate in.'

Just like most luxury brands, Selfridges also understood that it didn't have to put products in windows to sell, but you did have to have an interesting story to tell if you wanted people to notice you and engage with you over and over again.

I asked Linda about Selfridges' success around awareness-raising of climate change: 'That was radical and inspiring' she said [talking about Project Ocean and Project Earth], 'it helped people to understand and learn about sustainability by feeling it, seeing it, tasting it, reading it, and experiencing it. Project Earth was a multi-sensorial feast of cues and nudges that enabled anyone that worked at Selfridges or engaged with Selfridges to understand what was important to us and what we were challenging ourselves with, simply by experiencing it on one of the channels.

'The thing is,' she continued, 'you have to be consistent in your actions when you communicate on sustainability. Every day, and at as many touch-points as possible, it is not only about what you say but it's how you go about doing it authentically. When you start that journey, it is important to understand that this is not a campaign. It is much more than that, it has to become the whole business strategy as this is about who and how we want to be in the world,' said Linda.

In 2024, the majority of luxury brands across all sectors are behind in the sustainability journey just like they were in their digital transformation. Embedding sustainability in the strategy of the business is a change management exercise that requires an intentional cultural change aligning budgets and production processes in order to truthfully transform the organization.

This is the very reason why luxury is behind the sustainability transformation curve – why would you disrupt what has been working so beautifully for over 40 years?

Sustainability is no longer a matter of the heart, today it is a matter of financial resilience, commercial risks and, ultimately, survival; although perhaps these risks are a little too far to see, it this does not mean that they are not there.

Luxury is in a privileged position to foster a climate for change and has the responsibility to lead the way, especially when it comes to innovation. But luxury is not alone when it comes to funding the change.

Working more closely with suppliers and helping this transition is an imperative that all companies must embrace sooner rather than later if we want to achieve the 2030 goals.

A great example of optimizing for sustainability is the America's Cup, founded by Larry Ellison, founder of Oracle. The cup is not just a sailing competition, it is a driver of sustainability, engineering, design and technology innovation, setting a new paradigm for the yacht industry. From innovative materials to improve wind performance to the use of hydrogen, from the use of AI in the design process to being a plastic-free team, the Cup strives to showcase what is possible for an entire industry.

Is the luxury industry a catalyst for innovation that then spreads elsewhere

The sustainability conversation concerns areas that are easy fixes with light capital investment, but those days are numbered.

The big-ticket items are still to be resolved, and this requires capital investment, something that investors and companies are not a fan of.

Re-shoring to maximize supply chain resilience, developing climate transition technologies and updating or adapting the machinery of traditional processes will require a mindset shift from I to we, especially when you outsource your supply chain.

Granted, this is not sexy to talk about but it is fundamental to make the shift that we ought to make. When we think about fashion, furniture, carpets, trainers (sneakers), bed linen, car seats, baby clothes, prams – in fact, any items that use fabrics – we can't avoid thinking about the dyeing processes.

In 2018, Quantis produced a report called 'Measuring Fashion – The Environmental Impact of the Global Apparel and Footwear Industries Study'. The report highlighted the high energy demand from the dyeing processes because it requires heating high amounts of water many times a day at temperatures over 130°C (Quantis, 2018).

This process is not just energy-demanding but also freshwater-intensive. The report also highlights the water and energy intensity of fabric production as the yarn preparation for that process uses a lot of water as part of the wet spinning process for both natural and synthetic fabrics.

If we are going to achieve net zero targets, companies will need to invest in systemically changing archaic machines across many regions including Italy, Portugal, France, the UK, China, India, Bangladesh, etc.

This is not going to be an overnight process. 'This could take at least 10 or 20 years and will require funding and rethinking relationships with suppliers. In addition, taxes on industrial water are getting higher as the era of water scarcity approaches and cleaning the chemical processes that put the water back into the system becomes expensive. Understanding what your biggest impacts are, whether your own or those of your suppliers, and investing in change is what will drive the industry forward,' said Nikita Jayasuriya, General Manager, Head of Europe of The Mills Fabrica, an incubator and investment fund for advanced sustainable innovations in the textile and apparel industry.

Trying to understand the luxury customers and the requirements of wider society is a hugely complicated balancing act. 'No company wants to go too fast or too far, for fear of losing clients or customers, or even their jobs!' Dame Polly Courtice shared with me, and I agree.

'What we may come to see is luxury brands really embracing the idea of corporate activism as a means of staying relevant to their markets', she added. 'Luxury is in an excellent position to change people's thinking and behaviours. To inspire that change is the power that the industry holds. Luxury companies are extraordinarily good at adapting, bouncing back and setting trends, but most importantly at creating consumer want and desire. So we know that they have the skills. But crucially, in changing the way people think, we have to move on from the mindsets that created the problems we face today. We need new mindsets for such an uncertain future.'

Can luxury apply those skills in the interests of society and nature?

Most companies are struggling to get the balance right, as it is not easy. There's something subtle about doing things differently. Changing behaviour today is about doing less rather than more, wanting less rather than more, and therefore producing less rather than more too. Bottega

Veneta is leading the way in this space, reducing its stock-keeping units and leaning into circularity.

Technology has brought us so many things which have made our lives easier and made us able to do things which our parents could not. We can optimize our time, if used wisely, get everything that we need at a click. It helps us calculate companies' ESG impact, calculate stocks vs location in real-time, understand our warehouses, etc.

Imagine our parents' generations, washing by hand and taking notes in a book, or simply waiting for a phone call by phoning a building on the off chance the person you wanted was in there. For the developing world, our lives, even though we think that they are somewhat imperfect, are what they want. Our lives are filled with luxury, from a Dior bag to a new TV and time to analyse how we feel.

Demand for luxury is never going to go away, but it is shifting geographies, Courtice explained. 'I'm not a techno-optimist in the sense that technology is going to fix everything. I do believe that there'll be rapid tipping points that can take us there more quickly than we ever imagined possible – in the way that digitalization has done. As we said before, change is not linear. The crucial thing, and often the hardest thing to transform, is human behaviour, although that too can change remarkably quickly with the right stimuli.'

I keep coming back to the fact that so much of how we respond to sustainability challenges is down to how we think and behave – our mindsets. You, me, us, society need to consider what kind of life, what kind of future we want for our children and our children's children. What will we need to do differently to secure it? Humans change when we are forced to change, when a crisis, trauma and/or tragedy arises. But the existential threats we face now are so great that we can't afford to wait, or to accept the inevitable. Nor can we use the same approaches that seem to have served us so well in the past. We have to face the fact that our future – indeed the very future of our species – is dependent on profound changes that we must make now. We are going to have to change everything about the way we live now, how we work, how we move around, what we eat and how we consume. Above all we are going to have to change the way we think.

Transforming the system is not a simple task, and it will only transform as a result of many drivers coming together. The current system has numerous vested interests, making it difficult to effect change, yet change is imperative.

The luxury industry has the potential to blaze a trail in innovative think-ing and implementation, given its creativity and ability to develop unconventional models, especially as its outputs are often smaller in scale compared to other industries. It is imperative that this approach be made systemic and inspiring enough to encourage non-luxury brands to embrace innovation as well.

The luxury industry has a unique opportunity to lead the way in sustain-ability innovation, by developing new markets, products and ideas that others can adopt through an open-source model. Rather than guarding their systems and risking poaching, luxury companies can make it part of their mission to share and teach others. For instance, Kering made its EP&L methodology available to the public in 2015 and actively supports collective initiatives like The Fashion Pact and the Watch & Jewellery Initiative 2023. Chanel has also made significant strides in sustainable practices by upgrad-ing its suppliers workshops and factories and enabling them to trade with everyone, not just exclusively with Chanel. These actions demonstrate the luxury industry's ability to make a systemic contribution towards sustaina-bility and innovation, which is well within reach.

Systemic change – what does it all mean?

When we talk about systemic change, we mean setting the cleaner and greener option as a default versus forcing consumers to make the choice. All these abstract concepts need to boil down to something tangible and real that people can actually do. Otherwise, people just feel disempowered. Some simple steps to transition to a new climate economy involve assessing the potential impact of the changes that the organization and its stakehold-ers will have to go through but also understanding the impact of not changing.

Change management will help successfully navigate transitions and achieve desired outcomes and financial returns. The pain point for organi-zations is that sustainability changes are not perfectly orchestrated. Usually, there are not enough resources or budget allocated for them. In some cases, people are expected to embrace sustainability in addition to their current roles and responsibilities, which is a significant demand. Despite many organizations setting sustainability goals and targets in recent years, few have provided a well-defined strategy and designated accountable individu-als for implementation and delivery. It is not solely the responsibility of the sustainability department to achieve these objectives. Rather, it is imperative for every member of the organization to understand their role in reaching these targets and to be cognizant of the funding allocated for their realization.

1 Communicate the company's ambition to every department in the organization.

2 Conduct an in-depth analysis of the current workforce composition to understand the existing gender representation across different levels and departments and identify where the gaps are.

3 Recognize and address any systemic barriers or biases – conscious or unconscious – that may exist within the organization's hiring, promotion and retention processes. This may involve examining job descriptions, interview practices and performance evaluation systems for any gender-based biases.

4 Develop inclusive strategies to attract diverse candidates. Consider expanding recruitment channels, engaging with diverse communities and organizations, and reviewing job advertisements to eliminate any gender-biased language. Implement blind resume screening techniques to mitigate unconscious bias.

5 Provide training to all employees across the organization. Offer mentorship and sponsorship programmes that can support the career growth of women and other marginalized genders.

6 As an employer, celebrate, value and respect diversity. Establish employee resource groups (ERGs) that champion gender equality and provide a platform for everyone to share experiences and ideas, encouraging honest and open conversation that creates opportunities for people to learn from each other.

7 Offer flexible work arrangements and policies that accommodate the needs of all employees, including working parents and caregivers. This can help people to balance their personal and professional lives more effectively.

8 Ensure that the leadership team is not just on board but also demonstrates a strong commitment to achieving the 50/50 target. Fostering an inclusive culture starts with leadership, but it is everyone's responsibility. Establishing diversity metrics, monitoring and reporting on them is a great way to know where you are vs your objective.

9 Collaborate with external organizations, industry groups and professional networks that focus on gender diversity and inclusion. Participate in initiatives and events that promote women in leadership and leverage external expertise to accelerate progress.

10 Analyse data on recruitment, promotion and retention rates to identify any gaps, review the effectiveness of your strategies, seek feedback and repeat.

Striving for a 50/50 gender balance is an ongoing endeavor that demands continuous commitment, ample resources, and necessary adjustments to overcome barriers and biases. Undoubtedly, it will remain an everlasting process that will demand collective efforts. Nevertheless, the outcomes will be worthwhile as the company will attract and retain top-tier talent while reaping the financial benefits of an inclusive culture.

When one thinks about system change, almost without fail the topic goes into supply chain transparency, but that is not the only process important for an organization or for the system itself. Logistics, animal welfare, gender pay gap, diversity, equity and inclusion – especially in leadership positions – and the mental health of employees are as important, amongst others.

What we learnt from The Macallan case study (Chapter 5) is that sustainability is about doing the right things, setting realistic goals in a realistic timeframe, allocating financial budgets and resources to go with them and ensuring that you have a clear roadmap to get from A to B. No two sustainability journeys are the same, no two companies will achieve the same outcomes in the same timeframe, even if they try. But what is quite amazing is how many companies don't actually have a clear mission and values aligned to sustainability. In recent years many companies are prioritizing incorporating sustainability attributes in their products and communicating those. It's important to note that this alone is not sufficient in creating a captivating brand story. Simply showcasing a product does not necessarily entice consumers to buy into the overall brand mission and values.

Let me share an example that I love: when President John F Kennedy went to visit the site of NASA's moon shot at Cape Canaveral, he bumped into a man sweeping the floor. When the President asked the man what he was doing, the man replied, 'I'm helping put a man on the moon' (cited in Guresu, 2022).

Building a strong company culture involves recognizing and valuing everyone's role in fulfilling the organization's mission, while also demonstrating how their actions contribute to something greater than themselves. Convincing individuals to make decisions that prioritize sustainability may seem at odds with their immediate objectives, such as increasing sales, but incorporating the organization's values and mission in that narrative can help people visualize how their short-term actions ultimately contribute to the long-term health and success of the company, its employees and the world at large.

'Belief is absolutely critical,' said Jenny Davis-Peccoud, Global Practice Head, Sustainability & Responsibility at Bain & Company. 'Companies have always resonated with the concept of purpose. The definition of purpose has evolved over the years, and most recently it's included contributions to society beyond a company's own consumers and employees. Connecting the purpose of your work with a contribution to humanity is a very powerful way to inspire, engage and mobilize people around delivering on these agendas.'

Hollywood, Universal and the power of young, bold, fearless women

Jaime Nack, President of Three Squares Inc., said that 'when we speak to boards of luxury companies, oftentimes board members will mention that they receive pressure from their children to do more on climate. They will say that my son or my daughter came home and pointed out how we as a business should be taking the climate crisis more seriously and doing our part. And, so board members are actually getting lectured at the dinner table first and then tackling the same issues in the boardroom.'

The way your company will create a fertile climate for change is to form positive relationships with those outside your company and ensure that all your messages and actions are totally consistent so they can tell a positive story about you.

Hollywood is determined to create a climate for change. Netflix and some of the other studios have started to add the sustainability narrative across many of their productions to educate talent and viewers about the importance of sustainable living. They are working on a blueprint to normalize electric vehicles for their movies, commercials and series. This is not product placement, this is just doing the right thing first and then working on how to maximize revenues as a secondary step.

Studios bring products to viewers' eyes in a subtle way by showcasing a lifestyle as old as Hollywood. This is why the US Surgeon General's Office has long warned of the causal link between smoking in films aimed at young people and the likelihood of youth tobacco use (Andrew, 2019). Featuring positive lifestyles has the same potential – this time for good, shifting talent and consumers' mindsets. It is no coincidence that the demand for EVs is skyrocketing because driving an EV is cooler than driving an SUV.

The entertainment industry has a lot of what we call 'invisible waste'. Hundreds of thousands of hours are made into 'digital content' whether films, ads, Instagram or TikTok shorts, etc; to put this in context it takes an average time of three to five months to shoot a full-length feature film and around four days for a 30-minute TV series episode. People are brought to a location, costumes are made, clothes are transported, used and maybe discarded, very good quality food and drinks are served, trailers and sets moved from A to B are more often than not powered by diesel, and just like that during the editing process, the director cuts a few scenes because certain elements don't work.

This means that many hours, days, months of digital resources are getting discarded at a click of a button literally. This is invisible – nobody is watching or talking about this, but it is very real, very resource-inefficient and very expensive for the studios, producers, brands and in fact everybody involved. I'm not suggesting we compromise creativity but what can studios, production companies, advertising agencies, brands and talent put in their riders and brief clauses to ensure that this is not overlooked?

I had the pleasure of speaking with Lauren Gloster Pendleton, Director of Client Accounts at Earth Angel. Earth Angel is a sustainable production agency dedicated to reducing the environmental impact of film and television production. In speaking about her role at Earth Angel, Lauren summarized, 'Our mission is to educate and engage the cast and the crew about sustainability on every production. At times, we have the unique opportunity to review scripts and incorporate behaviour-changing narratives in a visual way. For example, we aim to replace all single-use plastics both in front of and behind the cameras. We might suggest on-screen green messaging in other subtle ways such as incorporating a recycling poster in the background on a city subway scene. Such opportunities to embed behaviour changes in front of the screen can be incredibly impactful,' she said.

These small but effective behaviour changes are similar to those we've seen evolve in other ways over the years, like smoking on screen. Smoking, which was once viewed in a far more favourable, even 'sexy' light, does not sit nearly as well with many viewers these days. The cultural shift away from smoking has happened in many societies around the world, and Hollywood can effectively reinforce this larger shift by limiting or removing this perceived behaviour on screen.

In October of 2022, Good Energy Stories published a research project conducted in collaboration with The Norman Lear Center's Media Impact Project aimed at understanding and measuring the frequency that 36 key words related to climate change were mentioned in over 37,000 scripted TV episodes and films from 2016–2020. The results? Only 2.8 per cent of all scripts included any climate-related keywords and only 0.6 per cent of scripted TV episodes and films mention the specific term 'climate change' (Good Energy Stories and The Norman Lear Center's Media Impact Project, 2022). Television and films have an incredible opportunity to shift the landscape surrounding viewers' behaviours, attitudes and knowledge regarding climate change, which affects everyone in various direct and indirect ways. It is important to think critically about how we can address climate change through the content we see on our screens and our role in demanding such shifts.

But the impact of film and television is not just that you see on screen, it is largely what you do not see – and it is not just a carbon metric, although that is significant too. One of the magic tricks of film and television is to create something out of nothing; many things you see on screen do not actually exist. See a remote desert location? A robust team of production crew, production vehicles, diesel-burning generators powering air-conditioned trailers for cast and crew with catered food and chilled drinking water – to name a few – are all behind the camera making that scene possible. Those diesel-burning generators in turn have very real environmental and human health impacts. By incorporating sustainability in a meaningful way into the planning and execution of a production, the massive footprint of a film or show can be mitigated to varying degrees through the adoption of technologies like electric generators and solar powered trailers. Productions in New York, Los Angeles, London, Vancouver and other major cities with more robust infrastructure are more easily able to align with such options in addition to implementing other important measures like a comprehensive zero waste programme (composting, reusing and/or recycling) if a production team is willing to engage these technologies and measures.

I've asked Lauren how she and Earth Angel are achieving the steep changes we need to see in the film and television industry – 'Baby steps,' she said. She continues:

> Just like the luxury industry, a lot of the necessary actions require capital
> investment, buy-in from the decision makers, and shifts in business-as-usual
> behaviours and technologies, i.e. replacing diesel generators with electric and

hybrid options wherever possible. What is promising to see is when members of the cast and crew champion sustainability in their own right, as those are the most successful productions moving the needle towards the positive change that is possible. Of particular significance is when we work on a set where the lead talent advocates for sustainability both in front of and behind the camera as they have a unique and powerful platform to effect change.

I'm sure that you, as I was when I've spoken to Lauren, are curious to know the outcome of their work. Since its founding in 2013, Earth Angel has worked on many notable productions including *The Whale*, *Severance*, *The Amazing Spider-Man 2* and more. Over the course of more than 10 years, Earth Angel has helped to divert 19 million pounds (over 8.5 million kg) of waste, avoided over 3.8 million single-use plastic water bottles and donated over 365,000 pounds (165,561 kg) of materials.

What would have happened to these materials otherwise, I asked? 'Landfilled,' she replied. Without a material recovery plan, many sets are disposed of after a production wraps; scenery, building materials, appliances, lighting, furniture, wardrobes, household items and decor, electronic waste, the list goes on! Without a plan, these items frequently end up in landfill. What we do is work with the relevant departments to identify and recover as many materials as possible on a production, oftentimes donating it to organizations in the community, thus investing in the local infrastructure. Similarly, catered food can be donated to local shelters and organizations rather than sending it to the landfill. With every production, and every cast and crew member that embraces these incremental changes, we can collaboratively work towards reducing the environmental impact of the film and television industry.

Scope 4, Avoided Emissions, is something people often don't think about, but in fact, could be argued to be the most important scope not just for carbon accounting but for water, waste, energy, plastic, materials and money, just to name a few. Scope 4 represents how we can avoid emissions and measure the outcome of our potential actions, instead of measuring the impact of our actions. Scope 4 gives us agency to be proactive in understanding our role in carbon emissions versus being reactive to what has already been done, serving as an effective tool in informing positive behaviour changes at the onset. Shifting our thinking in such ways is something that will no doubt see acceleration as we approach the end of this decade.

FIGURE 7.1 Earth Angel's impact since 2013

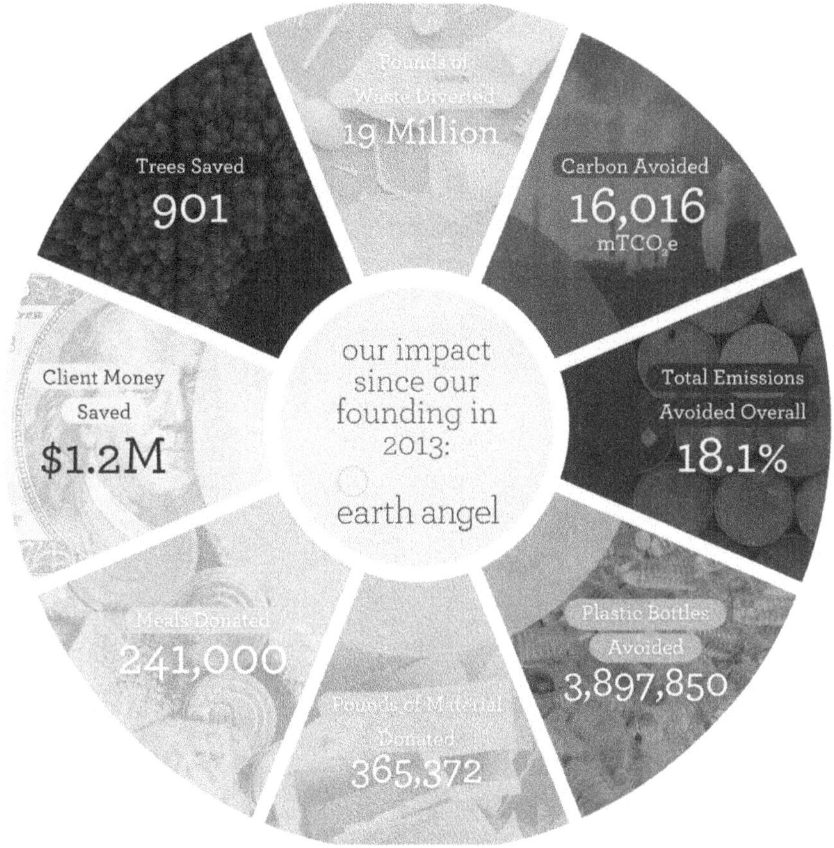

Pounds of Waste Diverted
19 Million

Trees Saved
901

Carbon Avoided
16,016
mTCO₂e

Client Money Saved
$1.2M

our impact since our founding in 2013:

earth angel

Total Emissions Avoided Overall
18.1%

Meals Donated
241,000

Pounds of Material Donated
365,372

Plastic Bottles Avoided
3,897,850

Earth Angel (2023)

My Future – Watch (these are Billie Eilish song titles)

Billie Eilish, one of the highest-earning artists right now, and her mother, Maggie Baird, are both environmentalists, committed animal activists and vegans. For every part of her business, Billie has written environmental policies that outline her social and environmental expectations.

These policies affect how her tour is operated, the transport, the venues that she performs, merchandising contracts, wardrobe, hair and makeup and her stylist, just to name a few.

You can't work with Billie Eilish unless you have read and agreed to her social and environmental requirements and principles. For example, no animal products in her hair and makeup, fully vegan meals and no animal products in her wardrobe.

When she performed at the O2 Arena in London, she turned it into a vegan, fully plant-based venue for a week.

When you think about the impact of that, even if it's only one week out of the year, it's unprecedented.

I'm sure that concessionaires fought back and said there's no way we can do this, we can't source that quantity of plant-based meals. People complained, but they did it.

When you do something like that – once you show to others and to yourself that it can be done – Billie is hitting and breaking ceilings that have never even been touched with confidence, conviction and commitment. All of her fans supported it, and hopefully, many artists, and actors will follow.

Another band that is doing their bit is Coldplay – whether you love his music or not – we need to recognize that Chris Martin has been an environmental activist for a long time. In the UK alone, live concerts generate 405,000 tons of CO_2 – which is approximately the equivalent of 4,131,314 Olympic swimming pools.

Coldplay's tour rider is built on three principles:

- Reduce the tour's CO_2 emissions by 50 per cent
- Reinvent: by supporting innovative technologies that can reimagine a greener music industry
- Restore, by funding nature- and technology-based projects

'We're very conscious that the planet is facing a climate crisis, so we've spent the last two years consulting with environmental experts to make this tour as sustainable as possible, and, just as importantly, to harness the tour's potential to push things forward,' the band wrote when they launched the tour on their social media channels (Coldplay, 2021).

What is the impact of your vinyl collection?

Sticking with the music theme, the return of vinyl has been hailed as a return to an age where quality of sound is valued over the easy access, poor quality audio of digital. It's also good for musicians, as songwriters and performers earn more from vinyl sales than streams on Spotify or YouTube. But have you ever thought about how your vinyl collection may harm the environment? In recent years, the sustainability of this format has been put under the spotlight, as vinyl is – eek – plastic.

The good news is that companies such as Evolution Music have launched their first bioplastic vinyl record that produces less toxic emissions than PVC. ElasticStage, a start-up working on using less energy, no PVC and less harmful chemicals to vinyl, just raised £3.5 million to scale up their technologies. They aim to eliminate the use of harmful chemicals, use less energy and no PVC – offering a sustainable solution to creating vinyl (Paul, 2022).

Culture eats strategy for breakfast

So true, no matter how strong your strategy is on paper, the culture will dictate its success or failure. But why is culture considered to have such power?

Culture sets the tone for how things are done in the company and shapes employees' mindsets and decision-making. When people feel emotionally connected to an organization, they will go that extra mile, which counts for a lot. In today's rapidly changing business environment, companies need to be agile and adaptive to remain competitive, so a culture that is open, transparent and honest and promotes innovation, learning and collaboration enables people to respond to new challenges and opportunities. Culture often outlasts individual strategies, as strategies come and go, but a strong culture provides stability and a sense of identity that transcends and remains focused on its mission and maintains a consistent direction.

What all of these examples highlight is that creating a climate for change and fostering a culture of sustainability and innovation is crucial. When everyone within a company, movie set or music tour crew is genuinely committed to the mission, driving positive change becomes possible. While having a strategic plan is crucial for establishing objectives and identifying the appropriate course of action, it is the underlying culture that ultimately shapes the implementation and long-term endurance of these strategies.

Culture in action

A super sports car company – that I have promised not to name on record – has not yet transitioned to produce cleaner vehicles. The company conducts an employee survey once a year, and this year, they have added social and environmental questions to the survey to gauge the sentiment of employees towards sustainability topics.

Some of the results were mesmerizing, including the fact that over 50 per cent of their employees wanted EV charging stations at work. In other words, the results of the survey showed that most people in the organization were working on a product that they don't want themselves.

What does this teach us? Firstly, it is important to have a decarbonization plan because sooner or later, everybody will be there and secondly, it is rather important to know what your people think about you and how you can retain them and incentivize them.

Anonymized employee surveys are a really good way to gather feedback and insights from your employees regarding their thoughts and behaviours related to sustainability practices in the workplace. Here are some suggestions:

- Begin the survey by providing a brief explanation of what sustainability means to your company and why it is important.

- Include questions to gauge employees' awareness and understanding of sustainability principles, such as what your mission is and what your sustainability initiatives, goals, targets, etc are. This will help you identify the areas where your employees need more information or skills and training, or both.

- Ask employees about their current practices and behaviours related to sustainability, such as recycling, water conservation and energy management at home and then inquire about their involvement in sustainable initiatives and whether they feel empowered to contribute at work.

- Inquire about any perceived barriers or challenges employees face when trying to adopt sustainable practices at work, such as infrastructure, resources, training or awareness. Understanding these challenges can help you address them and provide support where needed.

- Dedicate a section of the survey to invite employees to share their ideas and suggestions for improving sustainability in the workplace.

Include questions that measure employees' attitudes and level of engagement towards sustainability initiatives. This can help you understand the level of buy-in and commitment within your teams, identify potential changemakers and uncover opportunities for improvement.

Once the survey is complete, analyse the data and identify key findings and trends. Share the results with employees, along with an action plan outlining how the organization will address the feedback received. Regularly communicate progress and updates to maintain transparency and accountability.

What would you know about the people in your organization if you were to run a survey with sustainability topics?

Sustainability and innovation are good for your top and bottom line and to attract and retain the best talent. But be aware that when you get the best talent, and they start seeing inconsistencies between what you say, what you do and how you do it, you might lose them quickly.

The climate for change is here to stay, sustainability, innovation and ESG are areas that can no longer be ignored in any business and in any industry, and yes that includes luxury.

Are you ready to create the climate for change?

References

Andrew, S (2019) On-screen smoking in PG-13 films has doubled since 2010, CDC says, *CNN*, 1 November, https://edition.cnn.com/2019/11/01/health/tobacco-use-movies-increase-trnd/index.html (archived at https://perma.cc/38YA-NVPW)

Coldplay (2021) 'Coldplay Music of the Spheres World Tour', Instagram, 14 October, www.instagram.com/p/CVAh8KpoRRH/?utm_source=ig_embed&ig_rid=d0975c7a-03fa-4fc6-9be7-a0cd8b35cbc0

Good Energy Stories and The Norman Lear Center's Media Impact Project (2022) A Glaring Absence. The Climate Crisis is Virtually Nonexistent in Scripted Entertainment, October, https://learcenter.s3.us-west-1.amazonaws.com/GlaringAbsence_NormanLearCenter.pdf (archived at https://perma.cc/MM2L-E5Y2)

Guresu, G (2022) Well, Mr. President, I'm helping put a man on the moon', LinkedIn, 4 February, www.linkedin.com/pulse/well-mr-president-im-helping-put-man-moon-gabriela-guresu/?trk=pulse-article_more-articles_related-content-card (archived at https://perma.cc/K8ZT-8A5S)

Paul, M (2022) elasticStage tunes in £3.5 million to modernise vinyl production, Tech.eu, 15 August, https://tech.eu/2022/08/15/elasticstage-tunes-in-ps35-million-to-modernise-vinyl-production (archived at https://perma.cc/U68K-4YS2)

Quantis (2018) Measuring fashion. Environmental impact of the global apparel and footwear industries study, https://quantis.com/wp-content/uploads/2018/03/measuringfashion_globalimpactstudy_full-report_quantis_cwf_2018a.pdf (archived at https://perma.cc/VZY9-CLXM)

SocialStatus (2023) Facebook organic reach rate benchmark, monthly historical data, www.socialstatus.io/insights/social-media-benchmarks/facebook-organic-reach-rate-benchmark/ (archived at https://perma.cc/DK5J-ZGPR)

Townsend, S (2023) *The Solutionists: How businesses can fix the future*, Kogan Page

08

Successful storytelling

Back to the future

Back in the mid-1950s, mainstream advertising was a simple tool to influence people. The market was less fragmented, people read newspapers rather than smartphones on their commute, TV viewers spent time watching ads rather than clicking past them and families would chat together at the dinner table or around the TV, making the media a shared rather than solo experience.

Most advertising had positive and engaging storylines, setting out to build dreams and desire. One of the most famous ads from this Golden Age is Coca-Cola's 1971 Hilltop, which saw young people of different races and nationalities singing in unison about a positive future. The ad said nothing about the product.

Coca Cola has consistently associated itself with communicating pleasure, joy and happiness and it remains in the top five most well-known brands in the world.

Negative narratives, conversely, don't sell anywhere near as successfully. They are hard to engage with and people want to switch off as they feel hopeless. When you fear something you can either run away from it or face it and the majority of humans are wired to run, Susan McPherson, author, founder and CEO of McPherson Strategies, an impact communication agency, told me.

'I remember 10 years ago,' she said, 'when senator James Inhofe from Oklahoma stood on the floor of the US Senate with a snowball in his hand and used it to claim "there's no global warming, you see?" It was a difficult narrative to counter, not because it was true but because the story we told about global warming was negative.'

The storytelling about our warming planet carried such a sense of doom that people expected the markers of this event to have been chaos – floods, disasters, a global catastrophe in real time. We have not seen that. Instead, we have seen smaller episodes popping up all over the globe that most people find hard to connect to. Why would a flood in London and a fire in Spain be part of the same problem? When people struggled to see how the storytelling around climate chimed with their own personal experience, they tuned out. 'Only now this narrative is becoming more personal, especially from a US perspective,' according to McPherson.

The narrative of climate change has failed to connect with its audience at scale, in order for them to take meaningful consistent actions. Companies working to bring about change struggle to effectively communicate the true impact of their efforts in terms that are easily understood by the general public. The challenge lies in bridging the gap between the technicalities of the myriad of sustainability topics and the layman's perspective.

How can the luxury industry reimagine themselves in order to remain relevant to people?

In this chapter I will explain why and how luxury brands need to understand their new story.

Explaining how a product is complying with legal restrictions is not good enough, there is no dream or desire in that.

It is simple…

It's not only about what you say, but how you say it is equally important.

It's not just your advertising but every touchpoint with the consumer and all stakeholders.

It's not about trumpeting short-term gestures, it's about the life you lead.

Behave like a hero. If we have heroes, we want them to live like heroes. We want them to live greater lives than we could dream of living.

Luxury brands are the heroes of the consumer world. The stories they live and tell should be 'immortal'.

Today, luxury brands talk about craftsmanship and design but that story is too simple for companies that have diversified into many different markets and far beyond the story of the talented craftsmen and women working in harmony with the natural world.

In his book *Sapiens*, which was first published in 2011, Israeli historian Yuval Noah Harari describes the cognitive revolution that took place in our species some 70,000 years ago. Before then, homo sapiens were weaker than the many other species of human that co-existed alongside us, especially Neanderthals. A human group was limited to around 150 people, also called Dunbar's number after the British anthropologist Robin Dunbar, who proposed the theoretical limit in the 1990s.

Harari (2015) explains that homo sapiens rose to the top of the food chain, wiping out all other human species along the way, because they learned how to tell stories. It's a story that convinces people they belong to a nation or believe in an ideal. When a story unites two, then four, then eight groups of 150 sapiens, they can bring a bigger game to the fight. At the very heart of our being lies the importance of stories. Our neurobiology has hardwired us to feel connected through these narratives.

Stories make that connection bigger, deeper and memorable. Milo Cress started the Be Straw Free campaign in 2011 to raise awareness about plastic waste when he was just nine years old. Through the combination of a YouTube video of a marine biologist extracting a straw from a tormented sea turtles' nose (Figgener, 2015) and the #StopSucking social media campaign which kicked in around 2015, chains like Starbucks switched from plastic straw to paper ones. By 2020 the UK had banned plastic straws, cotton buds and single-use stirrers.

The problem was strikingly visual and easy to understand, the solution was in everybody's reach and one could see the difference that they could make by making a different choice very quickly – it was easy and it felt good. We changed the narrative, the product and the behaviour in less than 10 years. Success!

Stories have the power to transform our lives and enable us to see and/or reimagine the world in a different way.

There's evidence from neuroscience that suggests that when telling a story and somebody is listening to the story, our brain patterns begin to mirror one another. We are connecting, both emotionally and at a physical level (The Health Foundation, 2016).

Luxury narratives are becoming outdated as people who buy luxury are getting younger and they see the world in a different way to the older Millennials, Baby Boomers or Gen X.

The generations of Gen Z and Alpha are marked by their unique media consumption habits and priorities. They value experiences over material possessions and while they do place an emphasis on creating shareable social media moments, they are also discerning when it comes to choosing those experiences and brands. They consider a brand's alignment with their personal values and beliefs on social and environmental issues to be of equal importance and the brand or experience itself.

Luxury shouldn't play catch up

When we think about luxury brands communicating on sustainability, the closest comparison is thinking about how luxury embraced technology. The companies were slow to the party.

It took the pandemic to prompt luxury to lean into e-commerce, enabling anyone anywhere to buy luxury brands from the comfort of their sofas, but when it comes to sustainability, we have started seeing green shoots. One can only find a small section dedicated to the topic on many brands' websites; although there are some notable exceptions, for the majority, almost all the communication comes from the distant holding group rather than the labels that people desire and identify with.

The thing is that people before did not question sustainability and luxury, it was their experience of the brand, or the absence of it, that created this myth on sustainability. But as luxury brands are diversifying and playing on other territories that are perhaps more affordable, luxury will need to start becoming a lot more transparent.

As people watch luxury brands diversify, a quiet revolution amongst consumers has started. People have started to question the price tag vs their claims of craftsmanship, hand-made items or the perpetuation of tradition. Just as many luxury brands are expanding their operations to mass luxury, like eyewear, perfumes, hotels, haircare, furniture and experiences, so the question about sustainability is higher in consumer minds.

In an interconnected world, generations have become more comfortable moving through the digital and physical worlds to a point that today there is no more distinction between the two. Gen Z consumers represent over $360 billion of spending power in disposable income, according to a Bloomberg report (Pollard, 2021). They are technology native, hyper aware of advertising – including influencers – and highly educated. They trust third party validations – such as certifications and peer recommendations. Importantly, that no longer includes influencers per se – younger consumers know that they are paid by brands.

Although there is a lot of historic research that says luxury brands should keep their magic and avoid entering the sustainability discussion, the reality is that this bubble is closer to bursting. More expensive does not mean socially and environmentally sound and the assumption that sustainability is embedded in the price tag is a myth being unveiled.

Quality, craftsmanship and branding are drivers today but inclusive communication and accountable outcomes will be tomorrow's drivers.

The material risks for the luxury industry

In the near future, the material risks for the luxury industry include inequality and communications, aka storytelling – both visual and behavioural. It is a dissonant narrative if a company says that it invests in nature, cares for its people and uses sustainable packaging but then spends millions sponsoring fossil-fuel-heavy Formula One, which does not sit well with younger consumers. Likewise, when they overdress the shop windows or hire painfully skinny models regardless of their gender, it is hard to claim they are people-kind.

Elisa Niemtzow, Vice President, Consumer Sectors and Global Membership BSR, told me that wealthy people did well during the pandemic and, since 2020, the richest 1 per cent of people have captured 63 per cent of all new wealth.

In a world where global inequality is increasing, the pandemic has made the world's poorest more vulnerable and inflation is outpacing wage increases. This means questions are being asked about the social acceptability of luxury. Niemtzow said, 'The luxury industry has a strong track record on topics like job creation and regenerative practices, but the sector does need to communicate that it's creating long-term value. Luxury consumers see luxury as having a unique influence, so it is well placed to make strong contributions to positive change, in line with the vision of exemplarity the sector embodies.'

When talking with Dean Sanders, founder and Chairman of GoodBrand, a corporate sustainability innovation consultancy that's now part of the global sustainability activation group Anthesis, we discussed the role of luxury in the future and what would – in the not too distant future – give luxury brands a licence to operate beyond the aesthetic of the product? Of course, aesthetics is incredibly important, but when a handbag costs the equivalent to a month's salary, it is time for luxury to start justifying its role in the world. 'Luxury margins should allow brands to aim for Net Positive impact.'

Is it luxury's mission to better the quality of life for people or the planet? 'In my view, and this is a broad generalization,' he continued, 'the luxury behaviour and mindset need a thorough overhaul towards progressive, aspirational values.'

So luxury storytelling may be about quality and craftsmanship or service and excellence, but in 2024 the questioning of the role of luxury in consumers' lives will become louder. The younger generations are inquisitive and outspoken and they have already started to ask these questions.

Today people have an idea of how luxury brands will make them feel, especially in relation to others' opinions, but this is also changing, as they are discovering that they don't need things to make them feel special. As a result, their relationship with brands is changing and people expect different behaviours. Not that long ago, beauty brands just needed great packaging and great claims. Today people expect brands to be considerate with minimalistic packaging, outstanding formulation and to deliver visual results.

Unless luxury is able to change the narrative to one that is more open and inclusive or can give clients clarity on what their specific value creation model is, brands will struggle to capture the minds and hearts of their future consumers.

People don't spend a lot of time analysing what they will buy – with the exception of cars, a home or furniture. AI and algorithms nudge us towards the brands that we see in our social media feed. This is why creating positive narratives and content that resonates with your audience is a great tool to create desirability still today.

This is the very reason why content creators – aka influencers – exist. Brand's storytelling must be clear about what kind of emotion it would like to spark in the viewer and what action/feeling it would like the person to have. This is why choosing your content creators carefully is so important. This approach helps brands to differentiate themselves in a rather cluttered and noisy environment. Luxury brands create their value through their stories.

Yes, it's the story not the product – just like Coca-Cola.

Today the most successful brands focus on excellent storytelling and how they communicate their story.

If a story is no different from other brand narratives, there is no way to price it differently.

People decide what they are going to buy when they are online searching. Brands that centre their storytelling around conventional values have little chance of engaging digitally with their audiences. On the other hand, companies that tell their story in an emotional way with absolute clarity of what role they play in their audience's lives are perceived to have extreme value.

Now is an invaluable opportunity to shape the world we want. An extraordinary chance awaits us to conceive a reality where we prosper as we forge ahead. Although companies can exhibit both fortitude and hesitancy, the idea of change often invokes trepidation due to the perception of forfeiting something, rather than realizing potential gains. It is imperative that we focus on narrating the tale of our journey towards a brighter future that we all want to be part of. There are already many great innovations that at scale will curb our emissions, replenish our soils and clean our waters... but there is a $7 trillion gap in 2024 to develop those – mainly in capital investment. I see this as a golden opportunity.

So what's missing? According to McPherson it's people – people coming together across borders and across socioeconomic classes. In other words, luxury brands are part of a wider system. This can't just be the luxury brands, we need collective action to succeed.

I think it is really important to start with knowing ourselves first and connecting with our values, whether as individuals or companies. Mission values are the key ingredient to make valuable connections or partnerships. If we can build connections beyond the tight group of people we already know or feel comfortable with, that requires stories.

The growth of the luxury market is not driven by the 1 per cent

Surprised? Don't be. The growth of the luxury market is mainly driven by the growth of the middle classes in emerging markets, particularly in Asia, India, MEA and other emerging countries. It is also driven by those outside the 1 per cent as a result, ironically, of inequality.

Naomi Muggleton is Assistant Professor of Behavioural Science at Warwick Business School and lectures on The Economics of Wellbeing on the undergraduate programme. Her April 2022 research on workplace inequality showed it is associated with status-signalling expenditure. Muggleton and her research colleagues combined the payroll data from more than 680,000 people at 32,000 organizations with digitally derived spending information for a 10-month period in 2019 to see how income inequality affected spending (Muggleton et al, 2022).

They looked at two dimensions of income inequality: the distribution of workers' salaries in the firm they work at using the Gini coefficient and where a person's salary ranks compared to others in their firm. The results provide a compelling case for status anxiety being a contributor to the negative outcomes linked to income equality.

They also highlighted a connection between income inequality and luxury goods spending. They found that given the same salary and purchasing power, the higher the inequality in a workplace, the greater the proportion of income spent on luxury goods rather than on discretionary items or necessities.

In 2023 luxury in Europe is stagnating and the US is growing but again not as much as before. Dina Khalifa is an experienced academic in the areas of luxury branding and marketing with more than 10 years of teaching experience in both the UK and Egypt. She has a PhD from Cambridge University in luxury brand marketing with a focus on consumer responses to identity threats and social exclusion and clearly is the best person to answer this question.

'When we look at activism, for instance Black Lives Matter, black and ethnic consumers statistically tend to be of lower socio-economic classes in comparison to their white counterparts. So we were interested in seeing which topics are important in which markets and how consumers react when luxury brands address this topic. We also tried to find out their attitude towards the brand and perception of the luxury brand's power, prestige and status and all these factors. And we have seen that there are regional differences, like in the US where Black Lives Matter is the focus,' Khalifa said.

When luxury brands embrace activism and address these inequality issues, it is perceived as positive and removes any negative association with luxury. 'We also see the different ways brands tackle these topics – if it's just an Instagram post, if they make a statement or if they take more action by supporting grassroots led organizations,' she added. 'So there was of course more support for the brand that took the extra action.'

She pointed out that topics such as Black Lives Matter were not perceived as a priority in Asian countries, where their own regional topics were to the fore. Indeed, if a brand makes a public stand or takes an action on a topic which may not be relevant to Asian consumers, it could backfire.

She worked on a study in the UK to ask consumers about which topics luxury brands should address to tackle inequalities and what their attitude towards the luxury brands being inclusive and trying to address inequalities would be. 'We found that the UK consumers have negative attitudes,' she explained. 'They don't believe that luxury could be inclusive, and this was particularly among consumers from lower socio-economic backgrounds – which is not surprising, and also more among those who do not buy luxury than those who buy luxury, which is again not surprising. Researchers call this the clean luxury fallacy. Those who buy luxury think it's clean because it's so expensive and they paid so much that means it's doing everything right.'

So, the negative attitudes are mainly held by those who do not buy luxury. The most important way, as far as they are concerned, for luxury to become inclusive was to look inside its own business – workers' rights and supply chain followed by race and gender.

People in the UK also see there's an intersectionality between environment and social, according to Khalifa. LGBT rights and public health and wellbeing wrap up the list of actions luxury brands should correct to become more inclusive.

Hence, I would like to discuss activism.

Corporations have to become activists. Activism can change consumer sentiments and behaviour at the same time.

For clarity, I don't mean activism in its disruptive form but activism in proactively trying to change consumer sentiment, attitudes and behaviour and making it easier for them to understand topics or issues through educational programmes, creative narratives and a change of business model so they can experience the brand differently.

The next material risk for luxury brands

Marketing and advertising is under the spotlight as never before, especially for brands marketing clothes and beauty products. Concerns regarding the casting of size zero models have driven the industry towards inclusivity, embracing a wider range of models' size, shape, and skin colour. Failing to consider diversity across gender, sexuality, age, disability and religion opens a brand to protest and attack – not just from the excluded groups, but from consumers across the spectrum for whom this is increasingly unacceptable.

In the case of Balenciaga, February 2023 saw the brand fall out of the Lyst Index's Top Ten Hottest Brands for the first time. The Index is a quarterly ranking of fashion's hottest brands. Balenciaga has dominated the list since it launched in 2017 but extensive criticism of its controversial advertising, problems within store, behaviour by staff and antisemitic statements by brand ambassador Kanye West, aka Ye, has damaged what appears to be an unassailable position. The brand has since created a group level 'brand safety' team to avoid future scandals (Martin, 2023) but has unfortunately continued to witness a decline in sales for two consecutive quarters.

As I'm writing this book in the summer of 2023, the sentiment behind the brand is divided amongst its fans, although the brand is not completely cancelled. It certainly has not been forgiven and people are shying away from wearing the brand with the same pride that they used to only a few months ago – even if they own it.

The promotion of unrealistic beauty standards by brands, often exaggerated through advertising and social media, can harm the psychological and physical wellbeing of vulnerable individuals, particularly minors.

Companies have the power to actively combat racial, gender and socioeconomic stereotypes and defy societal norms by prioritizing inclusivity in their portrayals of individuals and the choice of influencers as role models. By consciously working towards a more diverse and representative representation of people, companies can play an important role in challenging and dismantling these harmful stereotypes.

Remaining silent is not a viable choice any. For most individuals, luxury brands products, and lifestyles, along with their corresponding image, fall beyond the reach of financial feasibility. As brands, they transcend the commonplace, resulting in heightened scrutiny and susceptibility to targeting.

A good example of this happened on 13 April 2023 when French protesters broke into the LVMH headquarters during the nationwide protests over raising the pension age to 64 years old. 'You're looking for money to finance pensions? Take it from the pockets of billionaires,' said the Sud Rail trade unionist Fabien Villedieu, as the building filled with red smoke from flares (Chrisafis, 2023).

LVMH, parent company of Fendi, Celine, Krug Champagne, Louis Vuitton and Dior, was founded by chairman Bernard Arnault who, at the time of writing this book, is the richest person in the world. Was the attack reasonable?

In today's polarized world luxury brands across all sectors must be incredibly sensitive to the way they react to such social change.

Many companies have been criticized for engaging in superficial support for social causes on social media, whilst having no ethnic diversity at senior leadership level, or failing to actually address their sustainability or the environmental outcomes of their actions, raising concerns about the authenticity and effectiveness of their commitments and communication.

The dance with paradoxes continues, and no brand can be seen to capitalize or take advantage of mainstream social issues without walking the talk. Setting and reporting publicly on the outcome of sustainability goals and targets is essential – for example how many hectares of forest have been preserved, how many women have been trained in new skills and how many new jobs have been created.

The emotional potential

Luxury is in a fortunate position – it comes with 'feel good' pre-installed. Purchasing a luxury item has always been a pick-me-up and can give us the feeling that we are worth more, albeit perhaps temporarily, with many people having what is called psychological ownership. This feeling of a sense of control over an object or even a particular space emphasizes the emotional and cognitive attachment that people develop towards something that they perceive to have a personal connection with, and the feeling that their sense of identity increases.

This could be one of the reasons why the demand for luxury products has been on the rise since the pandemic, a trend that is very possibly going to be leading the industry for the foreseeable future.

So as luxury rides this wave, how about if companies play a role in helping us to imagine a collective positive future and a world of possibilities? The media market I described at the beginning of the chapter came at a time of huge optimism for the future and its domestic consumer potential. *The Jetsons* is the kids' TV version of this – a cartoon where a family living in a sci-fi future had flatscreen televisions, smart watches, video calls, drones, holograms, digital newspapers and even automatic vacuums. Back then this was radical, back then this was luxury and still is for certain parts of society.

What would we put in our version of *The Jetsons* today?

Now is the time to explore the business model of the future. This is the time to align people from all corners of the earth into a collective vision where we live at one with nature and our social communities, and better yet, work towards regenerating these systems.

It is time to talk up aspirations that appeal to values – for example, how kind you are is a more engaging and important narrative than how thin you are. The disposable plastic society the Jetsons spawned must become a society where reusing a dress is as good as buying a new one – just like Nicole

Kidman re-wearing the garment from a Chanel advert she appeared in nearly 20 years ago for the 2023 Met Gala.

These narratives will resonate far better in times of social unease and crisis, and rather than purely promoting products, they also offer experiences and services which provide opportunities for additional revenue streams. Just like when the Model T or the iPhone were created, they were at the beginning of a huge explosion in economic potential in the platforms for travel and communication.

We need to examine how the 'platforms' of our future support various combinations of business models. Companies that demonstrate a lack of empathy and social consciousness will over time fail to resonate with their 'tribes 'and their reputations may well fall flat.

On the other side, there are profits waiting to be claimed.

Activism as storytelling

Tommy Hilfiger first launched the 'Moving Forward Together' campaign in September 2020. The company has been campaigning around diversity, equality, inclusion and sustainability. Moving Forward Together is a campaign where people become involved digitally to co-create new clothing using leftover fabrics.

After its success, they decided to partner with learning platform FutureLearn, to offer a series of free digital learning courses about different topics such as community building and LGBTQ+ allyship. The brand also hosted live talks on social media empowering followers to drive social change, but their work does not stop there. They fund and support start-up businesses that have a positive social impact.

When I think about activism another brand that comes to mind is Selfridges under the leadership of Anne Pitcher, former CEO of the Selfridges group, as well as Linda Hewson, former creative director, and Daniella Vega, former Chief Sustainability Officer. They were an unbeatable team, challenging convention and reimagining the retail experience.

Selfridges had a sustainability culture well before sustainability was a common term. In 2011, they launched Project Ocean – a storewide takeover where, among other things, Selfridges banned the sale of endangered fish and created a marine reserve in the Philippines. Since then, they have been pushing the conversation forward and made bold commitments to turn the tide on plastic pollution and invite people and partners to do the same.

Here are some of the highlights from Selfridges:

- Founded The Marine Reserves Coalition with leading charities.
- Banned the sale of shark oil (squalene) from beauty halls.
- The first to ban single-use plastic water bottles, saving 3.4 million bottles from sale since 2015.
- Stopped selling plastic microbeads in beauty products and plastic straws in our restaurants before it was legislated.
- Banned single-use beauty wipes in 2016 – this has only been legislated in 2023.
- Removed all plastic-based cosmetic glitter.
- Launched 'Bright Young Things' – giving airtime to young independent designers such Sealand and Zero Waste Club.
- Launched 'Bright Old Things' – celebrating older creatives.
- Supported the Black Lives Matter movement.
- Project Ocean became Project Earth where they announced an ambitious target to have 45 per cent of transactions come from circular products or services including resale, rental, repair, refill and recycle – by 2030. They launched Reselfridges as a vehicle for this.
- They are driving a transition in the food halls and restaurants to ensure that everything is palm-oil free, has less packaging and comes from certified sustainable sources.
- And when it comes to mindsets, they are committed to building an inclusive retail culture in which teams, communities and customers put the health of people and planet first.

Anne Pitcher told me, 'Hewson is one of a kind. Fearless when reimagining retail as they saw the store as a social centre powered by imagination, curiosity and creativity. Selfridges is still on a journey to transform the way people shop, eat and live.'

Anne is softly spoken and empathic with a great sense of style and a witty sense of humour. She explains that the team found their voice as a response to customers' dislike of the store selling fur and exotic skins, with the activist community coming after them. 'In the very early years, we took the decision not to sell those anymore,' she explained. 'It felt uncomfortable as it was and it was a big business, but it was a very speedy decision because it just felt wrong from the inside, wrong to do and wrong as well from our customers' perspective. We were really one of the very first retailers to do that.'

The reaction from customers was amazing, she said, and it felt like that they saw us as a brand that they could speak to. 'And so the journey really began because after we stopped selling foie gras, we began to realize that if we wanted to touch the hearts and minds of our customers and our own teams, we needed to talk to them and care about the things that they cared about.'

After Selfridges said no to fur, Kering and Chanel followed and now faux fur as the default is normalized, at least in Europe. The store hosted the educational and gastronomic WastED – Dan Barber's pop-up restaurant using food waste to create a feast and teach about food waste in the most delicious way imaginable. There was Shakespearean theatre, celebrations of new and upcoming artists and designers, supporting and championing causes that people care about. Daniella Vega, who wrote the first sustainability strategy for the company, coined the phrase 'buying less but buying better' nearly 10 years ago. Hewson brought it to life.

'We did this in a light-hearted way, enabling the audience to enjoy the conversation as opposed to instilling fear,' Pitcher added. 'People shy away if you do fear, but I think if you embrace the conversation in a way that has energy and allows people to think then you can bring the right attitudes and responses. My other big learning was that every time you talk about big topics, you have to break them down, and break them down again so people can imagine them or relate to the information, or they will switch off. Anne believes that you have to be on a journey, commit to the journey and accept that you can't fundamentally get off it.'

Every time the team came to her with a suggestion, she admitted she was often nervous, sometimes reluctant and sometimes downright uncomfortable.

She confided in me that she always excelled when facing challenges. The prospect of overcoming a difficult obstacle motivated her to work harder, resulting in her best work.

She shared the plastic story, the time when Selfridges committed to stop selling single-use plastic. Starting in 2015 with plastic bottles – at that point they sold over 1 million plastic water bottles a year. That commitment meant removing £1 million a year in turnover.

'We sought input from a diverse team,' she said. 'Their suggestion was to implement a freemium approach by giving away water while selling the reusable containers. This resulted in a significant increase in our water sales revenue.'

At a certain point, a unique opportunity arises to not only start a conversation that piques the interest of your customers or potential customers but also turn a problem into a profitable success. This pivotal moment marks a turning point for any business and must be embraced, Anne said.

Many organizations encounter difficulty in aligning their sustainable journey with growth, but initiating this process early on can result in substantial commercial benefits. By identifying reduction opportunities in areas such as carbon, water, waste, packaging, and logistics, businesses can delineate clear cost advantages as they strive to optimize for sustainability. Combining both approaches will provide organizations with a competitive advantage and a stronger financial position.

The trick is knowing how you grow your business by caring about the way you do business. For Anne, this had to do with how to acquire and retain customers. Whilst people do return to department stores, they often limit their visits to single brand stores. 'We wanted to prove that more customers were attracted to our brand because of the actions that we took and they spent money because of those actions, which was more valuable than any comparison to a digital marketing customer acquisition strategy,' she explained.

Selfridges did just that in 2020 during lockdown. They launched Project Earth, acquiring more customers through their sustainability narrative than through any other part of the business. Those people converted more frequently at a higher price point than any other metric in the organization.

'People were excited and inspired by what we had to say,' said Pitcher. 'They wanted to learn and we provided the platform for learning and understanding. We also provided the products and services beautifully curated under Project Earth coupled with the conversation that met their needs.'

Selfridges exists to make the world a little bit brighter; they believe in the power of collaborations, that collective optimism can kick start radical change towards a sustainable future for people, communities and their customers.

I hope I have inspired you but please do not attempt to create an activist campaign to resonate with these consumers. This may, if you are not genuine and consistent about what you stand for, backfire and you may be accused of virtue signalling as a means of profit instead of genuinely raising awareness. If you are thinking about hiring influencers – although effective today – the winds of change are there too as you need to look for content creators with engaged audiences not vast number of followers.

Eat, sleep and care

It is not a secret that the hospitality industry is an active contributor to the climate emergency as they produce large amount of waste and CO_2 and consume a vast amount energy and water; having said that, they are in a great position to act as a model of sustainable living, setting examples and showcasing what is possible to 'live well' and 'do good'. When people stay in hotels, whether for business or on holiday, they feel that the hotel has 'got their back', they can relax because everything around them is being taken care of and in general their mindset is open and receptive.

The hotel industry has been forced to reimagine themselves as they had no choice, especially during the pandemic. Mixing hospitality, hotel services, residences and wellness centres is not uncommon, and very recently hotels and airlines are taking this trend to a new level offering their guests the possibility to rent their wardrobes, shoes, jewellery, cars, etc. These services are not exclusive to VIPs as all guests can access these services, however the VIP experience has been reimagined to new levels. Some hotels have a pre-booking app or virtual concierge offering their guest the ability to pre-book a car that picks them up from the airport, have their room at arrival, customize all the room choices such as a selection of their favourite drinks and food being available in the room, or showcasing of local brands if they chose the 'surprise me option', and make reservations in a selected, highly curated list of restaurants and members' clubs, including a money-can't-buy section to access shows or events that are normally sold out.

Pre-booking your experiences is a great way to manage resources from the hotel perspective, have an additional revenue stream and enhance the guest experience.

I had the pleasure of interviewing Jennica Shamoon Arazi, owner of the Marbella Club in Spain. The Marbella Club is one of the best-kept secrets, one of the most renowned hotels in the region for its facilities, service and quality. Their clientele grows year on year through word of mouth, and includes Mick Jagger, Bruce Willis and Naomi Campbell as some of their guests.

Jennica's positive and can-do attitude are unmissable, she believes that the hospitality industry is in a great place to set the tone when it comes to sustainability without compromising the guest experience.

'Although it is not always easy, patience, education and taking people through the [sustainability] journey have been our key levers for success, and guests are ready to come on this journey with us,' Jennica said. 'Every department in the hotel got the "memo", budget support and training to integrate social and environmental sustainability practices into the everyday running of the business and into our guest experience. It's been a rather rewarding journey. We create a guest experience that is authentic, luxurious, thoughtful, consistent and inspiring combining high levels of service with sustainability at the heart of it.'

People behave differently in hotel rooms, she explained. The state they leave their rooms in and the things they throw away would raise anyone's eyebrows. She found that communicating the Club's sustainability commitments and actions in the rooms – 'little touchpoints' she calls them – have an impact in a very positive way.

'Perfect is the enemy of good,' she said. 'Sustainability is a journey, not a destination and I must admit that at the very beginning of our journey it was like trying to turn a supertanker, but everybody in the team made it simple as they embraced the change with open arms, and although we are not perfect, we have a plan and the belief that great service combined with social and environmental sustainability play a pivotal role in the luxury hospitality industry.' The Marbella Club has been awarded with the Butterfly Mark powered by Positive Luxury for their journey towards social and sustainability excellence.

A bit closer to home in the UK is Whatley Manor in the Cotswolds, where, just like the Marbella Club, their team is fully engaged and committed to the sustainability journey and it is very much part of their day-to-day running of the business.

The hotel has heavily invested to be carbon neutral by absolute reductions in 2035, single-use-plastic-free by 2023, and are working with their suppliers to accompany them on this journey, having a coherent and integrated approach downstream and upstream without compromising the guest experience; if anything, enhancing it is not just their ambition but a reality.

The hotel is surrounded by 12 acres of land, a mixture between gardens and forest which they work hard to ensure flora and fauna indigenous to where the hotel is based is reintroduced, conserved and preserved. They ensure that the food that they serve is seasonal, local when possible and they hold their suppliers to the highest standards of quality and sustainability.

Sue Williams, General Manager, told me that for her and her team 'sustainability is not an add on but the way that we do business'.

Hotels just like the other luxury segments shy away from actively communicating their sustainability efforts. Mainly because the language of sustainability is complex and the assumption is that the guest would not like to know, which is clearly an oversight.

But communication and innovation sometimes go together especially when you think about holiday destinations. In Lanzarote, Spain, for example there is the Underwater Museum, the only one in Europe. The museum has incredible sculptures by British eco-sculptor Jason deCaires Taylor. The sculptures are cast in pH-neutral cement, which provides a surface for coral growth and regenerates the marine ecosystem. This is a great initiative that has brought Lanzarote to the fore as a destination.

Word of mouth is a very powerful tool for hotels, and this is all about the guest experience, which needs to be uncompromising from a quality, service, comfort point of view, yet the devil is in the details as they say. For luxury hotels it is not about communication, it is about signalling and discovering, and enabling their guests to realize that their positive experience has ripple effects in the local community, local schools, parks, beaches, economy and ultimately nature. When staying in a hotel, we can directly contribute, through the hotel's actions, to positively affect society and nature. We, together, have the power to reimagine our experiences, we just need to do it consistently.

Changing the narrative

Paul Hawken (2017), an American environmentalist, entrepreneur and author, stated that, 'climate science contains its own specialized vocabulary, acronyms, lingo, and jargon'. This language comes from policy makers and scientists so it is straight to the point, and very specific. Just like any jargon it's difficult to understand and hard to communicate to the wider public.

The language barrier creates friction and distance. Some environmentalists feel that if the points made are not scientifically explained they have no value, and the public feel powerless to understand what they are supposed to be doing as it is all rather pessimistic, confusing and unachievable.

There is also the challenge of localization – adapting to different regions or countries making it tangible to their culture and context.

The opportunity for the climate narrative is to move from a 'tragedy' narrative such as Romeo and Juliet to a 'quest of voyage and return' type narrative like Indiana Jones where we all get to play 'Indie'. An ordinary person, with extraordinary determination, who is not invincible, experiences setbacks, makes mistakes but it is resilient and relatable. Their perseverance leads them to success, just like so many stubbornly optimistic reimaginers working in this field.

Sarah George, Deputy Editor of Edie.net, the sustainability media brand, agreed that climate change is overdue a change of narrative. Today, sustainability directors move from activists to activators. Pre-Covid most sustainability officers would have had to build consensus amongst the board as part of their job to convince them that the climate crisis was a real thing and it was imperative for the company to take action, from a moral, risk, resilience and profitability perspective.

'Today the board is coming to them and saying we need a new strategy, we need net zero by this date, we need to be net-positive by this date,' she explained. 'And can you please do it straight away? This does not mean that sustainability teams are getting enough time, money or resources to think about storytelling or new technologies or changes to processes.'

This is a good first step but clearly not enough. What Sarah is also seeing from where she sits is that the public has not missed the constant doom and gloom headlines. There is now acceptance that this is a problem, but people feel powerless to do anything. This can lead them to pointing the finger or being anxious.

So the appetite for the narrative to shift from the problem to the solutions is there. I think storytelling for a lot of companies is still very much trial and error, what marketing and the comms teams need to consider now is how much information is TMI (too much information).

The information from brands to consumers needs to be succinct and digestible but also provide evidence to back it up so that they're not greenwashing. Thinking about journalism, there is a pathway that you can be trained as a climate journalist, but now there are also training courses to learn about 'solutions journalism'. This means there is an appetite to learn how to create public understanding while delivering positive social change.

We need to talk about transition and adaptation – these are not easy. They take time, intention and money but there is no other choice.

What is asked of us all, and especially of the people in leadership positions, is to reimagine the world we would like to live in and the world that we would like to leave behind. We can be gloomy or optimistic, and borrowing Christiana Figueras' line – I choose optimism.

We must start with a narrative that motivates and inspires people and businesses to do what it takes to make the world we need. We must reimagine business, relationships, collaboration, connections, wealth, power, joy, time, space, nature, value, what constitutes a good life and reimagine what really matters.

People don't feel connected with the climate agenda because there is no immediate response or feedback loop. We only change when we can see the results.

As David Attenborough said, we have the technology, we have the knowledge, and we have all the solutions – we just need to have that collective vision of how all will fit all together.

Positive narratives are used to draw attention to a desired behaviour, and reinforce behaviour in a constructive way. Statistics and data help monitoring and understanding supply chains and/or other organizational levers, but those coupled with positive narratives can have the power to motivate and change minds and hearts.

Belinda Parmar, OBE, is the founder and CEO of The Empathy Business. Belinda talks about the jargon of sustainability, which often includes terms that dehumanize people or actions, as they seem small against a giant context of complexity. Belinda said 'Empathy is not synonymous with sympathy. We don't really know how other people feel. We are just projecting. To reassure people that their concerns are heard the best way is to practise active listening and create a sense of belonging among employees, suppliers or in fact anyone.'

This is the type of leadership that we need in order to be able to move through the transition smoothly. Good leadership combined with a growth mindset is a great recipe for success.

The media often portrays climate change and sustainability through a lens of fear, leaving us feeling helpless. Imagine if instead we embraced a unified vision for the future, redefining the stories around manufacturing, consumption and, most critically, our symbiosis with nature. Influencers play a pivotal role in changing the narrative. Nowadays the influencer movement has been facing backlash for a while as people are aware that influencers are paid by companies to plug products and many are not to be trusted if not authentic.

Having said that, social media stickiness has not slowed down, and influencers and their followers continue to enjoy a strong bond, mainly because, unlike companies, they can be spontaneous and share what is important to them without restrictions. They feel approachable and real.

I had the pleasure of speaking with Doina Ciobanu, a content creator, model, sustainability advocate and influencer – although she does not feel comfortable with the latter label as she feels it's associated with a lack of integrity and mindfulness about the world. 'On the other hand, Michelle Obama is an influencer, so if you are calling me an influencer as a person that has influence then I'll take that,' she said smiling.

Doina has collaborated with many brands including Louis Vuitton and Monica Vinader. Her passion for sustainability is a mix of 'my heritage, Moldova, and my knowledge of the harm of single-use plastic,' she explained. 'I could not just sit still; I had to do something about it. That is why I've used my personal brand to raise awareness. It is a very difficult space to navigate, full of contradictions and increasing complexity that cause it to change so fast.'

Doina said it is a privilege that many don't understand because 'my grandparents and the village in Moldova where they live, they do not think about it.'

'They actually live sustainably, because that's a default means of traditional living, survival, and thriving,' she explained. 'But they've never thought of that as a distinct choice they have to make; it's not a conscious choice, it's just the only way they can survive on their limited budget. Full use, re-use and recycling are just a natural part of her day.'

Doina also chooses optimism as she can see incremental change coming from people like you, me and any one of her growing 1.5 million followers. She found that in her years of posting and engaging with people, we are not designed to see ahead to 2050 and be worried about that future today. We can't comprehend that time distance at an emotional level. Personal accountability, on the other hand, is easy: just switch off your light, turn off your router, take shorter showers, say no to freebies that you will throw away and be mindful about your purchases.

From another perspective

Sustainability and ESG does not affect everybody in the same way, and this is one of the reasons why when in conferences and/or round tables I abstain from commenting when radical views of what others should do are expressed. Nothing is as simple as 'they should not... or they should...'.

Being from the Global South, I've learned to 'speak' and understand 'both languages'. As I would like to think of myself as a 'mediator', in the next few paragraphs I will do my best to neutrally explain the context.

The Global South is in a different stage of economic development. The United Nations uses the Human Development Index (HDI) to define a country's stage of development based on four indicators: life expectancy, adult literacy, school enrolment and standard of living measured by the country's Gross Domestic Product per capita (National Geographic, 2022). Therefore, the set of priorities and narratives are different from the Global North. Please allow me to explain that when I talk about the Global South, I've deliberately excluded Japan, Israel, South Korea, Australia and New Zealand, as although they are geographically in the Southern Hemisphere their economies and rate of development are on par with the Global North.

The term climate justice is used in Latin America to express the need of the Global North to pay for their environmental debt to the Global South in order to help them remedy the effects of climate change caused by the extraction and depletion of natural resources. In Africa, it is a well-known fact that they would also like to freely pursue prospecting and extraction of fossil fuels to develop their economies or if not be properly compensated for the cost of not doing so.

For the Global South it is a luxury to think about climate change as their everyday life is riddled with economic challenges that they have no control over, such as inflation. Companies also often face different economic challenges, such as poverty, unemployment and limited financial resources, which unavoidably will affect the levels of investment and the areas of sustainability investment – more often than not leading with social good instead of environmental initiatives.

Maslow's Hierarchy of Needs, proposed by US psychologist Abraham Maslow in 1943, is an oversimplified but still useful way to think about the way people think depending on their financial security. At the bottom is securing food and water – meeting one's physiological needs. Once secured, we move to shelter and safety, then to finding belonging and love, and only then do we have the space to consider our own self-esteem and the aesthetics of the world around us.

Luxury still has a huge role to play in developing economies. The influence of luxury is off the scale, as buying luxury brands gives people the illusion of belonging to the upper echelon and be part of the Beyonce, Shakira and/or Messi clan.

The total global revenue in the luxury goods market amounts to around $354.80 billion in 2023 and expects an annual growth of 3.38 per cent (CAGR 2023–2028) (Statista, 2023a). The Latin America luxury market is expected to have an annual growth of 1.36 per cent and Africa a 1.32 per cent annual growth (CAGR 2023–2028) according to Statista (2023b, 2023c). This includes automotive and hospitality which are the fastest-growing segments in both Latin America and Africa.

When I interviewed Argentinian journalist and broadcaster Marysol Antón, when asked about how companies, government and people are tackling sustainability topics in the Mercosur, she deflected to share that Argentina's inflation had hit the interannual value of 157 per cent in June 2023. She paused and took a deep breath as we intentionally decided not to go down that rabbit hole. 'Sustainability is new to Argentina,' she continued, 'I would say that in Buenos Aires, only since 2022 companies have started to talk about ESG, and mainly these are international companies with a presence in the country instead of home-grown ones, although there are financial incentives to do so such as better financing and better rates.'

'Argentina is a little bit like Italy and Spain,' said Marysol.

> Our economy is mainly dominated by SMEs (PYMES). There are approximately almost 2 million SMEs in the country with a population of almost 46 million people. The turnover of these companies ranges from 78 million to 4 billion pesos which is the equivalent of £240,000 to £12 million. These companies are the ones that are perhaps the ones most involved in sustainability practices, giving jobs or apprenticeships to vulnerable people within the communities they operate. Buying small and buying better is what drives the movement in Argentina that leads with aiding to solve social issues instead of environmental ones. People today, especially Gen Z, talk about sustainability, but it is very hard to live it as the infrastructure is not there.

There are three EV stations in the country and EVs or hybrids are a luxury. Recycling is almost non-existent: only 8 per cent of total waste is actually recycled vs 44 per cent in the UK. To put it in context, Marysol said, over 40 per cent of people live in poverty and can't afford the basics. Water and electricity are a luxury, not only due to affordability but also because the government rations them.

When I asked about environmental issues, she shared with me that Indigenous people are being made destitute from their land in order to mine lithium to sell to the Global North. Lithium is buried under some of the largest salt plains with a backdrop of outstanding beauty. Where is the international community?

We in the Global North have the 'privilege' to be given the opportunity to think about sustainability. It is a privilege that many don't understand because in the Global South – the majority of people do not think about it because survival comes first.

Karen Hanton, MBE, is a serial entrepreneur and founder of toptable, Europe's number one restaurant booking website sold to Opentable.com, and PetsPyjamas.com, the first travel company entirely dedicated to dog friendly travel.

'I was brought up on a Scottish croft and looking back, I think we were always conscious consumers and conservationists before sustainability as we think of it today was really a thing,' she said. 'Growing up we had enough but nothing extra, and as children we were made fully aware of the need to look after our small farm and animals that sustained our family of five. Waste was kept to an absolute minimum with recycling and repurposing a way of life. I am still very conscious of outcomes and do my best to live by many of those same principles. I invest in entrepreneurs who are doing some fabulous things that can be part of the solution, as I truly believe that the human race has it within its control to slow down negative impact, even at this late stage. Small, collective actions would literally make a world of difference.'

We need a cultural reset. It is easy to blame our needs and wants on social media but perhaps the hard truth to accept is that social media is a reflection of today's society, exposed and open for everybody to see.

Dame Polly Courtice told me:

> When we engage in discussions about the social and environmental challenges that we face, and consider how we might solve them – in effect the storytelling that we use – there is the usual spectrum of opinion, with deep pessimism at one end, and action-oriented optimism at the other, and people often gravitate to one end or the other. I often find myself veering between the two, and I know others do too. But in the end, I am not comfortable dwelling for long at the pessimistic end, even though there is good cause. And, strangely, it's almost a comfortable place to be. But hopeless despair doesn't change much. And more importantly there are millions of people around the world who do not have the luxury to sit around and indulge in intellectual pessimism. That galvanizes me.

As I contemplate the dire consequences of further global warming, my thoughts turn to the countless individuals in underdeveloped nations who will bear the brunt. These resilient souls are simply doing the best they can to survive.

'The way stories are being told is changing – the who, the where and the how,' said Kodzia Edenharder, co-founder of *Haus von Eden*, a sustainable lifestyle and design magazine. 'Today, the role of the media is to empower and educate people, while pressurizing the industry to foster their sustainable transition,' Edenharder believes.

For storytelling to be successful it needs to be consistent and without dissonances, the content needs to be honest and authentic and the medium needs to be genuine and inspiring but most importantly needs to understand the context in which the story is told. Climate change is giving people, especially the younger generations, a sense of anxiety and fatalism, both in the Global North and South, that makes it hard to understand what there is to look forward to. We need to move from just talking about climate change and start talking about innovation, climate adaptation and transition to a liberating future where anything and everything is possible.

So many opportunities lie ahead of us, socially, economically and environmentally, that the future, seen through a positive narrative, could be exciting, accelerating and rewarding. It is a revolution, but through this revolution we become more ourselves, not less. There is no question of stopping short, striking a compromise or standing still. Nothing ever stands still. We must add to our world or lose it. We must do better or fail completely. We must go forward or backward. I believe in optimism, and I believe that we shall go forward, faster – together.

There is so much to celebrate, as there has been so much progress globally, although I do get it, hard to see at times, and yes there is still a long way to go but sustainability is a journey, every day is a chance to make changes and reimagine the world that we live in and that starts with what you chose. I chose to believe that the journey itself is part of the reward, even if at times it feels hard and unfair.

Are you ready to reimagine our world?

References

Chrisafis, A (2023) French protesters storm luxury group LVMH offices before pensions ruling, *The Guardian*, 13 April, www.theguardian.com/world/2023/apr/13/macron-returns-to-more-protests-in-france-on-eve-of-pensions-ruling (archived at https://perma.cc/4UZE-ZSSR)

Coldwell Banker Global and WealthEngine (2019) A look at wealth 2019: Millennial millionaires, https://blog.coldwellbankerluxury.com/a-look-at-wealth-millennial-millionaires/ (archived at https://perma.cc/62J4-ZJ6G)

Figgener, C (2015) Sea turtle with straw up its nostril – 'NO' TO SINGLE-USE PLASTIC, *Sea Turtle Biologist on YouTube*, 11 August, www.youtube.com/watch?v=4wH878t78bw (archived at https://perma.cc/65NB-5QBM)

Harari, Yuval Noah (2015) *Sapiens: A brief history of humankind*, Harper Perennial, New York

Hawken, P (2017) *Drawdown: The most comprehensive plan ever proposed to roll back global warming*, Penguin, New York

Martin, H (2023) Balenciaga: one of many racist high-end luxury brands, *The Boston Political Review*, 14 March, www.bostonpoliticalreview.org/post/balenciaga-one-of-many-racist-high-end-luxury-brands (archived at https://perma.cc/T96B-TNJJ)

Muggleton, N, Trendl, A, Walasek, L, Leake, D, Gathergood, J and Stewart, N (2022) Workplace inequality is associated with status-signaling expenditure, 8 April, PNAS, www.pnas.org/doi/10.1073/pnas.2115196119 (archived at https://perma.cc/GB99-VT4H)

National Geographic (2022) Encyclopedic Entry: Development, 13 May, https://education.nationalgeographic.org/resource/development/ (archived at https://perma.cc/LM57-6JDS)

Pollard, A (2021) Gen Z has $360 billion to spend, trick is getting them to buy, *Bloomberg*, 17 November, www.bloomberg.com/news/articles/2021-11-17/gen-z-has-360-billion-to-spend-trick-is-getting-them-to-buy#xj4y7vzkg (archived at https://perma.cc/YZ36-SEUR)

Statista (2023a) Luxury Goods – Worldwide, www.statista.com/outlook/cmo/luxury-goods/worldwide (archived at https://perma.cc/B5BV-YB6Q)

Statista (2023b) Luxury Goods – South America, www.statista.com/outlook/cmo/luxury-goods/south-america (archived at https://perma.cc/8GV6-HEKW)

Statista (2023c) Luxury Goods – Africa, www.statista.com/outlook/cmo/luxury-goods/africa (archived at https://perma.cc/7EBF-URK5)

The Health Foundation (2016) The power of storytelling, 12 December, www.health.org.uk/newsletter-feature/power-of-storytelling (archived at https://perma.cc/9GEP-QGGR)

09

How can innovation get
us out of this 'hot' mess?

I've started this journey by saying that luxury companies are not obsessed with tradition but instead are investing in innovation and innovative strategies, leaning into technology upstream and downstream and keeping their finger on the pulse of new market trends.

In this journey, I have also learned that in a not-too-distant future, most brands will need to behave like luxury brands, as the prices of raw materials, from glass to wool, from water to cotton, will become more expensive year after year. As our climate is becoming more unpredictable and people expect more from their employers, and the world at large, things that once were acceptable are no longer ok. Owning the raw materials will be as precious as the brand itself.

Since 2020 our world is being redefined and the status quo challenged, and things that we thought were impossible. Even the concept of the impossible is up for being reimagined.

Reimagining collaboration is key to co-create solutions and drive innovation, which involves partnering with customers, suppliers, startups and academia, and in this way, businesses tap into the collective expertise and accelerate the pace of innovation. In the previous chapter we touched upon the great opportunity that circular models present. Businesses can reimagine their operations to minimize waste, promote reuse and recycling, and design products for longevity and easy repair. By adopting sustainable practices, businesses can reduce environmental impact, enhance resource efficiency, create new revenue streams and have driven net positive social and environmental outcomes. Reimagine traditional work structures and embrace flexible work models. This includes remote work, flexible hours, and work-life balance initiatives. Prioritizing employee well-being, fostering inclusivity, and creating a positive work culture can boost productivity, attract top talent, and drive innovation within the organization.

Reimagining business requires a mindset shift, a willingness to challenge the status quo, and an openness to embrace innovation and change. By redefining business models, leveraging technology, and prioritizing purpose and sustainability, organizations can position themselves for long-term success in a rapidly evolving world.

Deemah AlYahya, Secretary-General of the Digital Cooperation Organisation (DCO), expects the digital economy to contribute 30 per cent to the global GDP and create 30 million jobs by 2030 (Devi, 2023). To date, the digital economy has grown 2.5 per cent faster than the GDP of the physical world over the last 10 years, according to the World Bank (Devi, 2023). A report by Arup and Oxford Economics (2023) estimates that green solutions could be worth $10.3 trillion to the global economy by 2050, equivalent to 5.2 per cent of the global GDP that year.

Many see the green transition as a cost. There will be costs, true, but the value of the opportunity to reimagine our world and invest in green solutions is a chance that should not be missed. We have seen a blueprint for this back in the 1970s with the birth, rise and growth of the digital economy. If you had been in California back then when Steve Jobs and Steve Wozniak were looking for investment from banks to build their microcomputer business, would you have been one of the many bank managers who thought their device costly and inconvenient? Would you be like Don Valentine, founder of Sequoia Capital, who passed on investing? Or would you have the vision of Mike Markkula, the retired marketing manager who recognized their potential?

Arguably the green transition will be bigger in economic terms and more impactful than the digital revolution. I still remember the sceptics back in my early 30s, at the beginning of the digital revolution, ruled by fear of change, blind to the fact that there was no way back to an analogue, controlled world. Instead of reimagining their industry or business and understanding what they could gain, they wasted precious time focusing on what they could lose. Don't miss out. Be Markkula, not the bank manager.

There are huge opportunities to invest in innovative solutions that can transform the way we live and will transform the lives of us all, very soon to be 10 billion. From investing in sustainable mobility or renewable energy, including green hydrogen at scale, to digitalization, SMART infrastructure for waste and water management, including renovations and conversions of buildings, the transition to a circular economy, biodiversity, land and ecosystem restoration and decontamination, up-skilling and reskilling is getting society ready for this transition.

The natural reaction of people when we see or hear something new or creative is to deny it, rubbish it or run away from it – things that are new, different and cause change are exciting from afar. But agile transformation is key to keeping ahead in these uncertain, yet extremely competitive times.

When we talk about innovation, agility is a means, not an end in itself. One needs to consider what is really working and keep those things ring-fenced. In organizations, people may feel reluctant to change but it is important to distinguish the difference between fear of the new and antici-pating blind spots. Supply chain transparency is a much-needed makeover, agile or breakthrough innovation can be a catalyst for change at scale from a social and environmental perspective.

Legislation is now driving this change in many industries, including the fashion industry, and in June 2023, the EU started to consider legislation for the beauty industry similar to what the fashion industry is going through right now.

When is TMI is in fact too much information

When companies talk about transparency, it can be in many different areas, from packaging to store/hotel design/redesign, formulations, ingredients, materials, carbon footprint, carbon removals, experience design, hotel management, etc. In order to achieve transparency, what strikes me is that eco-design and/or sustainable design is at the beginning of the transparency journey – whether products or experiences. This means considering the envi-ronmental and social impact of the product/experience at every stage of the development and throughout its lifecycle, including the end of life or end of the experience/stay, whilst celebrating its social and environmental outcomes.

Beauty

When it comes to the beauty industry, for example, this should deliver a very well thought-through guideline of what you would like that product to achieve, what are the must not haves, what are the compromises and for how long, what is the health and safety of the product, where the ingredients come from, what is the social impact, energy and water consumption both upstream and downstream. 'Consume Responsibly' is very much part of the product impact piece, just like 'Drink Aware' is to the drinks industry.

Just like the fashion sector, the beauty industry, another highly unregulated industry, is about to be regulated by the EU. At the time this book is being published, ongoing public consultation on revising the cosmetics regulation to better align with EU sustainability goals, and tightening the requirements around cosmetic products, labels and artwork is happening.

With this in mind, cosmetic companies with global product lines in the hundreds could face significant challenges to identify, update and re-issue all affected products to achieve the level of compliance required with any new or amended regulations.

Some of the areas under revision are chemicals, ingredients, communication and information, including digital product labels, to name a few. In 2022, the US updated the Modernization of Cosmetics Regulation Act of 2022 (MoCRA) for the first time in 80 years. This is a step in the right direction for consumer safety because it expands the authority of the US Food and Drug Administration (FDA) over beauty and personal care products. This means that the FDA is now allowed to recall products that are deemed unsafe.

The bill requires companies to disclose to the FDA – although not to consumers – fragrance ingredients that are common allergens, and to maintain records showing 'adequate substantiation' of the safety of cosmetic products and ingredients, among other provisions, Vogue Business reported in January 2023 (Cernansky). It is a must for beauty businesses to invest in innovation both upstream and downstream, from packaging to refillable, from ingredients to consumer use.

Companies like La Prairie Switzerland are aware of this coming change. 'We have internal governance structures for our group and external advisors. What we've done is set up an external advisor network to have input from people from a wide range of backgrounds, from newcomers and NGO startups to much more experienced people integrating sustainability strategies in business, including the luxury industry,' said Leigh Pezzicara, Vice President of Sustainability at the luxury beauty brand. 'So we try to tap into the resources and expertise in this broader sustainability world to keep us sharp, to challenge us and to make sure that we're not just internally focused, but that we're aware of opportunities for innovation and stay up to date with cross-industry sustainability trends,' she explained.

Cécile Lochard, a sustainability veteran, and author of *Luxury and Sustainability: A new alliance*, has worked in the field for 25 years firstly at HSBC and then WWF and now heads the sustainable development department at Guerlain. Cécile has also set up an external and independent 'sustainability board' to help the Maison define, deploy, innovate and promote strategic sustainability initiatives. Guerlain is the first beauty brand leaning into transparency, with a tool that enables people to see where the raw materials and packaging come from, ahead of legislation. Traditionally, the beauty industry has a well-documented dependency on the liquid plastic, fossil fuel and chemical industries.

Many companies today are investing heavily, ahead of the legislation in innovation. Genomatica, a biotech company that creates a sustainable alternative to oil-based surfactants from the transformation of plant sugars by living microorganisms, was founded by L'Oréal, Kao and Unilever.

The new ingredients will contribute to L'Oréal's 100 per cent eco-designed formulas and ingredients goal by 2030. Another good example is GFBiochemicals, whose company mission is to turn agricultural waste into a fossil fuel replacement. They produce levulinic acid, often found in beauty products for conditioning and softening of the skin, as well as acting as a preservative, derivatives from biomass – a renewable energy source, generated from burning wood, plants and other organic matter, such as manure or household waste.

I spoke to its co-founder and CEO Mathieu Flamini, a former Arsenal football player, who said:

> Plant-based alternatives to oil-derived chemicals will be transformative to many industries from cosmetics to paints. We want to be the Intel of the chemical world. As you know, he continued this is a transformative decade and policy is on our side, as the EU is clamping down in hundreds if not thousands of harmful chemicals and urging the industry to replace them with something cleaner. Also, we have the 'fan' on our side – drawing an analogy from his football days – people are more aware than ever about nanoparticles and/or any other chemicals that harm them and the ecosystem.

Chanel backed Evolved by Nature, a green chemistry company that develops sustainable silk. The application of this fabric is beyond fashion and can be used in cosmetics and medical products. They also invested in Sulapac, a Finnish company that is developing a biodegradable alternative to plastic that is used in Chanel's No. 1 perfume caps. PolymerExpert, a French company that creates natural cosmetic ingredients, launched Estogel Green, a 100 per cent bio-based oil rheology modifier derived from castor and rape-seed oils. This ingredient can be used to suspend particles such as pigments, glitters and mineral filters, and stabilize emulsions.

Biotherm, a L'Oréal company, has their own permanent lab outside of Paris, to focus on biotech and biofermentation. The company partnered with Carbios to enable infinite recycling of beauty packaging; although this technology is still in early-stage development it can be highly scalable. Another way that beauty is innovating is the use of '2 in 1', and although not a new concept, it is a nascent one when it comes to beauty. People want to shorten their beauty routines and save time and money.

Dibs Beauty launched a 2 in 1 bronzer and blush stick, for example, which is one of the favourites for many TikTokers. The same applies to fragrances, as companies are seeing the rewards of 'fragrances with benefits', such as mood-enhancing properties.

People expect more from beauty businesses, and expect benefits that go beyond the product itself, for example how the product makes them feel as well as how they make them look. When we think about fashion, we think about the beautiful, finished products but most of what we wear starts at the soil or the lab. Whether cotton or leather or wool or viscose, the earth nurtures our garments.

So why has legislation become so buzzy, you may ask? The new legislative frameworks enable comparability between companies, which in turn will guide investors to make better investment decisions, not depending on blended scores but on actual comparable data across E, S and G topics. Whereas right now investors rely on rating companies or certification frameworks that are not comparable.

When it comes to retailers, companies have to complete a retailer's questionnaire that is unique to every retailer, mostly at brand level. The pain point of this is not only the fact that companies need to spend a lot of time ticking boxes, but also because this exercise does not accelerate the transition that requires companies to be positively good. All this means is that bigger companies, in both size and economic impact, will have a bigger sway with suppliers to influence change, leaving smaller brands in a weaker position to be listed on those retailers.

For many years we all were craving consistency and comparability – we have it – it's called CSRD, TCFD, ISSB and the outcome of these is really to understand what the net positive outcomes of businesses is. Of course, companies can always ignore these and pay the fine, as this behaviour has been normalized; however, the price of that will now be around 5–10 per cent of the total global turnover of the business. This is a high price to pay for 'indiscretions'.

CASE STUDY
Premium drinks

One of the biggest material risks for all industries is water. Although we have water everywhere, the best way to think about this topic is like we think about our banks. The surface water, the water that we see in lakes and rivers, including rainwater, is our current account, and the groundwater is our savings account. When we talk about water poverty or water scarcity, it is because companies borrow water from our 'savings account' depleting the water tables at speed, without us noticing it.

There are businesses like Chêne Bleu, an award-winning winery based on the Dentelles de Montmirail, a small chain of mountains in Provence, France, that not only thinks about water but holistically about the entire ecosystem. La Verriere Estate is one of the only untouched natural biospheres in Europe. It lies at 550 metres (almost 1,800 feet), making it one of the highest vineyards in the Vaucluse region, and in the South of France. UNESCO names the region a Biosphere Reserve as they recognize the biodiversity value of this secluded terroir.

The estate is surrounded by a pine and oak forest that protects the vines from pollution, making it a wildlife haven. Back in 1993, Nicole and Xavier Rolet found the house and the vineyards in a derelict state.

The couple brought the estate to life creating a modern winery combining the handcrafted traditions of winemaking with sustainable organic and biodynamic practices to create an award-winning wine. The Rolets nurture not only the soil and the terrain but also their teams, made up of friends and family, local experts and international consultants with a passion for wine, nature and the pursuit of excellence.

To regenerate the vineyard, Chêne Bleu, instead of bringing commercial clones, uses the traditional system of massal selection, replanting new vineyards with cuttings from old vines from the same (or nearby) property. Chêne Blue separates the vineyard into mini parcels, which they treat individually, to capture the identity of each different section of the soil.

They do not use fertilisers or chemicals in the soil and ensure that sheep manure, food compost and very small doses of sulphur and copper are used to nourish the terroir. The whole estate is managed in accordance with biodynamic principles, which are about managing the soil and the vines in accordance with the influence of the phases of the moon, and it involves treating the soil with small doses of natural treatments.

The same principles are used in the cellar racking of the wines, and of course, when tasting. The Estate is a healthy living system that promotes cross-pollinating plants and wildflowers. The result is bee heaven – the bees love the chemical-free ecosystem, and the results speak for themselves if you try their honey.

Their wines are PEFC (Programme for the Endorsement of Forest Certification) certified as their forest is managed actively in conjunction with the National Forest Protection Agency, Ecocert, French Organic certification and the Butterfly Mark certification powered by Positive Luxury for meeting the highest standards of verified ESG performance.

When you meet the Rolets, there is no question of the passion and care that they have for nature, their employees, their family, their community and the world, as it can be tasted in every drop of Chêne Bleu.

Chêne Bleu (2021a, 2021b)

Some great innovations coming from Italy can be seen in a company called Drype, which is aiming to solve the issue of transporting drinks. The company distils the ingredients, adds the alcohol and bottles it. The only thing missing is water, which one can add. This is a great solution for cruises and planes where the relationship between weight, fuel and CEO is significant. The company does not reproduce the cocktails that we know, but they combine new flavours achieving tasty results.

Until now, the luxury industry has been reluctant to engage in the sustainability conversation, yet they will not be able to avoid the transparency and accountability conversation as it is part of current and future legislation as well as consumer expectation. Peer-to-peer accountability is something that we have started to see.

Open innovation

Leaning in to open and breakthrough innovation will help the industry to start making the changes that they need without hurting the core business. Traditional innovation is a way of innovating or conducting early-stage R&D, which prioritizes proprietary knowledge and full ownership and control.

The open innovation approach, on the other hand, comes from a trend in scientific research where you do not just turn to one expert or one lab, but instead open the problem you're trying to solve up to anyone who has a potential solution, which is beneficial for innovation and accelerates the pace of the evolution of ideas.

'If you need a solution and you don't know the journey to get there, open it up, and the power of the crowd, rewarded with the right incentive models, most certainly will give you the answers. You essentially are paying for success as opposed to praying for success,' said Paul Bunje, President of Conservation X Labs, a technology and innovation company working to prevent the sixth mass extinction. Since 2015, they have run 12 open innovation competitions, plus five other open innovation programmes (including mass collaboration), and they supported more than 130 solutions to solve some of the most challenging problems the world has seen to date.

There still is a lot of space for innovation, particularly in the luxury industry – whether it is fashion, jewellery, cosmetics or drinks. On the cosmetics side, there are many increasing opportunities for synthetic biology, which is a field of science that involves engineering biology for useful purposes to have new abilities. For example, they can play a meaningful role in taking petroleum out of the system, by engineering microbes to grow the very specific compounds that you need in a closed-loop system environment that could even potentially be solar-powered. There is a great opportunity to innovate with Cyanobacteria, a division of microorganisms that are related to bacteria but are capable of photosynthesis.

They are among the oldest photosynthesizers, the so-called chemotrophs, which use chemical energy, e.g. from vents in the ocean floor and are probably among the earliest living organisms to have evolved. Paul has spent much of his career working at the intersection of climate change and energy transition, but today, as co-founder and President of Conservation X Labs together with his partner and CEO Alex Dehgan, running open innovation competitions allows him to draw from a large pool of people around the world to find new solutions to very specific problems, something that is not only at the core of his company's mission but also his own.

They ran two rounds of the Artisanal Mining Grand Challenge, accelerating solutions for people and the planet. The first was global and addressed multiple minerals. The second, which concluded in December of 2022, was focused on gold from the Amazon basin. Altogether, they awarded more than $1.5 million dollars in prizes and opportunities to support entrepreneurs, researchers and innovators from all different corners of the world, to find solutions for artisanal and small-scale gold mining that are better for people, nature and communities.

Minerals, including rare earths and gold, go into high technology components. Gold is one that has the biggest imprint on jewellery and other luxury items from your mobile phone to your EV car – as the tech industry is the one driving the most demand for gold. Furthermore, jewellery uses a variety of artisanal mining metals and gemstones, while the mineral ingredient mica is crucial to almost all makeup products. Some 15–20 per cent of the sourcing of gold, cobalt and palladium come from these informal, often illegal mining operations in places like the Amazon, the Congo Basin, Indonesia and elsewhere. As a result, not only are Indigenous communities affected but the rapid degradation of nature and the ecosystem is also a major factor of concern.

Current negative political, ecological and health effects associated with artisanal mining include child labour, forced labour in mines run by nationalized armed forces, widespread poverty in resource-rich lands, birth defects, cancer and other illnesses, polluted water and decrease in biodiversity in microorganisms, plants, animals, and fish and aquatic animals. In the Amazon for example, the topsoil has been completely stripped because that is where the gold is.

As a result of gold mining models in the 1850s with mercury, amalgam, cyanide, etc, hundreds of hectares of formerly virgin rainforest are covered with toxic waste. The result of this type of operation is a moonscape of contaminated toxic pools of water in completely barren soil. The miners are the ones exposed to mercury during the gold mining process, Paul said. Mercury amalgamates to the gold, extracting it from the sandy ore. Burning off the mercury with blow torches is one method that then leaves the gold purified. The mercury goes through the air as an aerosol as well as through the water to eventually reach the ocean.

Paul elaborated, '37 per cent of all the mercury pollution in the world is attributed to small-scale and artisanal mining, which I didn't know about and was quite surprised.' The problem wasn't the sea per se, but it was these mines in the middle of the Amazon, and as a result, you can't eat certain types of fish like tuna, as they have the highest concentrations of mercury. Tuna is perhaps one of the most expensive top predator fish that bioaccumulate mercury in their bodies.

The older the fish, the larger they are; therefore, some of the most expensive sushi in the world will have some of the highest concentrations of mercury.

The supply chains are sometimes intentionally opaque – it is informal and unregulated and sometimes even illegal, as a lot of these minerals also go through the same trade networks that also work in weapons, drugs, human trafficking, wildlife trafficking and diamonds.

The primary source of the problem lies on the demand side that is driving the destructive mining practices. Specifically in countries like the US and the UK, there is often high consumption and demand for various goods and materials, including electronics, automobiles and jewellery, which require minerals and metals obtained through mining. By decreasing our consumption, we can help minimize the extent of destructive mining practices. You can't blame the people; they need to get out of poverty, so banning these practices is not an option.

At least 40 million people currently rely on artisanal mining as their main source of income. When you include their dependents, the number of people relying on ASM is over 100 million, Paul explained.

The question is, how do you help them to extract the gold and the mercury without damaging nature and the people living in these communities? But the problem does not end there, it is also about how you help the forest grow back.

Conservation X Labs ran a couple of challenges and ended up with some remarkable innovations that included everything from new forms of mercury-free mining, native bamboo restoration projects and breeding bamboo species native to the Amazon that would start the succession of the natural restoration process of the forest and kickstart it in a much faster way from decades to two years kind of thing. Solvers in Conservation X Labs' Artisanal Mining Grand Challenge also developed AI and software solutions to be able to see where people started to cut down the forest and identify the sites of new mining operations. Thus, it could be possible to formalize the awarding of mining concessions so that the mining process is formal and regulated.

I've also spoken to Devin Nieusma, Textile Circularity Challenge Manager at Conservation X Labs. Devin is as enthusiastic as Paul about the mission and the impact of the organization. 'This new challenge is aiming to help fashion companies to transition to a circular economy faster, and that means keeping materials in circulation for longer, these challenges take a while to scope, research, scope and fund,' she said. 'But when you start seeing the applications coming in and the challenge starting to take shape, it is the most rewarding thing ever to be working on solutions that will shape my feature.' The future is very exciting as in a very short time organizations are starting to look for solutions and leaning into innovation.

AI is going to revolutionize things for consumer brands, not only because you're going to have better intelligence about consumers, but also because your companies will be able to start to crack open supply chains in a way that you never had before and understand where things are coming from.

Breakthrough innovation

Machine learning algorithms can interrogate data and understand complex patterns in a way that we don't have other tools to do. Nike, for example, unveiled the ISPA Universal Shoe, made using an injection moulding process that utilizes Bio-EVA foam derived from sugar cane and combines 3D printing, AI design and eco-friendly materials. Every single fibre is laid precisely where it needs to be at exactly the right point.

We have within reach technologies from a chemistry perspective where you can do pretty much anything in a lab, without testing on animals or damaging the natural world, including making burgers, diamonds, coral, leather and even replacement human organs. Unlocking sustainable growth through innovation is something that many luxury businesses have started to do.

I came across Sustainnovate.co, a company that works at the intersection of open breakthrough innovation and professional development helping organizations generate, commercialize and scale-up ideas turning them into revenue-generating opportunities, fast. Urgent sustainability actions are imperative to turn opportunities into growth, moving beyond gradual improvements to reimagine products, services and business models. Innovation and collaboration enables organizations to move further – faster.

The company specializes in helping organizations articulate their pain points – and find solutions behind closed doors. These solutions can then be either used internally, open sourced or sold to replace an existing material or process. Publicly acknowledging that there may be a problem with your products, process or overall business model invites stakeholder scrutiny and backlash, especially if there is not a solution in sight. Sustainnovate.co takes pride in helping companies to concretely define their problem and in keeping their work at the 'edge' of the organization and outside the public domain. Innovation is a reiterative process, that takes time.

'The first step to drive breakthrough innovation into your business is to create a fertile ground for people to try new things and fail quickly,' said Chantal Gaemperle, Group Executive Vice President Human Resources and Synergies at LVMH.

Gaemperle said:

> In 2017, DARE (Disrupt, Act, Risk to be an Entrepreneur) was born to give LVMH employees a voice and a platform for their ideas to be heard following an agile – start up – methodology. In such a sizeable group like LVMH – 75

Maisons (brands), 200,000 employees – cultivating an entrepreneurial spirit, giving employees a chance to contribute allows to stay agile and close to our founding values. DARE is about that, and it showed great benefits for business and people development. It mobilizes senior executives as coach and mentors of the projects selected, thus giving COMEX members a pulse of the organization, staying close to people. I have been a sponsor from the beginning, proud that the program was born and developed in HR.

I was invited as an entrepreneur mentor from the beginning of the programme and gave my support to the programme for three years. The methodology used was similar to the Stanford d.school about fast prototyping and testing and preparing their pitch to get funded. For the last five years the DARE community had over 720 people attending the events and more than 30,000 active people on the platform and LVMH funded 52 projects to date.

As an example, these are four projects that the group founded, which are successfully running:

- Nona Source was the first online resale platform which re-values dead-stock fabrics from the Group's Fashion & Leather Goods.
- Maisons Shero, an internal digital platform created to empower LVMH women and men through learning modules and inspiring content with the goal of boosting gender equity, such as articles, videos and podcasts.
- The Inclusion Index, an observatory and accelerator of diversity and inclusion initiatives within LVMH.
- Heristoria, which curates and sells iconic millesime pieces from LVMH Maisons.

Why did DARE work so well? Firstly, culture is the one thing that brings together all the Maisons within LVMH – whether fashions and leather goods, wines and spirits, hospitality, etc. Secondly, the initiative illustrates the power of teams, gathering diverse profiles and experiences, participants working not only on their ideas but contributing to those of others and ultimately the performance of the group. DARE is now a worldwide diverse and motivated community that they nurture and will keep growing: creativity and innovation have always been rooted in the group's DNA.

Paul Bunje agreed with the LVMH approach: 'Nobody wants to disrupt the core of the business, yet you are responsible for creating the disruption within your company. This is a lot better than somebody else disrupting you.'

What cannot happen is to ignore the problem because you don't have the solution yet. Breakthrough innovation is a relatively low-cost exercise that can help organizations grow and evolve without hurting the core of the business, plus you can use this as an incentive for your high-performing employees.

Give them two years, cordoned off with a budget, a clear task and parameters, and track their progress. By making this a separate business, not integrated into the quarterly reporting or with any financial KPIs associated with it until the point of market release, you have the best opportunity to create something truly amazing.

Often the smartest people leave organizations to solve problems related to their jobs. Imagine if they could do that within your own structure. As LVMH just proved, it can be a real success.

The light bulb moment

A great example is Philips Lighting. Philips is responsible for creating the LED light. The story fascinates me. Once upon a time, the white light-emitting diode was invented by Nobel Prize for Physics winners Shuji Nakamura, Isamu Akasaki and Hiroshi Amano. Their innovation enabled the birth of the LED light bulb, creating efficient lighting in terms of energy and costs as well as being lower in light pollution. Furthermore, LEDs can be charged using solar power enabling the Global South to be able to access 'clean light'. Philips created an 'edge organization', as Paul Bunje describes it, and set off. For context, at that time, Philips was the largest producer of incandescent light bulbs in the world. Very quickly, this edge organization created a great LED product, significantly better from a performance perspective in a whole host of ways, drove down the price and within no time the edge organization was the biggest contributor to Philips Lighting's bottom line.

Their innovation was so good that they completely disrupted themselves and every other area of their business as this innovation drove efficiencies on flatscreen TVs, computers, etc. Philips did it right, because they have a growth mindset, and therefore their people have a growth mindset too.

You would never be able to do that within a company where the managers are interested in protecting their KPIs, instead of wanting to make the company better as they won't want to invest in an LED project that's going to reduce their sales of incandescent bulbs because they won't hit the numbers, and this type of mindset is really damaging for businesses.

Jewellery and watches

Another good example of innovation is Daumet, a French materials science company. The company was founded in Paris by Cyrile Deranlot and Albert Fert, 2007 Nobel Prize for Physics, acting as scientific advisor. The pair developed a unique technology in advanced metallurgy, intended originally for microelectronics but which then found its first big market in the jewellery and watch industry. As of today, Daumet is the only supplier in the world able to offer white, durable non-allergic gold, according to Forbes (Girod, 2020). Typically, watchmakers are faced with the dilemma of choosing between whiteness and eternity, a challenge even for renowned brands like Rolex. However, Daumet has successfully resolved this trade-off, achieving a solution that was deemed impossible by many, until now. The company has been awarded the Butterfly Mark for their journey towards social and sustainability excellence.

Hospitality

The travel and hospitality industries have been 'flying under the radar' when it comes to sustainability expectations compared with the fashion industry, yet, they are in a privileged position to be a catalyst of change, running 'model hotels' to showcase sustainable living in harmony with nature. As different and big as the world may seem, what every destination has in common is human activities, sometimes the people themselves are the threat. Overtourism is not a new phenomenon. In 2017 the local residents of Barcelona, Venice, Amsterdam, Dubrovnik, Iceland and Skye protested so much that these destinations either increased their visa fees or restricted the number of visitors to attractions such as Machu Picchu and Angkor Wat. The influence that the industry has on their guests is huge. Just to give you an example, Loxe, a US-based startup, developed a mobile key solution that will help hoteliers save money, cut the use of single-use plastic and gain better data from customers, while at the same time cutting the number of elevator trips for guests in a not-so-great mood, when you get to your room and find out that your card is demagnetized or you lost it sometimes in your own bag – or maybe that is only me.

TablePort is a contactless solution for ordering and paying at restaurants and hotels, reducing the wait time for customers, and making orders and bill settlements fast, easy and saving on paper. Considering that there are around 368 billion credit card transactions a year globally – the paper of those plus the receipts from the merchant, well, that is a lot of paper!

Nonofique is a microfiltration company that managed to remove the microfibers from textile water waste. Granted that most hotels outsource their laundry today, however there is a trend to bring the laundry in-house as not only will it save you money but also reduce your Scope 3 emissions. But all converge at the front of the house with a unique experience, outstanding customer service, quality and comfort.

Sustainability actions peppered throughout the guest experience are incredibly powerful; in fact, it is more important than any piece of advertising, as it can drive word of mouth. The industry as a whole still remains shy of truly leaning into the sustainability transformation, mainly because the margins are tight, it requires a capex investment, there is a misconception that guests don't really care about it and sustainability is perceived as a cost, not an investment. The winners will be the ones that dare to think differently. Six Senses as a company had sustainability in their DNA since their inception, and although for a few years they did not lean into it, now they are working to bake it into every hotel and every experience. Most of their properties, for example, host an organic garden, where they compost and help build healthy soil. Their gardens and landscapes are made up of local and non-invasive plants; many of them serve as ingredients for their restaurants and spa treatments. They invest in R&D to ensure they can explore how they can keep their habitat healthy for all species.

Here are some quick wins for hotels but you can also implement these at home to save you money and make the world better:

- Installing smart thermostats in each room enables people to customize their temperatures with a cap in order to optimize efficiency
- Recycling options in guest rooms
- Locally sourced foods and products
- Free access to bicycles
- Eliminating single-use plastic, including shower cups, wrappers, bottles, etc
- Creating paperless environments

- Sourcing from sustainable suppliers
- Purchasing from white chemistry cleaning supplies
- Developing recycling programmes

Fashion

Stella McCartney founded her brand in 2001 – she was an outlier for many, but in my eyes a trendsetter. The designer built the first cruelty-free fashion business, with women at the heart of its innovation.

Materials are a major area of innovation leading the change in luxury, especially in fashion but also automotive and soft furniture like sofas, rugs/carpets and chairs, although, unlike their fashion counterparts, they feature less under the spotlight. 'It's the material companies that really have an impact when it comes to the fashion industry as a whole. We must aim to replace the toxic materials first before we can do anything else. That's the key,' said Nikita Jayasuriya, General Manager and Head of Europe of The Mills Fabrica, a company that supports the pioneers of eco-solutions by showcasing them within their innovation gallery and experiential concept store called Fabrica X in Hong Kong and London.

The Materials Innovation Institute is another example of a network organization enabling the connection between industry and society in the development of new materials helping to reach scale.

But in order to do this, luxury companies will need to upscale their funding to biomaterials. Instead of manufacturing plants, animal skins or petroleum into textiles, sustainable materials can be grown from bacteria, yeasts, algae and fungi. Companies and designers around the world are already transforming the textile industry through biofabrication. Backed by the Hermès family, biotechnology company Mycoworks raised $125 million in 2022 to mass produce mushroom-based leather, a vegan alternative that requires only a fraction of the time, water and energy to grow compared to the resources required to raise cattle. Hermès has re-edited their 1997 travel bag with lab-grown mycelium in its lining.

Stella McCartney, Adidas and Lululemon have also invested in mushroom leather, developing products made from Mylo, the mycelium material developed by Californian company Bolt Threads, which unfortunately ceased production in June 2023 after failing to secure the funding necessary to scale (Chan and Webb, 2023). Balenciaga launched the world's first mycelium garment officially available to buy in stores in collaboration with Italian biotech firm SQIM as part of its Winter 2022 collection. Kering, who is a pioneer in sustainability, has created Demetra, an animal-free, leather-like material, after two years of research and development in their Gucci factory. But unlike their other companies, they have made Demetra available to anyone who is interested in buying it.

Kering also established the Material Innovation Lab, where designers from all over the world can explore certified sustainable fabrics and materials to use in their collections.

Biosynthetic silk, a sustainable material made from the same protein spiders use to create silk without harming any animals, is also on the cusp of becoming a commercial reality.

Biotech company AMSilk developed the high-performance fibre. Biosteel worked together with Omega, the watch company, on a luxury watch strap. Other product pilots manufactured from man-made spider silk include a prototype of Adidas' 'Futurecraft' shoe with Biosteel, the limited-edition Moon Parka, designed by The North Face in collaboration with Japanese textile research company Spiber, and a prototype Microsilk dress by Stella McCartney and Bolt Threads.

Another good example of innovation is German company Leuchtstoffwerk Breitungen GMBH, a phosphors and chemicals company that specializes in inorganic phosphors and optical materials for specialist markets in light production, diagnostics, product marking and the authentication of bank-notes and security documents.

Their technology is now used for cotton and other materials where you will be able to understand their provenance without human intervention by uploading the digital ID – this will get done as close to the field as possible.

These types of collaborations are the ones that we need to accelerate efficiency and transparency. In 2022, Fendi, an LVMH-owned company, announced a two-year collaboration with Imperial College London and Central Saint Martins to develop lab-grown fur.

Young reimaginers are coming to the forefront with fresh ideas that might have seemed impossible years ago – just because they dared to try and fail. Innovation comes from universities, startups and biology labs, in fact innovation comes from anywhere. Interdisciplinary designer and CSM alumna Jess Redgrave, for example, has developed a fibre for textiles, complete with natural dyes and a waterproof coating, made entirely from sunflowers. Redgrave's project combines fashion and science in a range of modular solutions for the textile industry that support agricultural food systems, protect biodiversity and contribute to climate protection.

'For fashion to have a future, there needs to be an imminent shift to regenerative practices,' she said, 'and when you want to get sustainability into the mass market, the aesthetic needs to be something that can be liked by everyone, not just a certain group of people.' As promising as it sounds, projects like Redgrave's are prototypes – the industry is still in its development phase and only a fraction of initiatives make it past the research and prototyping stage.

Although some luxury companies are already leaning towards material innovation, more funding is required to accelerate the change – brand support and investment are crucial to making innovative materials more accessible.

Fashion for Good is another brilliant source of innovation for the industry. It is led by Katrin Ley, fellow Young Global Leader, who has done a remarkable job in making this company a leader in the open innovation field, connecting people working in sustainable innovation with brands, retailers, manufacturers and funders to breathe life into new technologies and ideas. Kering, C&A and Chanel are some of the brands that are leaning into open innovation and collaboration. They are the founding partners of Fashion for Good accelerator Plug and Play, whose mission is to identify innovators and startups and give them access to capital to scale.

And just like that, we can reimagine cleaner materials to produce textiles that do not come from the soil or from fossil fuel derivatives, with less harmful chemicals, and which can be recycled into something else or the same thing – fully circular. With the rise of customer-centric luxury ecosystems, the linear business logic of brands needs reimagining.

The vintage renaissance or pre-love is a 'new' business model and here to stay. Positive Luxury and Bain & Co co-authored a visionary report back in March 2021 called 'LuxCo30, a vision of sustainable luxury'. When the report was written, people thought it was utopian; today, this thought is far from the truth and instead it became a comprehensive 'to do' list for organizations. It:

- Set a bold strategic vision and redefined the company's mission and values
- Established a transparent baseline for all key sustainability issues
- Defined science-based targets and qualitative objectives for positive impact by 2030

- Designed a portfolio of projects to realize the vision and objectives
- Identified defensive and offensive strengths
- Built commitment to sustainability among the leadership team
- Aligned the organization and operating model to the new challenges

What is vital is to approach sustainability in a holistic way across all stakeholders and all departments. 'You're never going to transform an entire organization with a "coalition of the willing". A coalition of the willing or the passionate or the interested may play a role in helping get things started and finding early proof points, but full-scale transformation requires embedding sustainability in how everyone works,' said Jenny Davis-Peccoud, Global Practice Head, Sustainability & Responsibility at Bain & Company.

'The problem I see with the sustainability departments today is that even if they do everything right, from identifying the right issues to set the appropriate goals, they are often detached from the business,' said Matteo Capellini, Expert Associate Partner in Milan at Bain & Company. He added:

> This has the fundamental consequence that operationalize sustainability (basically embedding in the day-to-day business decisions) is becoming the greatest barrier for achieving actual results. What I believe will happen is that sustainability will spread as a core competence across business and support functions, in a similar way to what happened with digital 20 years ago. At first it was only the IT Director with a small team, now digital capabilities are embedded in every team (marketing, commercial, etc). What complicates the situation with sustainability is that we are talking about a very multifaceted and complex topic, that encompasses many and very different problems, from decarbonization, to biodiversity, chemicals, social implications, etc. So most likely it will take more time and most companies will need external support to build that.

As Capellini suggested, the journey towards digitalization can provide a clear blueprint for transformation across the entire company and supply chain; as digital technology evolved, there came a point when the standalone digital teams had to become a companywide digital mindset:

> This holistic approach was the best way to move intent and targets into quantifiable action – then meaningful change and economic reward concluded the report 'LuxCo30. A vision of sustainable luxury' that I have co-authored with Capellini, Davis-Peccoud and Claudia D'Arpizio Partner, Milan from Bain & Co.

Reimagining shopping

As the luxury consumer gets younger, digitalization and personalization are becoming ever more important, and this includes social commerce, live-streams and pre-loved. People's expectation is that the brand recognizes them as trusted customers regardless of the medium, online or in store, and they will receive recommendations according to their previous purchases and taste.

Reimagining people-centric digitalization is a pain point for luxury as consumers are getting younger, and their expectations and demands are higher; they know no boundaries between the digital and physical world. For most Gen Z the luxury digital experience does not match their physical one. They would like the fluidity of Netflix, a wide well-displayed assortment of clothes, shoes, etc at the speed of Amazon. Consumers become channel agnostic, increasingly expecting luxury brands to communicate and sell using different physical and digital channels, according to a survey on luxury consumption and distribution presented by Boston Consulting Group (BCG) (2021). Consequently, luxury online shopping can be seen as inadequate.

Apple is helping Burberry reimagine its retail journey by creating R Message – a by-invitation-only chat that store staff use to manage inventory and receive company news. R Message will enable store employees to communicate directly to VIP customers, book appointments, send personalized recommendations and share products that are in stock in order to make the suggestions. R Message will enable Burberry to offer its custom-ers a unique and customized service in order to foster loyalty.

Brand membership is another great concept that has not yet taken off at scale in the luxury business, however it's brewing. What I mean by brand membership is anything that will keep the consumer engaged with your company for longer. Apple does it rather well with Apple Care, selling more memory for your iCloud storage.

Brand membership could be a great way to merge the physical and digital world with the sale of NFTs, and increase customer engagement through circular business models. In the gaming world, for example a Gucci handbag, sometimes costing you more than physical items in the real world, sold a 4-minute-film as an NFT for $25,000, and in Roblox, a famous gaming platform, a handbag sold for 350,000 Robux, the Roblox currency, which is around $4,115, 700 times more than someone would have paid for it in the real world.

Dressing your avatar in designer clothes is something that has captured the imagination of many luxury brands, from Balenciaga selling character skins on Fortnite to Ralph Lauren launching digital clothing on Zepeto, a South Korean platform. Morgan Stanley analysts estimated in November 2021 that metaverse gaming and NFTs could make up 10 per cent of the luxury brands addressable market, at a valuation as large as $50 billion by 2030 (White, 2022), as consumers are changing; this is possible even if you can't quite see it or understand it. Other luxury companies do not have the same confidence in circular business models and opt for sector diversification and focus on maximizing their returns on a linear model, at least for the time being.

American luxury department store Nordstrom aims to offer its New York customers an unforgettable luxury experience by offering an extensive food-and-beverage service. Customers will be able to choose from a selection of food and drinks and it will be brought to them as they try things on.

Breitling has opened in many Asian countries, such as China, Indonesia and Korea, a new destination for watch lovers. The boutiques have a cafe and food service where you can sit, chat, lose time or buy timekeepers.

On the subject of watches, Supernova, a startup currently raising seed investment, is breaking new ground – not only with its futuristic, extremely lightweight watch equipped with an augmented intelligence system and using an everlasting energy source, but also with its business model. They are working towards having its customer as founding partners, a club member, an ambassador, a creator and an owner to help a younger generation of wealthy individuals to connect with high horology via a new set of values and communities.

Chanel opened a new Paris flagship that will be the testbed for new digital capabilities to create immersive and interactive experiences in partnership with Farfetch. Augmented reality will deliver a more personalized experience, leaving no doubt that the next generation of luxury retail will be digitally enhanced. The store is reimagining the future of luxury retail with a high human touch and the use of digital.

Zelig is the brainchild of Sandy Sholl, former CEO of Madaluxe Group. Zelig is a groundbreaking technology that enables people to try on and style clothes in seconds via online retail experiences. It will contribute to significantly reducing the 92 million tons of clothing that end up in landfills by hugely reducing returns and eliminating waste. Zelig will cut the fashion industry's carbon footprint and change the way we consume and wear fashion forever.

Another example is Aura Blockchain Consortium, which was launched by Louis Vuitton, Prada and Cartier to enable people to access the product history and ensure the authenticity of their goods. This is becoming particularly valuable as the resale market is growing to track the authentication of the product and reduce counterfeit.

Korea is at the leading edge of robotics, digitalization and AI. When you think about robotics, think about human-like machines, which look and feel very much like us, with soft skin and gentle mannerisms. I have seen robots making cocktails, and after a few, you can't distinguish whether your waiter is human or not. Another interesting innovation is smart mirrors at the point of retail. Smart mirrors can interact with you, take your measurements, analyse your skin type and make recommendations on the kind of treatments and/or special routines for the type of skin and the type of damage that your skin may have. As image recognition is very much part of this 'mirror' experience, it remembers you, your taste, and size and makes recommendations based on what you bought last year.

Personalization and digitalization are also an interesting intersection, where machines can understand your scent and suggest matching and complementary scents that will accentuate your presence in a room. Those customized perfumes could have added pheromones or any other properties that are wellbeing-enhancing.

Digitalization and transparency are two sides of the same coin, and multi-brand retailers are now forced to increase the end-to-end visibility of the type of decisions they made to curate their offering. Sustainability and ESG decisions are among these, both at the company level as well as the product level. The New York State Senate unveiled an Act in January 2022 requiring fashion retailers to publicly set and track ESG targets, including employee wages, greenhouse gas emissions and the use of recycled materials, as well as conducting supply chain mapping with a minimum disclosure of 50 per cent of their suppliers across Scope 1, 2 and 3. People are more aware of 'greenwashing' than ever before, and certifications with no real action behind them are becoming detrimental for brands. Furthermore, circular supply chains will become the norm – especially amongst the younger generations, involving them as a protagonist of the brand story and making the consumer accountable for the role they play in the journey of the product – from purchase, care and end of the life in the hands of that person, before the product is re-sold, rented, leased or simply gifted.

Making circularity a reality

There are many companies adopting a circular mindset. For example, Steven Webster, who in 2017 created RESET, an extension of their bespoke jewellery service for repurposing unused jewellery into a newly, reimagined, design. Created as an intimate consultative design experience, Stephen brainstorms ideas with his clients and then works his magic by redesigning old pieces of jewellery into something new and fresh, giving old stones and metals a second life. RESET aims to retain the sentimental value that is held in gold, platinum, diamonds, gems, etc and reimagine them for their next journey.

'The whole concept of circularity is going to be a game changer. An apparel CEO once said to me, "Our business is about selling more stuff to more people more often – and this is just not sustainable",' Davis-Peccoud recounted. 'As circular business models start coming into the luxury space, we'll see growth that isn't reliant on selling more new stuff but finding ways to extend product lives, create experiences or engage consumers in non-material ways.'

Levi's just opened a new concept store in Soho, London, with sustainability and consumer first. Levi's message to us all is to love what we wear and to ensure that the product lives for longer – they will play their part by repairing, reimagining and recycling the garment. A new collection, 'Levi's by Levi's', is made from returned and faulty products.

When we think about luxury, we think about heritage, but all brands started small and created that heritage with the passing of time. Combining new and old codes of luxury and emphasizing its innovation may be the new way to reimagine luxury and keep it relevant while playing up an updated luxury code of excellence, consisting of the beauty and design of the exceptional products or experience, rarity, craftsmanship, customer service, eco-design, circularity marrying exceptional customer service and technology. Each person, each generation, each company creates its heritage, this newly reimagined luxury will be the custodian's culture and our natural world.

Are you ready to reimagine innovation?

References

Arup and Oxford Economics (2023) The Global Green Economy
  Report, www.arup.com/news-and-events/green-transition-creates-103t-
  opportunity-for-the-global-economy-by-2050-a-new-report-finds#:~:text=A%20
  new%20report%20from%20Arup,move%20quickly%20to%20capture%20
  them (archived at https://perma.cc/N9QX-X4W3)

Boston Consulting Group (2021) True-Luxury Global Consumer Insights, June,
  https://web-assets.bcg.com/f2/f1/002816bc4aca91276243c72ee57d/
  bcgxaltagamma-true-luxury-global-consumer-insight-2021.pdf (archived at
  https://perma.cc/8ZMX-7YYY)

Cernansky, R (2023) The US beauty industry is largely unregulated. Is that starting
  to change?, Vogue Business, 26 January, www.voguebusiness.com/sustainability/
  the-us-beauty-industry-is-largely-unregulated-is-that-starting-to-change
  (archived at https://perma.cc/6X34-4BHS)

Chan, E and Webb, B (2023) Stella McCartney-backed leather alternative Mylo
  halts production, *Vogue Business*, 30 June, www.voguebusiness.com/
  sustainability/stella-mccartney-backed-leather-alternative-mylo-halts-
  production-bolt-threads-kering-ganni-adidas-lululemon (archived at https://
  perma.cc/4RXD-2RXL)

Chêne Bleu (2021a) Welcome to Chêne Bleu, www.chenebleu.com/labor-of-love
  (archived at https://perma.cc/S53C-SJHK)

Chêne Bleu (2021b) The Vineyard, www.chenebleu.com/the-vineyard (archived at
  https://perma.cc/3FQZ-422G)

Devi, A (2023) DCO 2030: Digital economy to contribute 30% of global GDP and
  create 30 million jobs by 2030, *IT edge!*, 5 February, https://www.
  edgemiddleeast.com/business/dco-2030-digital-economy-to-contribute-30-of-
  global-gdp-and-create-30-million-jobs-by-2030 (archived at https://perma.cc/
  K8BH-MYK3)

Girod, S (2020) Discover what inspires today's luxury entrepreneurs, *Forbes*,
  25 September, www.forbes.com/sites/stephanegirod/2020/09/25/discover-what-
  inspires-todays-luxury-entrepreneurs/ (archived at https://perma.cc/M9FD-AYFS)

Positive Luxury and Bain & Co (2021) 'LuxCo30. A vision of sustainable luxury',
  www.positiveluxury.com/2021/03/10/luxco2030/ (archived at https://perma.cc/
  ZB56-8PEJ)

White, K (2022) From tradition to digitization: modern innovation secrets of
  luxury brands, PatSnap, 12 April, www.patsnap.com/resources/blog/from-
  tradition-to-digitization-modern-innovation-secrets-of-luxury-brands/ (archived
  at https://perma.cc/EWZ2-C82N)

10

The inspiration chapter

It is possible to reimagine business. Regardless of your size, industry, location or sector, sustainable innovation is key to unlock business resilience and the enabler for your tribe to keep growing.

Although the luxury industry is 'small' in economic terms compared with other industries, it is not when it comes to influence. The luxury, entertainment and hospitality industries are in a privileged position to lead the way because of their image, influence, desirability, margins and their aspirational positioning.

When meeting with investors, to my surprise, there are still many sceptics of the financial opportunity businesses that put nature and people at the core of their strategies really present, but the good news is that ESG metrics and the new reporting directives will enable investors to be a little bit more 'certain' about what they are investing in as it will be easier for them to carry out climate due diligence as they carry out financial ones. From 2025 there will be little room for ambiguity.

Sustainability and commercial success are not a trade-off – the two go hand in hand. I met Eva Kruse, Chief Global Engagement Officer of PANGAIA, a company on a mission to build an earth-positive business. The textile tech brand and fashion label balances sustainability with design, creating sustainable loungewear. Its goal and philosophy is to give back more than we take in and to inspire and accelerate a positive future for Earth by creating value that improves the quality of life for people, animals and plants.

The company was born as an enabler to transform the fashion industry through material science and innovation creating better products and materials with less impact on the planet delivering true industry transformation. The company is driven by three core impact pillars: planet, people and positive change. They are dedicated to preserving biodiversity, taking action on climate change, ensuring water health and reducing waste. Additionally, they prioritize elevating human potential by valuing human rights and driving positive change within their community. Through their commitment to giving back to both people and the planet, PANGAIA aims to create a better future. The company's third pillar focuses on innovation, particularly in materials and circularity. True to its slogan, 'Powered by Nature. Delivered by Science', the company is committed to responsible material and process innovation while extending the lifespan of its products, materials and resources to optimize the entire production process and product lifecycle for sustainability.

'Every material that we bring to market has less impact on the planet because at the heart of what we do is material innovation. Reimagining a less extractive economic system is what we strive for,' explained Eva. 'I like to think that we are a solutions company. We invest in innovative materials to scale up faster and we also create our own.'

The company develops and works with a handful of innovative and cruelty-free materials that can be part of the solution for the industry:

- FLWRDWN™: A plant-based fossil fuel-free alternative to animal down combining wildflowers, a biopolymer and cellulosic aerogel.
- C-Fiber™: A bio-based Seacell™ fibre combining eucalyptus pulp and seaweed powder.
- Frut Fiber™: A bio-based fibre utilizing food waste, turning bamboo, banana and pineapple leaf fibres into a cotton-like innovative fabric.
- Plnt Fiber™: A bio-based fibre using renewable, fast-growing plants such as Himalyan nettle, bamboo, eucalyptus and seaweed.
- Peppermint oil: A durable odour control finish and broad spectrum anti-odour treatment that enables garments to stay fresher longer.
- Nettle and hemp denim: Plant-based materials made using Himalayan nettle or hemp blended with organic cotton and treated with peppermint oil.

Creating sustainable fashion and developing new environmentally friendly materials, PANGAIA is both a B2B and a DTC company. 'We created a brand to showcase the material science put into actual desirable products: to show how a company can be driven by design and great material innovation and deliver both profits and a positive outcome in our world,' said Kruse.

This type of innovation is not exclusive to medium-sized businesses, established companies like YSL Beauty, a brand from the L'Oréal family, are also innovating. Marie-Pia Schlumberger, Sustainability Director at L'Oréal Luxury, exudes enthusiasm and positivity when speaking about 'reimagining luxury beauty'. For her, it means redesigning products to achieve lower environmental impact while maintaining top performance and desirability, redefining cultural codes to make sustainability glamour, and reinventing habits to create beauty experiences that are more mindful of the 'planetary boundaries'.

This is what the 23 brands of L'Oréal Luxe's portfolio (as of June 2023) are working on within the framework of L'Oréal for the Future, the sustainability programme of the French cosmetic giant, which has set up measurable objectives for 2030 to shift its ways of operating across four domains – climate, water, biodiversity and resources – as well as to support its stakeholders, and to tackle the most pressing social and environmental issues the world is currently facing. To ensure the achievement of these goals, L'Oréal Luxury brands have been collectively transforming themselves based on common quantitative KPIs, all the while staying true to each of their unique DNA.

CASE STUDY
'Change the Rules, Change the Future' – YSL Beauty

In today's world there are many new challenges and opportunities for businesses to reimagine a future that is sustainable, regenerative and fair. 'YSL beauty has rewritten the rules so they can change the future. Their mission, vision and values are aligned with their sustainability strategy, reimagining the way they do business and deliver value to all stakeholders and nature. Their strategy "Change the Rules, Change the Future" aims to just do that,' said Marie Pia.

M. Saint Laurent defied the rules of the past, broke existing codes of fashion and reimagined the future to transcend heartsets, mindsets and, why not, generations. YSL Beauty is a changemaker who dared to rewrite the rules of business to change tomorrow's future.

Their strategy has *three* pillars: 'Abuse is not Love', their social pillar; 'Rewild our Earth', their environmental pillar; and 'Reduce our Impact', their innovation pillar. With strong commitments, the brand's strategy is already delivering tangible results today.

Since 2014, YSL Beauty has been working on sustainable sourcing and boosting biodiversity while empowering communities of women. The brand aims to provide them with access to entrepreneurial opportunities that will improve their financial independence and autonomy. The Ourika Community Gardens, an area of over 20,000 m^2 at the foothills of the Atlas Mountains in Morocco, is the home of more than 200 botanical species used in YSL Beauty products, and is at the heart of the brand's sustainability strategy. The Ourika community gardens are a place to observe, cultivate and protect nature to better enhance and restore it. They represent a vision of the future of beauty.

The botanical collection conducts experimental research to develop new ingredients. Furthermore, YSL Beauty has launched its global social impact programme – Abuse is Not Love – fighting against and preventing intimate partner violence (IPV), the most common form of violence against women. Lastly, their Rewild Our Earth programme is designed to protect and restore nature's most threatened areas while the Reduce Our Impact programme, rooted in innovation, dares to reimagine processes, and explore bold ideas, to uncover new possibilities.

Moreover, YSL Beauty align their actions to contribute to the United Nations Sustainable Development Goals (SDGs), a call to action to governments and business to contribute to end poverty, protect the planet and ensure that by 2030 we live in a just and prosperous world.

Strategies aligned with planetary boundaries

Planetary boundaries are thresholds within which humanity can survive and thrive. YSL believes they should never be crossed, which is why they are working to transition their business operations to conserve and rewild the world, leaning into the planetary boundaries' cornerstone of their sustainability targets for 2030.

In 2024 you will see the brand ahead of legislation, communicating transparently the social and environmental footprint of all skincare. This is a huge step for a brand that has so many products, and if this was not enough, here are some of other concrete actions that YSL is taking:

- Reducing greenhouse gas emissions by addressing the carbon emissions of all activities (Scopes 1, 2 and 3), starting with products.
- Optimizing their value chain from the sourcing of natural ingredients to product formulation, packaging design, in order to minimize the environmental footprint on natural resources and ecosystems.
- Reducing the environmental footprint: 100 per cent of their skincare serums and 50 ml creams are refillable. The iconic LIBRE Eau de Parfum is refillable.

- Limiting their environmental footprint by focusing on green sciences, preserving biodiversity through responsible cultivation methods and reducing the environmental impact of their formulas through green extraction and green chemistry.

- Using crop and soil science techniques to support farmers and communities to grow raw materials in the most efficient way and pioneering regenerative agriculture at scale.

- In retail and e-commerce, all stores are created following internal guidelines based on LEED Silver Design Criteria which guarantees their sustainability credentials. Furthermore, the brand is reimagining e-commerce by reconfiguring all direct e-commerce packaging, reducing carton weight and transport volume, plastic-free gift boxes, limiting the number of documents in each package, FSC-certified cardboard, removing magnets across packaging and POS and thriving to make e-commerce more circular.

Positively impacting our world

The brand mission, which goes across all levels in the organization, supports projects that specifically contribute to positively impact the planet but also people.

YSL have:

- Offered sustainability training: 100 per cent of YSL's beauty teams based at their HQ receive sustainability training every year. Furthermore, 100 per cent of their beauty advisor training managers are upskilled on social and environmental issues to ensure teams are knowledgeable about these topics.

- Launched their 'Abuse is Not Love' programme in 2020: this initiative, which shares information about nine signs of abuse, has reached over 400,000 people in over 33 countries as of June 2023.

- Educated employees: through the brand's 'Abuse is Not Love' initiative, YSL has educated over 9,000 employees worldwide on violence against women and how to identify or provide resources to those experiencing abuse.

Wild at heart

Conserving and preserving our world is imperative but not enough. We need to think about net positive outcomes, not just about impact.

At YSL Beauty they believe that letting nature 'alone' enables the natural processes to share the land and the sea for the ecosystems to be restored in order to create more biodiverse habitats.

Some 75 per cent of the earth's ecosystems have been degraded by human activity. To create a future we can live in, YSL Beauty created a global programme, Rewild our Earth, to protect and restore nature's most threatened areas in partnership with the NGO Re:wild.

In four countries, representing four biodiversity hotspots around the world (Morocco, Madagascar, Haiti and Indonesia), YSL Beauty cultivates ingredients which have successfully been rolled out over the course of 2022. Madagascar is one of the countries where vanilla and geranium are sourced. These ingredients are found in many of the YSL Beauty fragrances.

The brand engages the communities where they do business in the rewilding revolution, which includes protecting and restoring 100,000 hectares by 2030, which is the equivalent of 186,873 football pitches. To date, over 16,000 hectares of land and water that were protected and/or restored and 134,000 trees were planted in all four areas in 2022.

Armani Beauty – a vision for the future

Armani Beauty is another beauty brand positively contributing to reimagining the future. They recognize that climate change is one of the most pressing challenges for mankind, which is why they actively invest in reducing their impact and their carbon emissions by developing products that are refillable and designed to last and by conserving endangered forests in Zimbabwe, Peru, Brazil, Guatemala and Indonesia, where they source some of their raw materials.

The brand not only thinks about the health of the planet but also about their people. As we have witnessed in the last few years, water is a scarce resource, especially in the Global South. Giving access to clean and safe water to the most deprived communities around the world is at the core of their strategy. By 2025, it is estimated that half of the world's population could be living in water-stressed areas. The United Nations recognized access to water and sanitation as a human right in 2010. Since then, Acqua for Life, Armani's floral water initiative focusing on universal access to drinking water in water scarce regions, has helped over 530,000 people and has invested more than 14 million euros in water projects in 21 countries. By 2030, Armani Beauty aims to be a source of clean water for 1 million people.

Lastly, they think about their products. The brand is working on using ingredients that are bio-based, derived from abundant minerals or from circular processes with efficacy and performance at the heart of it. Armani Beauty also focus on increasing their use of recycled glass, plastic, metal and light packaging from product development all the way to the final consumer packaging. All their products are packaged with certified FSC/PEFC boxes.

'One of my personal favourites,' said Marie-Pia, 'is MY WAY perfume. It has an innovative refillable bottle enabling people to be part of the solution for reducing environmental impact.'

She continued, 'But it's not the only example! All the fragrance best-sellers of L'Oréal Luxe brands are now available in a refillable format: this is how we are reimagining luxury beauty!'

Something old, something new, something borrowed, something blue...

The oldest jewellery house in the world, Garrard, is also reimagining themselves. Garrard was founded in 1735 by George Wickes. Within the year, he received the firm's first royal order, which was placed by Frederick, Prince of Wales. In 1782 Robert Garrard joined the business and became a partner in 1792. In 1843, Garrard was awarded the Royal Warrant by Queen Victoria, and at the end of the century made many tiaras for the British Royal Family, including the Imperial Crown of India and the Fringe Tiara, which Queen Elizabeth wore on her wedding day. In modern history, Garrard made the world's most famous engagement ring for Princess Diana, now worn by Catherine, Princess of Wales.

Garrard is a luxury house on a mission to keep making history and transforming the luxury industry. The company is on the road to net zero by committing to reduce greenhouse gas emissions by 30 per cent by 2030 and has an apprenticeship scheme, which deliberately seeks out and encourages diverse talent.

Garrard launched Something Borrowed in 2023, a sustainable fine jewellery rental service that enables people to hire a selection of exquisite jewels for moments when people want a special piece of jewellery but prefer not to buy one – particularly around the bridal market. Garrard has taken the opportunity to turn rental into an experience, where you and three people can enjoy a glass of champagne in the coveted Queen Mary Room where Queen Victoria had her Consort Crown fitted in advance of the 1911 coronation. This is a relatively new concept for the jewellery industry, which the visionary CEO is keen to push. I had the pleasure of interviewing Joanne Milner, CEO of Garrard, who shared with me that 'In terms of circularity, we're not selling a product that has a short shelf life – we're selling things that last forever.' 'But we have to support that as well to be even more sustainable as a business model, this is why we offer repair services,' she explained.

Anybody owning a piece of Garrard jewellery, whether they bought it, inherited it or acquired it through an auction, can have it serviced no matter how old it is. 'Sustainability is not just important to our customers, employees and suppliers but also the investment community,' Milner, who previously worked in private equity, commented. 'Sustainability metrics are important in defining the value of the business, but on a personal level, I care very much about this topic. I have a young son who questions ownership, why I buy a certain chocolate spread and tells me he would rather have an experience as a birthday present than a physical item. So, if only for him, I'm always look-ing at different areas of the business and ways in which we can actually help.'

Garrard has a timeless archive of jewellery from vintage tiaras that date back to 1910 to modern earrings and necklaces.

CASE STUDY
The power of partnerships

The secret source of life and business is leaning into partnerships and collaborations. As the old African proverb says, 'If you want to go fast, go alone, if you want to go far, go together.'

Partnerships enable people and companies to combine their strengths, expertise and resources to create synergies otherwise unimaginable, leveraging their unique capabilities of each partner, in order to achieve extraordinary results.

Collaborating brings fresh perspectives and diverse knowledge to the table, helping the exchange of thoughts and ideas breathing life to creative solutions. In 2020, Sabrina and Idris Elba created S'ABLE Labs skincare after they realized that there was a lack of wellbeing products aimed at them. They lean into their life partnership to create a business, a recipe made in heaven for the Elbas.

They noticed the current wellness industry was elusive and exclusive. To counteract this, they're co-creating caring products and experiences that work, welcome all and don't just follow trends. Healthy skin is important to overall wellbeing. Inspired by the power of strong partnerships, in their own words, Sabrina Elba said, 'Partnerships included more than just romantic couples but also friends, business, and like-minded people or companies that aligned to disrupt the status quo or just add to it'.

They called this Coupledom, a marketplace that offers products that work efficiently and effectively for partners of all kinds. From the outset, they aimed to create a community for partnerships from all walks of life to come together, to be inspired and educated through inclusive conversations and ethical products. 'We want to fill that space with a community of people who understand the importance of partnerships,' said Sabrina. Their brand's purpose is to make people feel so good; that way, they can treat one another and the planet better.

Purposeful Partnerships sit at the heart of the company philosophy. From supply chain partners (who they know personally) to their conscious-minded community, these lasting connections co-create products and experiences that work, can be shared and help to generate positive outcomes for everybody.

Products are made with care, designed to be shared and they challenge every process and ingredient to ensure they really work for all ethnicities, genders, ages and backgrounds. Unrestrained transparency from ensuring ingredients are ethically sourced to refillable packaging, S'ABLE Labs has an open sustainability approach. The brand is certified with the Butterfly Mark powered by Positive Luxury for setting measurable and achievable ESG targets in line with a transitional plan, monitoring and certifying its progress vs targets yearly to achieve its goals.

They say, 'We're not perfect, but care is at the core of all we do, without compromising efficacy or quality. We will never overpromise, but we'll always try to overshare. Within our storytelling, we are committed to having honest conversations that cut the BS.'

The end is just the beginning...

The future is here to be reimagined. We have the honour to be living through this transitional era, where the innovations of today will affect the generations to come, it is our duty to make the right choices – but what is right?

Santiago Gowland, CEO of Rainforest Alliance and fellow Argentinian, said, 'We got to a point where companies need to demonstrate that they are being part of the solution, not just less of a problem. Food companies can play a pivotal role in transforming agriculture from being the key driver of habitat loss to becoming the fastest and most scalable driver of tropical forests and soil regeneration.' 'We are about to enter a new era where organizations align what they do with a positive outcome. It is an inside-out approach. The impact that we want to have in the world is to give more than we take,' he concluded.

Reimagine a new business era, where companies that innovate to drive positive outcomes on people and nature win. Reimagine a world where the those companies who are unkind to people and nature face extremely high costs and the risk that they may not succeed in their endeavours. Accelerating regenerative value creation across the supply and demand P&L levers in business, from tangible to intangible assets (like brands) where 90 per cent of value according to S&P Global lies, will play a pivotal role in tackling climate, biodiversity and social development crises. We need to find a new architecture of value creation where a tree standing up is worth more than a tree on the ground; in other words, that there are real financial incentives for doing the right thing.

Of course, measuring impact is a great starting point, as change starts with awareness, but sustainability innovation will be the driver for business resilience and sustainable economic growth. Focusing on net positive outcomes to restore and regenerate our world and educate and empower our societies is a better way to reframe the problems and truly find solutions that are scalable and economically sustainable.

The luxury entertainment and hospitality industries can help us reimagine the narrative, culture, social norms and what acceptable cues mean. We can choose optimism and solutions vs pessimism and defeat.

Reimagining Luxury outlines a new way of doing business prioritizing innovation, people and nature whilst driving sustainable economic growth. This way of thinking will help companies to differentiate from one another beyond the language of impact and compliance, which is, of course, necessary but just the beginning of the journey.

We have moved from commitment to action and from transparency to accountability in such a short time. By 2025 companies will need to disclose their 'double materiality' – meaning what is material to a company, both in terms of its implications for the company's financial value, as well as the company's impact on the world at large. Being less bad is not an option anymore; being positively good is mandatory.

Reimagining Luxury focuses on positive social and nature-related outcomes referring to actions and projects that better the economic wellbeing of societies and restore, rewild and conserve nature. This does not mean charity – this is about using the business muscle and innovation budgets to create long-term benefits for people and our planet, whilst driving sustainable economic growth.

And for the time poor, below is a simple list:

1 Lead with authenticity.

2 What not to do is almost more important that what you do.

3 Brand agency – think brand activism and create influence inside and outside the organization.

4 Coherence across the entire business from your mission to your formulations, products, experiences, materials, business models.

5 Accept your imperfections and share them – honesty and transparency are key.

6 Innovate and fail quickly – it is better to regret something that you have done than something that you have never tried.

7 See things through multiple lenses – empathy is a key ingredient of leadership.

8 Sustainability is not a tool to recruit new customers or future employees – don't actively communicate, let your products, your services do the talking and enable people to discover. A big advertisement sharing how great you are won't do you any good, instead, invest your money in innovating for good and work with the right partners to so they can share your story.

9 Ask yourself what if – rehearse six impossible situations and how you would react in each of them.

10 Investing in regenerating and rewilding our world and ensure that the biggest carbon sink, our oceans, are also well looked after.

11 Perhaps sustainability is not why people buy but why people will stop buying – 'Buycotting' is the new 'Cancel'.

12 Doing no harm is a thing of the past; net positive outcomes is where the future is at.

13 People want to do good, but they also want to benefit themselves – don't forget that for social and environmental sustainability to truly work you need to think about the economic value.

14 Involve your tribe on your journey, especially when you are thinking about the net positive outcome that you want to achieve. I win–you win. Somebody wise told me that you have four types of relationships: ok–ok; ok–not ok; not ok–ok, not ok–not ok. Remember to master your ok–ok (easy enough to remember).

15 Word of mouth is the best way to 'advertise' – invest your money in making your business process and your products good for our planet and societies.

16 Don't think about what you can control, think about what you can influence.

17 Sustainability innovation is an integral part of the solution.

18 Driving net positive outcomes is the new black.

19 Sustainability is a journey – this change will take a lifetime or more.

20 Be a reimaginer, remain optimistic, and if ever in doubt, call a friend or a stranger – partnerships and collaborations are superpowers.

And finally think where you invest your time and money: if all the time invested in talking about sustainability was invested in innovating, maybe change would happen faster.

Dare to be a reimaginer?

INDEX

NB: page numbers in *italic* indicate figures or tables.

Printed in the USA
CPSIA information can be obtained
at www.ICGtesting.com
JSHW072050070324
58808JS00007B/24